Women in the Middle East and North Africa

RESTORING WOMEN TO HISTORY
Series Editors: Cheryl Johnson-Odim and Margaret Strobel

Women in Asia
Barbara N. Ramusack and Sharon Sievers

Women in Latin America and the Caribbean
Marysa Navarro and Virginia Sánchez Korrol, with Kecia Ali

Women in the Middle East and North Africa
Guity Nashat and Judith E. Tucker

Women in Sub-Saharan Africa
Iris Berger and E. Frances White

Women in the Middle East and North Africa

RESTORING WOMEN TO HISTORY

by Guity Nashat and
Judith E. Tucker

*Indiana
University
Press*

BLOOMINGTON AND INDIANAPOLIS

Maps from *The Middle East: Fourteen Islamic Centuries* (3rd ed.),
by Glenn E. Perry, ©1998. Reprinted by permission of Prentice-Hall, Inc.,
Upper Saddle River, NJ.

This book is a publication of
Indiana University Press
601 North Morton Street
Bloomington, IN 47404-3797 USA

http://www.indiana.edu/~iupress

Telephone orders 800-842-6796
Fax orders 812-855-7931
Orders by e-mail iuporder@indiana.edu

© 1999 by Indiana University Press

The paper used in this publication meets the minimum requirements of
American National Standard for Information Sciences—Permanence of
Paper for Printed Library Materials, ANSI Z39.48-1984.

Manufactured in the United States of America

Library of Congress Cataloging-in-Publication Data

Nashat, Guity, date
Women in the Middle East and North Africa : restoring women to history /
by Guity Nashat and Judith E. Tucker.
p. cm. — (Restoring women to history)
Includes bibliographical references (p.   ) and index.
ISBN 0-253-33478-0 (cl : alk. paper). — ISBN 0-253-21264-2 (pa : alk. paper)
1. Women—Middle East—History. 2. Women—Africa, North—History.
I. Tucker, Judith E. II. Title. III. Series.
HQ1726.5.N37 1999
305.4'0956—dc21   99-11042

1 2 3 4 5 04 03 02 01 00 99

To the memory of Marilyn Robinson Waldman,
1943–1996, gifted scholar and rare friend

GUITY NASHAT

To the memory of my mother,
Ruth Horsfall Tucker, 1915–1997

JUDITH E. TUCKER

CONTENTS

SERIES EDITORS' PREFACE

This book is part of a four-volume series entitled "Restoring Women to History": *Women in Sub-Saharan Africa; Women in Asia; Women in Latin America and the Caribbean;* and *Women in the Middle East and North Africa.* The project began in 1984, bringing together scholars to synthesize historical information and interpretation on women outside of Europe and the United States of America. Earlier versions of the volumes were produced and distributed by the Organization of American Historians (OAH) as *Restoring Women to History: Teaching Packets for Integrating Women's History into Courses on Africa, Asia, Latin America, the Caribbean, and the Middle East* (1988; revised, 1990).

These volumes are intended to help teachers who wish to incorporate women into their courses, researchers who wish to identify gaps in the scholarship and/or pursue comparative analysis, and students who wish to have available a broad synthesis of historical materials on women. Although the primary audience is historians, scholars in related fields will find the materials useful as well. Each volume includes a bibliography, in which readings suitable for students are identified with an asterisk. Each volume is preceded by a broad, topical introduction written by Cheryl Johnson-Odim and Margaret Strobel that draws examples from all four volumes.

This project is the culmination of many years' work by many people. Cheryl Johnson-Odim and Margaret Strobel conceived of the original single volume, extending OAH projects published in the 1970s and 1980s on U.S. and European women's history. Joan Hoff (then Joan Hoff-Wilson, Executive Director of the Organization of American Historians), Cheryl Johnson-Odim, and Margaret Strobel wrote proposals that received funding from the National Endowment for the Humanities for a planning meeting of eight other authors, and from the Fund for the Improvement of Postsecondary Education (FIPSE) for the preparation, distribution, and dissemination of the manuscript. Under the leadership of Executive Director Arnita Jones, the OAH took on the responsibility of printing and distributing the single volume. The FIPSE grant enabled us to introduce the project through panels at conferences of the African Studies Association, the Association of Asian Studies, the Latin American Studies Association, the Middle Eastern Studies Association, and the World History Association.

Because of the strong positive response to the single volume, Joan Catapano, Senior Sponsoring Editor at Indiana University Press, encouraged the ten of us to revise and expand the material in four separate volumes. In the decade or so since the inception of this project, the historical literature on women from these regions has grown dramatically. Iris Berger and E. Frances White added important new information to their original contributions. White was assisted by Cathy Skidmore-Hess, who helped revise some of the material on West and Central Africa. Barbara Ramusack and Sharon Sievers found new material for Asia, with certain regions and periods still very unstudied. Marysa Navarro and Virginia Sánchez Korrol, with help from Kecia Ali, reworked their previous essays on Latin America and the Caribbean. Guity Nashat and Judith Tucker developed further their material on the Middle East and North Africa from the earlier volume.

This project is a blend of individual and collective work. In the 1980s, we met twice to discuss ways to divide the material into sections and to obtain consistency and comparability across the units. Each author read widely in order to prepare her section, reworking the piece substantially in response to comments from various readers and published reviews.

Scholars familiar with each region read and commented on various drafts. For this crucial assistance, we wish to thank Edward A. Alpers, Shimwaayi Muntemba, and Kathleen Sheldon for Africa; Marjorie Bingham, Emily Honig, Veena Talwar Oldenberg, Mrinalini Sinha, and Ann Waltner for Asia; Lauren (Robin) Derby, Asunción Lavrin, Susan Schroeder, and Mary Kay Vaughan for Latin America and the Caribbean; and Janet Afary, Margot Badran, Julia Clancy-Smith, Fred Donner, Nancy Gallagher, and Jo Ann Scurlock for the Middle East and North Africa. In revising the introduction, we received useful comments from Janet Afary, Antoinette Burton, Nupur Chaudhuri, Susan Geiger, and Claire Robertson. Anne Mendelson ably copyedited the OAH publication; LuAnne Holladay and Jane Lyle copyedited the Indiana University Press volumes. At various times over the years, undergraduate and graduate students and staff helped with nailing down bibliographic citations and/or preparing the manuscript. These include Mary Lynn Dietsche, Geri Franco, Jill Lessner, Lisa Oppenheim, and Marynel Ryan from the University of Illinois at Chicago, and Carole Emberton, Maryann Spiller, and Esaa Zakee from Loyola University Chicago.

This project owes much both to the Organization of American Historians and to Indiana University Press. We thank the following OAH staff members, past and present, who contributed to the project in various ways: Mary Belding, Jeanette Chafin, Ginger Foutz, Brian Fox, Kara Hamm, Joan Hoff, Arnita A. Jones, Nancy Larsen, Barbara Lewis, Michelle McNamara, and Michael Regoli. Our editor at IUP, Joan Catapano, waited months on end for the completion of our work. Without her prompting, we would probably not have taken the initiative to attempt this revision and publication of separate volumes. We appreciate her patience.

From reviews, citations, and comments at conferences, we know that scholars, teachers, and students have found our efforts valuable. That knowledge has helped sustain us in those moments when each of us, having moved on to other scholarly projects or having assumed demanding administrative positions, questioned the wisdom of having committed ourselves to revising and expanding the original materials. This kind of scholarship, what Ernest Boyer calls the "scholarship of integration," is typically not rewarded in academe as much as is traditional research, what Boyer terms the "scholarship of discovery."* For this reason we are particularly thankful to the authors for their willingness to commit their minds and energies to revising their work. Although our effort to get ten authors simultaneously to complete all four volumes sometimes made us feel like we were herding cats, we appreciate the intellectual exchange and the friendships that have developed over the years of our work together.

Cheryl Johnson-Odim
Chicago, Illinois

Margaret Strobel
Chicago, Illinois

---

*Ernest L. Boyer, *Scholarship Reconsidered: Priorities of the Professoriate* (Princeton, N.J.: Carnegie Foundation for the Advancement of Teaching, 1990), 16–21.

AUTHORS' PREFACE

Because I grew up in Iraq, Iran, and Egypt, I was keenly aware of the disadvantages of the position of women compared to that of men in traditional Middle Eastern societies, but I had no idea how these inequities had developed. The research required to prepare my portion of *Women in the Middle East and North Africa* has given me a much better understanding of the problems women in this region have faced for centuries; such understanding will, I hope, provide insights into how this improper treatment of women can be redressed.

I have benefitted from the comments and writings of many colleagues, students, and other scholars. I am particularly grateful for the generous help of Fred Donner of the University of Chicago, JoAnn Scurlock of Elmhurst College, Erica Friedl of Western Michigan University, and Judith E. Tucker of Georgetown University. I would also like to thank Joan Catapano of Indiana University Press for her continued encouragement to complete this project. Cheryl Johnson-Odim and Margaret Strobel have been exemplary editors, and their steady support and enthusiasm made this project possible. They have given much time to the project and made excellent suggestions without losing their patience and good humor. Special thanks to Peg Strobel for asking me to write an article on women in the pre-modern Middle East. Susan Allan, of the *Journal of American Sociology*, also has offered extremely helpful comments.

Finally, I would like to thank Gary S. Becker of the University of Chicago, whose theory of the family helped me understand the role of women in the Middle East.

Guity Nashat

I first began this project over a decade ago and, as is the case with any synthetic effort, I have benefitted enormously from the help I received from a number of individuals. The field of Middle East women and gender history is, happily, a moving target: there are many areas of the past that researchers have begun to explore only recently and, of course, even larger areas that have received virtually no scholarly attention. I have been dependent on the good will and solidarity of my colleagues to help me track and integrate this shifting body of material.

I would like to thank, in particular, a number of individuals whose readings and reviews of this and previous versions helped me refine my work here, including Janet Afary, Leila Ahmed, Margot Badran, and Nancy Gallagher. Julia Clancy-Smith deserves special mention for providing much of the material, both text and sources, on women in North Africa. The writing of Part II also benefitted from ideas and comments made over the years by graduate students at Georgetown University, some of whom went on to become teachers and scholars in the field of Middle East gender history, including Beshara Doumani, Bruce Dunne, Mary Ann Fay, Ellen Fleischmann, and Mona Russell.

The collaboration with the other historians in this series—Iris Berger, Marysa Navarro, Barbara Ramusack, Virginia Sánchez Korrol, Sharon Sievers, Fran White—and, in particular, Guity Nashat, was a most positive experience. Our joint meetings, workshops, panels, and discussions over the life of this project helped immeasurably to broaden the frame of reference as we tried to trace that difficult line between the universal and the particular in women's experiences. This book is, in many ways, the result of what was an exciting and satisfying collective effort.

Joan Catapano, of Indiana University Press, took an early and personal interest in this project and helped convince us to undertake the revisions needed for a new edition. Cheryl Johnson-Odim and Margaret Strobel deserve major credit for this volume and the others in the series. They not only provided the vision and leadership for this project, but also took on the hard work of cajoling, pleading, and threatening us until we lived up to our promises. The job of editor for such a series is in many ways a difficult and thankless one, entailing hard and time-consuming detailed work on the one hand, and sustained intellectual guidance on the other. The grace, skill, and tenacity with which they labored in this feminist vineyard was very much appreciated.

Judith E. Tucker

GLOSSARY

B.C.E.: "Before the common era." Used in place of B.C.

Bridewealth: Gift from the groom to the bride's parents. Sometimes called "brideprice."

C.E.: "Of the common era." Used in place of A.D.

Chador: A long, black outer garment draped to cover a woman from head to ankles (but not her face), worn primarily in Iran.

En: High priestess.

Fiqh: Islamic jurisprudence.

Gedik: A license authorizing its holder to practice a particular urban trade, often retained within families through inheritance.

Hadith: The traditions of the Prophet Muhammad; cf. *sunnah.*

Harem: The separate women's quarters of a household.

Mahr: The money and/or goods given to the bride by the groom, which are required by Islamic law.

Matrilocal: Societies in which a married couple lives with or near the wife's family.

Matrilineal: Societies in which descent is traced through the mother.

Patrilineal: Societies in which descent is traced through the father.

Patrilocal: Societies in which a married couple lives with or near the husband's family.

Polygamy: The practice of having two or more spouses at the same time.

Polygyny: The practice of having two or more wives at the same time.

Shari'ah: The revealed or canonical law in Islam. Literally, "path."

Sufism: The mystical tradition within Islam.

Sunnah: The sayings and doings of the Prophet Muhammad, later established as legally binding precedents.

Talaq: One form of Islamic divorce, unilateral repudiation by the husband.

Tariqah **(pl. *turuq*):** A Sufi order; a religious fraternity whose members practice Sufism, or the mystical tradition within Islam.

Valide sultan: The mother of the reigning Ottoman Sultan.

Waqf **(pl. *awqaf*):** A religious endowment; private property entailed for religious or charitable purposes.

MAPS

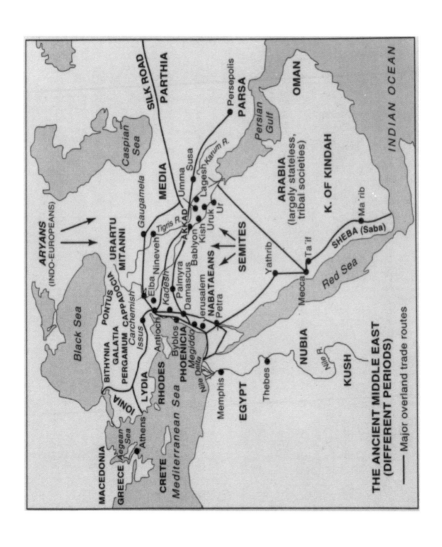

THE ANCIENT MIDDLE EAST
(DIFFERENT PERIODS)
—— Major overland trade routes

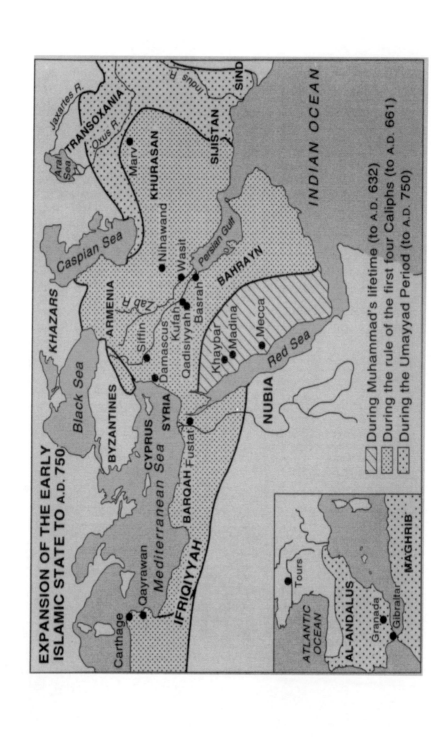

EXPANSION OF THE EARLY ISLAMIC STATE TO A.D. 750

During Muhammad's lifetime (to A.D. 632)

During the rule of the first four Caliphs (to A.D. 661)

During the Umayyad Period (to A.D. 750)

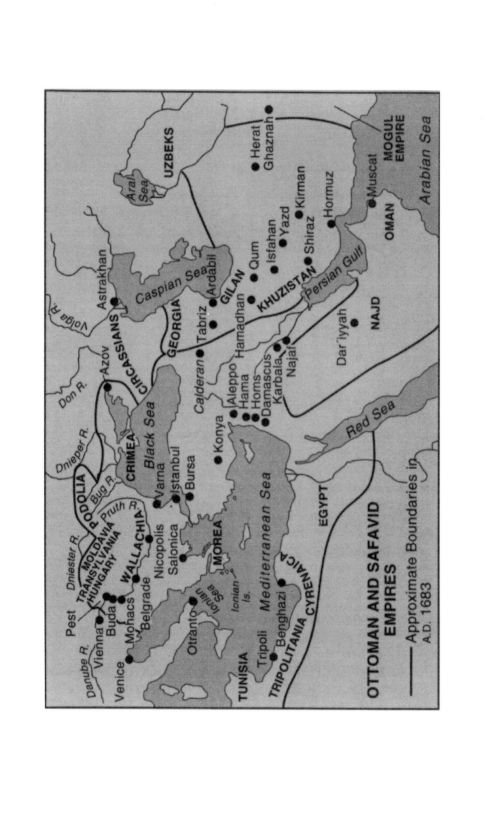

OTTOMAN AND SAFAVID
EMPIRES

—— Approximate Boundaries in
A.D. 1683

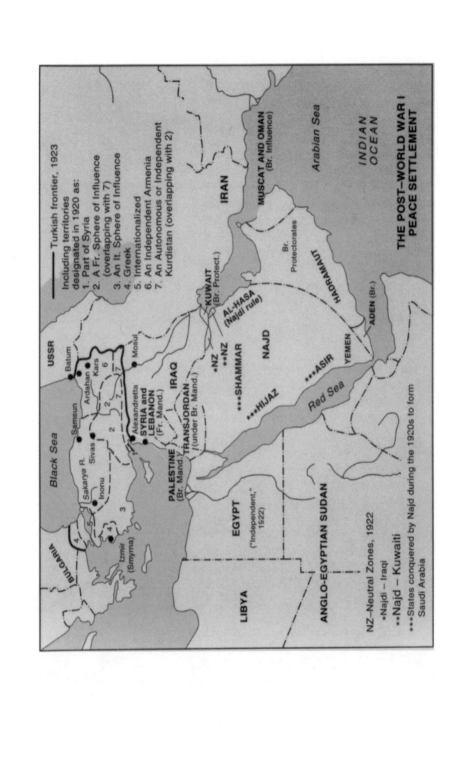

THE POST–WORLD WAR I
PEACE SETTLEMENT

Turkish frontier, 1923

Including territories
designated in 1920 as:
1. Part of Syria
2. A Fr. Sphere of Influence
   (overlapping with 7)
3. An It. Sphere of Influence
4. Greek
5. Internationalized
6. An Independent Armenia
7. An Autonomous or Independent
   Kurdistan (overlapping with 2)

NZ–Neutral Zones, 1922
*NZ–Najdi – Iraqi
**NZ–Najd – Kuwaiti
***States conquered by Najd during the 1920s to form
Saudi Arabia

Black Sea

USSR

BULGARIA

Izmir
(Smyrna)

Samsun

Sakarya R.

Sivas

Inonu

Ardahan

Kars

Batum

Mosul

Alexandretta

SYRIA and
LEBANON
(Fr. Mand.)

PALESTINE
(Br. Mand.)

TRANSJORDAN
(under Br. Mand.)

IRAQ

KUWAIT
(Br. Protect.)

AL-HASA
(Najdi rule)

*NZ
**NZ

SHAMMAR

NAJD

HIJAZ

ASIR

YEMEN

ADEN (Br.)

Red Sea

IRAN

MUSCAT AND OMAN
(Br. Influence)

Br.
Protectorates

HADRAMAUT

Arabian Sea

INDIAN
OCEAN

EGYPT
("Independent,"
1922)

LIBYA

ANGLO-EGYPTIAN SUDAN

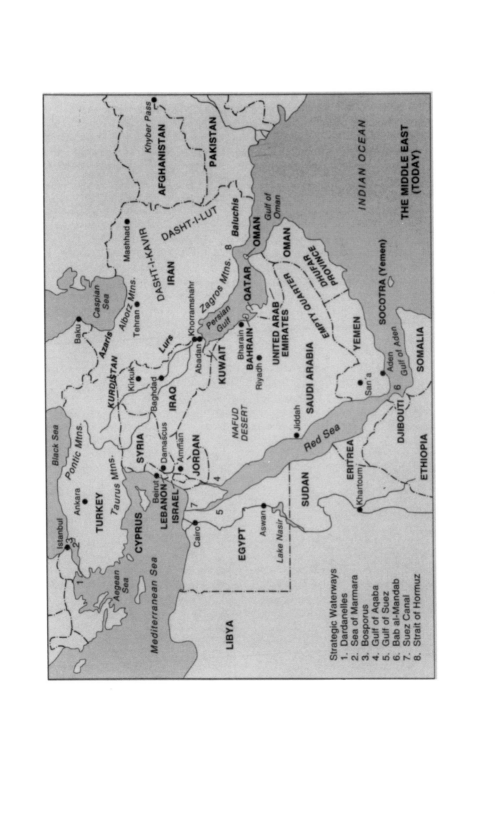

THE MIDDLE EAST
(TODAY)

Strategic Waterways
1. Dardanelles
2. Sea of Marmara
3. Bosporus
4. Gulf of Aqaba
5. Gulf of Suez
6. Bab al-Mandab
7. Suez Canal
8. Strait of Hormuz

CHRONOLOGY

632 to 661	Conquest of the Middle East by Arabian Muslims; rule of the righteous caliphs (four of Muhammad's major companions).
661 to 750	Emergence of the Arab Kingdom under the Umayyads; shift of political power from Medina to Damascus in Syria.
750 to 950	Emergence of the Abbasid empire; shift of capital from Damascus to Baghdad; conversion of the majority of the non-Arabian population of the Middle East to Islam; development of the *shari'ah*; spread of the veil and seclusion of women in urban areas.
950 to 1258	The beginning of Turkish tribal incursion into the Middle East; political fragmentation of the Abbasid empire; great flowering of Islamic civilization; downfall of the Abbasids (1258); rise of the Mongol-Ilkhanid state.
1258 to 1798	Rise of various Turco-Mongolian dynasties in the Middle East: the Mamluks in Egypt (1250), the Ottoman state (1299) in Anatolia; Ottoman conquest of Constantinople (1453) renamed Istanbul; the founding of the Safavid state (1500); Ottoman conquest of Egypt (1517); shift in the balance of power between the Muslim powers (Ottomans and Safavids) and Western European states; Napoleon's conquest of Egypt (1798).
1790 to 1870	The rise of European power and reforming governments.
1792–93	Ottoman Sultan Selim III institutes the *nizam-i-jedid*.
1794	Qajar dynasty in Iran established in Iran.
1798	Napoleon occupies Egypt.
1805–49	Muhammad 'Ali undertakes reform program in Egypt.
1814	British treaty with Iran, promising protection from Russia.
1821–29	Greek war for independence from the Ottoman Empire.
1826	Ottoman Sultan Mahmud II destroys the Janissaries.
1830	France occupies Algeria.
1838	Anglo-Ottoman commercial convention signed.
1838–61	Ottoman Empire undertakes reform movement called the *Tanzimat*.
1848–96	Reign of Nasir al-Din Shah in Iran.
1856–57	Anglo-Persian War.
1869	Opening of the Suez Canal.

1870 to 1900   European imperialism and revolt.

1871   Algerian uprising against French rule.

1881   ʿUrabi Revolt in Egypt.

1881–89   The Mahdi gains power in Sudan and leads revolt against Anglo-Egyptian forces.

1881   French protectorate established in Tunisia.

1882   Britain occupies Egypt.

1892   Tobacco strike in Iran.

1900 to 1917   Local elites press for independence.

1901–53   Reign of Ibn Saʿud, initially in Najd, later Saudi Arabia.

1906   Iranian revolution results in promulgation of constitution.

1909–11   Young Turk, Young Tunisian, and Young Algerian movements press for independence.

1914   Ottomans enter World War I on German side.

1916–17   Arab revolt against Ottoman Empire.

1917 to 1939   Renewed European domination.

1922   Declaration of Turkish Republic; League of Nations approves British mandate in Palestine and Egypt, French mandate in Syria and Lebanon.

1923–38   Presidency of Kemal Ataturk in Turkey.

1925–41   Reign of Reza Shah Pahlavi in Iran.

1940 to 1966   Independence and political transformation.

1945   Arab League formed; United Nations formed.

1947–48   War in Palestine and declaration of the state of Israel.

1952   Free Officer coup in Egypt topples monarchy.

1953   Overthrow of Mossadeq government in Iran with assistance from the United States.

1954–62   Algerian War of Independence.

1956   Suez crisis: Britain, France, and Israel attack Egypt.

1967 to 1995   Regional conflicts in global context.

1967   Israel defeats Arab states in the Six-Day War.

1973   War between an Egypt–Syria alliance and Israel.

1975–90   Civil war in Lebanon.

1979   Egyptian–Israeli Treaty signed.

1979   Iranian Revolution; overthrow of the Shah.

1979–88   Iran–Iraq War.

1987–92   The uprising, *intifada*, among Palestinians in the West Bank and Gaza.

1991   The Gulf War: the United States and its allies force an Iraqi withdrawal from Kuwait.

1993   Oslo Accords signed between Israel and the Palestine Liberation Organization.

SERIES EDITORS' INTRODUCTION

Conceptualizing the History of Women in Africa, Asia, Latin America and the Caribbean, and the Middle East and North Africa

CHERYL JOHNSON-ODIM AND MARGARET STROBEL

In this thematic overview* we hope to do, with beneficial results, what historians are loath to do: dispense with chronology and introduce several themes common to the histories of women in the "non-Western" world. A thematic focus will accomplish several purposes. First, we can discuss the significance of phenomena—for example, the existence of female networks and subcultures—so that the authors' references to such phenomena are given a broader context than the sometimes-scant evidence allows. Second, we can introduce and synthesize approaches and ideas found in feminist scholarship. Third, because regions often develop distinctive sets of research questions and ignore others, our overview may suggest new areas of exploration. Finally, we can suggest possibilities for comparative investigation.

We cannot here do justice to the specificity of the historical tradition in each region; readers may use the indexes of relevant volumes to locate elaborations on the examples cited below. Our themes highlight the similarities in women's experience across these very diverse regions, but the differences, not dealt with here, are equally crucial.

---

*An earlier version of this essay appeared in the *Journal of Women's History* 1, no. 1 (Spring 1989): 31–62.

The intellectual justification for addressing these four regions together rests on the assertion that most of these areas have experienced broadly comparable relationships with Western Europe and the United States in the past five hundred years. Although these volumes examine the long eras in each regional area before the last five hundred years, it is because of their histories of the last five hundred years that they are broadly viewed in the United States as "Third World," or "non-Western." We understand the need to problematize viewing *most* of the world's people, in all their diversity, in such "catch-all" categories and do not mean to claim the commonality of their relationship(s) with the West as the only reason for their appearance here.

It was difficult to decide on a common terminology that allowed us to keep from constantly listing the regions under consideration. "Third World" (despite some controversy) was often appropriate as a geopolitical designation, but it left out places such as Japan that are not generally regarded as Third World due to a high degree of industrialization. "Non-western" also seemed appropriate, except that after many centuries of contact, Latin American societies cannot legitimately be regarded as entirely non-western. Although we prefer not to refer to people by a negative term such as "non-Western" and are aware that terms such as "Third World" are problematic, we ended up employing both terms despite sometimes imperfect usage, in addition to the cumbersome listing of all four geographic regions.

A final word about terminology: we distinguish between "sex" as a set of biological (physiological) differences and "gender" as socially constructed roles that may build upon or ignore biological sex. Hence, in place of the common term "sex roles," in this text, we will instead use "gender roles."

THE CHALLENGE OF THIRD WORLD WOMEN'S HISTORY

It is important to avoid three common pitfalls: interpreting women as the exotic, women as victims, and women as anomalies. Stereotypes regarding the non-western world (particularly those labeling it as "primitive," "backward," or "barbaric") are very prevalent in our society and frequently provide the only knowledge many North Americans have about other cultures. The roles, positions, and statuses of women in non-western societies are often as central to those stereotypes today as they were when European colonizers first pointed to women's "oppression" in Africa, Asia, Latin America and the Caribbean, and the Middle East and North Africa as partial justification for their own imperialist designs. "Brideprice," women as "beasts of burden" and female genital mutilation (FGM) in Africa, *sati* and foot-binding in Asia, *machismo* in Latin America, female hypersexuality in the Caribbean, and the harem and seclusion of women in the Middle East frequently represent the extent of the Western public's exposure to the lives of women in these regions. It is in fact such images of women that help fuel our pictures of these societies as exotic. Feminist historians challenge this notion of the female exotic by placing cultural practices in an appropriate sociocultural framework and by looking at a multitude of women's activities over the broad scope of their lives.

Women, just because they are women, have undeniably been disadvantaged in their access to political and economic power. Where the fact of being a woman intersected with belonging to a racial, ethnic, religious, or other minority, or with poverty or lower-class status, women could be doubly or triply disadvantaged. But women have never been a monolithic group even within the same society; class, race, and/or ethnicity could have consequences as significant for women's opportunity and status as did (does) gender. Women's history, however, is not primarily a history of disadvantage and degradation. Such a "victim analysis" fails to present a picture of the variety of women's multiple statuses and relationships (including those with other women), the dynamism and creativity of their activities, and their importance in various cultures.

Women's agency and initiative, as well as their subordination, must therefore be explored. Integrating the histories of women in Africa, Asia, Latin America and the Caribbean, and the Middle East and North Africa in part poses the same challenge as that of European and U.S. women's history: the expansion and transformation of conceptual categories that, in explaining male, rather than integrated, human experience, have treated women as anomalies. For example, political history has tended to focus on activity in the public sphere and on office holders, both of which highlight male experience. The evidence demonstrates that women also have exercised power. Historically, however, it was most often within gender-segregated settings that ordinary women were able to exercise their greatest degree of power and decision-making. And, when they acted collectively, women could exercise considerable power even within male-dominated societies. Individual women—for example, Eva Perón—were often important political actors and exerted influence, both inside and outside of formal political structures. Because women's political participation did not always appear in obvious places or ways, it has been regarded as peripheral or absent, a view that ignores the complex processes through which power is exerted in societies. An investigation of gender relationships can add a critical element of analysis to our scrutiny of history and to definitions and explanations of the operation of political power and the conceptual category of political activity.

In addition to challenging definitions of what constitutes political history, the study of women can reveal important insights into the study of an entire region. For example, if one looks at the actual impact of Confucianism on women's lives in East Asia, the system of teachings becomes a much less monolithic historical force than it has hitherto been considered.

Similarly, looking at gender clarifies our understanding of Latin American society. Scholars have long studied the development of racial division there, yet gender and class were central to that development in several ways. Sex both opened and closed racial barriers: sexual activity across racial lines was legitimized through the practice of concubinage and was sanctioned because of the unequal sex ratios among the colonizers. But concubinage, while protecting status differences between the colonizers and the colonized, also resulted in a mestizo and mulatto population whose existence undermined racial barriers. Thus the control of (female) sexuality was linked to the control of racial purity.

In the Middle East, aspects of women's position that are at the core of historical and contemporary Islamic society (e.g., seclusion and veiling) have their roots in pre-Islamic practices. Hence, Islam can be seen not only to have introduced important changes in the Middle East, but also to have built upon existing practices; the introduction of Islam does not mark as sharp a break as some scholars have claimed.

In the study of Africa, the recent emphasis on examining gender has transformed our understanding of the Atlantic slave trade, a topic of longstanding importance in African historiography. Scholars had noted that African males outnumbered females on the Middle Passage, but why this was the case received little attention. As scholars began to problematize gender roles within Africa—and noted the extraordinary role women played in agriculture—some came to view the Atlantic slave trade as being partially shaped by the desire of African slave-owning societies to accumulate female labor.

The act of including women in the histories of these regions represents a more profound challenge than the "add women and stir" approach, as it has often been identified. The mere insertion of famous women, like the insertion of only "exotic" and hurtful practices, gives a distorted and inadequate history of the bulk of women's experience in a given society.

Just as adding information about women challenges the existing histories of Africa, Asia, Latin America and the Caribbean, and the Middle East and North Africa, so too does adding information about women from these regions challenge the writing of women's history. Because the oppression of Third World women is the result of both internal sexism and externally induced dynamics (e.g., mercantile capitalism, colonialism, neo-colonialism), being citizens of the Third World is as crucial as gender. Therefore, studying women in the Third World means studying not only a less powerful category within society, but also a category within societies that have often been dominated in the international arena. Thus, some things that oppress(ed) women also oppress men (slavery, indentured labor, alienation of land from indigenous owners or conversion of land to cash crop production, export of raw natural resources and import of finished products made from those resources and even of food), though often in different ways. And many issues that are not obviously gender-related, such as lack of self-sufficiency in producing staple foods and provision of water, bear their heaviest impact on women who are disproportionately charged with providing food and water.

Finding women in the histories of the non-western, just as in the Western, world requires persistence due to the silence or obliqueness of "traditional" historical sources such as documents written by historical actors themselves. The roles of women in agriculture, health, crafts, religion, politics, the arts, and other arenas have often been regarded as negligible, exceptional and infrequent, or irretrievable for other than the very recent period. However, far more is available than one may think; much of it lies hidden in non-obvious sources: oral testimony, mythology, life histories, genealogies, religious records, missionary and explorer accounts, archaeological excavations, language, legal codes, land tenure arrangements, oral and written literature, or cultural lore and fable. For women's histories, case studies often come after the general treatise, which frequently concentrates as much on exposing the lacunae and generating hypotheses as on synthesis. The historical literature on women in Africa, Asia, Latin America and the Caribbean, and the Middle East and North Africa has greatly increased in the years since these essays were first published, and that has led to their revision. Still, a great deal remains to be done. These general overviews are meant to acquaint scholars with the possibilities as much as to show what has been done.

THEORIES THAT EXPLAIN THE
SUBORDINATE STATUS OF WOMEN

Trained to look to the specifics of place and time more than to the creation of theory, historians have often left to anthropologists the task of theorizing about the origins of women's oppression or the factors that account for women's subordinate status. One basic division runs between biologically oriented and socioculturally oriented theories. The former finds significance in a relative universality of physical characteristics among humans and of a gender division of labor that assigns men to certain tasks and women to others, a division that sometimes characterizes the public sphere as a male domain and the private sphere as a female domain. This commonality is attributed to genetic or physical differences.

Environmentalists stress the equally apparent diversity of humans, physically and culturally, and claim that biology alone cannot cause this diversity. Moreover, they view "natural" features of society as fundamentally culturally and ideologically determined. Even childbirth and lactation, they argue, do not predestine women to stay at home; rather, societies can devise a division of labor that enables such women to be mobile.

Embedded in these positions are views about the appropriateness of men's and women's roles. Biologically oriented theories tend to assume that gender differences are best not tampered with. Sociocultural theories tend to see the pattern of women's subordination as subject to change; thus, the search for the causes of women's oppression becomes linked to the possibility of creating gender-equal societies. If the universality of women's subordinate status can be proved untrue, then the possibilities of creating gender-equal societies are strengthened; hence, some scholarship focuses on the search for matriarchies, or for gender-equal societies, past or present. While most scholars find evidence lacking, the discussions of matriarchy and gender-neutral societies have raised important questions about the relationship between the actual power of living women in a particular society and (a) kinship and residence patterns (e.g., matrilineality and matrilocality), (b) social structure and mode of production (e.g., patriarchy, pre-industrial), or (c) the ideological representations of women in art, ritual, or belief systems.

Another approach to the issue of the causes of women's oppression links women's power or lack of it to economic forces. Research in this area has generated questions about the link between gender inequality and levels of production or technology, class formation, women's and men's control of the products of their labor, etc. Furthermore, these theorists dispute the universality of the notions of public and private, arguing that these categories follow historically from the development of industrial(izing) societies. In the modern period discussion of women's oppression in postcolonial Third World countries must take into account the effects of colonialism and neo-colonialism on the construction of gender. In several places colonialism and neo-colonialism marginalized women in the economy, displaced them politically, cooperated with indigenous males to keep women socially subordinated, or increased the social subordination of women themselves.

Feminism challenges both European colonial and indigenous patriarchal ideologies regarding women. The relationship between Western and non-western feminist thought has often, however, been adversarial. In part the tension between the two groups results from the explanation given for the oppression of women. Many non-Western women (even those who identify themselves as feminists) object to Western feminist theories that posit men as the primary source of oppression. Recently this debate has generated theories that focus on the interrelationship of multiple forms of oppression, such as race, class, imperialism, and gender.

THE INADEQUACIES OF THE CONCEPTS
OF TRADITIONAL AND MODERN

The concepts of "traditional" and "modern" are often both ahistorical and value-laden. It may be legitimate to talk about ways people have done/do things "traditionally" (evolving at some unspecified time in the past) or in the "modern" way (coming into use relatively recently). However, for Africa, Asia, Latin America and the Caribbean, and the Middle East and North Africa, often the term "traditional" describes everything in the long eras before European intervention, and the term "modern" describes those phenomena following European intervention. This establishes a false dichotomy, with all things indigenous being "traditional" and all things Western being "modern." This usage often implies that the traditional is static and the modern, dynamic; it fails to portray and analyze each regional history within the context of its own internal dynamics, in which encounters with the West prove to be only one element among many. Such a view also obscures the fact that most societies were not isolated and had contact with other peoples before Western contact, that they are not homogeneous, and that several traditions often co-exist (to more or less peaceful degrees) within the same society or nation-state.

Sometimes this ahistoricity results from equating "modernization" with higher levels of technology; sometimes it is cultural arrogance and implicitly defines "modern/western" as somehow better. Since colonialist ideology in Africa, Asia, and the Middle East often used indigenous "oppression" of women as a justification for intervention in these societies, colonizers promoted the belief that the arrival of Western civilization would improve women's lives. For example, in India in the early nineteenth century, one of the central arguments British officials employed to legitimate political control based on the use of military force was that British policies would "improve" the status of Indian women. Thus the colonizers made women central to the politics of colonialism.

The study of the lives of Third World women, in fact, challenges the legitimacy of the notion of a strict dichotomy between traditional and modern. Women's lives, especially, show that traditional cultures in these regions are not static, monolithic, or more misogynist than Western culture, and that there is no automatic linear progress made in the quality of women's lives by following a Western pattern of development. Regional studies provide evidence that the "traditional" ways of doing things, especially in the political and economic arenas, were often less inimical to women's collective interests than the "modernization" that colonialism purported to export.

The concept of tradition has also sometimes been used as a rallying point in anti-colonial liberation struggles. That is, by conceptualizing their struggle against European domination in "anti-western culture" terms, various peoples have politicized the return to tradition as a liberating strategy. Because this "return to tradition" was often formulated during eras of high colonialism, when the promotion of Western culture was inseparable from the colonial presence, women were as central to the vision of tradition that emerged as they were to justifications for colonialism. Even after the colonial presence was gone, Western culture still symbolized continuing economic dominance. Gandhi claimed that women's superior ability at self-sacrifice made them better practitioners of *satyagraha* or non-violent resistance. In response to French cultural imperialism, wearing the veil became a political act of resistance in Algeria. Similarly, veiling became identified with opposition to Western influence and to the

Shah in Iran. In the 1970s, Mobutu Sese Seko of Zaire (now the Democratic Republic of the Congo) constructed his policy of *authenticité*, a major tenet of which was a return to the "traditional" value of women as mothers and housekeepers who obeyed male relatives. These are but a few examples that show women have often been on the losing end of a return to tradition—a "tradition" misused by ideologies of both colonialism and liberation. A view of culture as dynamic, as well as a better understanding of women's roles in the pre-European-contact periods, can help demythologize the concept of tradition.

RELIGION

Religion has been a source of power for women, or a source of subordination, or both.

Religious authorities have often functioned as politically powerful figures. In Inka society, women played important roles in the religious structure, even though male priests held religious and political power. As virgins, or *aqlla,* they were dedicated as "wives of the Sun" to prepare an alcoholic beverage for religious rituals and officiate at the same. Even in less-stratified societies of a much smaller scale, indeed perhaps more often in these societies, women acted as religious/political leaders. Charwe, a medium of the spirit Nehanda, led resistance to British colonialism in late-nineteenth-century southern Rhodesia. In the eighteenth century, the legendary Nanny drew upon her mediating relationship with ancestral spirits in leading her maroon community in Jamaica. Even where they did not hold religious office, women exercised power through religion: in peasant and nomadic regions of the Middle East, women continued, into the twentieth century, to control popular religious activities and thus to exert influence through their intercession with the supernatural.

Religious beliefs may point to the equality of women as sacred beings or the importance of female life force. Female clay figurines suggest the worship of female deities in Egypt around 3000 B.C.E., but we can infer little about the lives of women in general. Full-breasted female figurines, presumed to be fertility goddesses, are associated with the Indus Valley in South Asia around 2000 B.C.E. Aztec religion embodied many goddesses associated with fertility, healing, and agriculture. The presence of such goddesses did not signal a society of gender equality but rather one of gender complementarity, as in the Inka case. One of the largest temples in Ancient Sumer, at Ur, was headed by the priestess Enheduanna, who was also a renowned poet and writer.

On the other hand, religious beliefs may both reflect and reinforce the subordination of women. Women in many religious traditions are seen as polluting, particularly because of those bodily functions surrounding menstruation or childbirth. In West Africa, Akan fear of menstruating women limited even elite women's activities: the *asantehemaa*, the highest female office, could be held only by a post-menopausal woman from the appropriate lineage. Even though such beliefs may ultimately derive from women's power as procreators, women's status as polluting persons can restrict their activities and power. Moreover, traditions that stress the importance of male children to carry out ancestral rituals—for example, those in Confucianism—contribute to the negative valuation of female children and women. Other customs repressive and/or unhealthy to women—for example, *sati*, ritual suicide by widows—are sanctioned by religion. Finally, the traditions of Christianity, Confucianism, Hinduism, Islam, and Judaism all legitimate male authority, particularly patriarchal familial authority, over women: Christianity through biblical exhortation to wifely obedience, Confucianism in the three obediences, Hinduism in the Laws of Manu, Islam in the Qur'an's injunction regarding wifely obedience, and Judaism in the Halakhah Laws.

However much these traditions carry profound gender inequalities in theology and in office, these same traditions spawn groupings that attract women (and other lower-status people). In India, the Gupta period, in which the Laws of Manu increased restrictions on Indian women, also witnessed the rise of Saktism, a cult derived from pre-Aryan traditions that envision the divine as feminine. In this set of beliefs, the female divinity appears in three major incarnations: Devi, the Mother goddess; Durga, the unmarried and potentially dangerous woman; and Kali, the goddess of destruction. Subsequently, in the Mughal period in South Asia, women in search of help with fertility or other psychological problems flocked to devotional Hinduism, becoming followers of *bhakti* saints, and to Muslim Sufi holy men. Women in the Middle East and in Muslim parts of Africa were also attracted to these mystical Sufi orders, which stressed direct union with Allah and believed there were no differences between men and women in their ability to reach God. Among syncretic Christian offshoots in Africa, women play much more central, albeit often expressive, roles.

SEXUALITY AND REPRODUCTION

Many theories about the origins of the oppression of women see control of female sexuality and the reproductive process (or female procreative power) as central. For this reason, it is useful to examine basic questions, if not patterns, in societies' construction of female sexuality. Just as gender is socially constructed, so too is sexuality—that is, which sexual practices (and with whom) were considered socially acceptable and which were considered deviant are specific to time and place, and often contested. Scholarship on homosexuality, for instance, is in its infancy in many of these histories, particularly that regarding lesbianism. Some scholars, though, posit the harem or *zenana* as a site of lesbian relationships.

Throughout history, societies have generated ideological systems that link female identity to female sexuality, and female sexuality to women's role in procreation. Thus one reason for controlling women's sexuality was to control their role in procreation. Women were aware of their important role in the procreative process, and sometimes used such sexual symbolism as a power play. African women on several occasions utilized sexual symbolism to protest threats to themselves as women. For example, in the Women's War of 1929, Nigerian women challenged the offending officials to impregnate each of them, drawing upon an indigenous technique to humiliate men: they were protesting men's right to interfere in women's economic power and thus women's obligations as wives and mothers. In 1922, Kenyan women, by exposing their buttocks at a public protest of colonial officials' actions, challenged their male colleagues to behave more "like men," that is, more bravely.

Religions project varied views of female sexuality. Islam acknowledges women's sexual pleasure, as it does men's, while advocating that it be channeled into marriage. In contrast, the Mahayana Buddhist views female sexuality as a threat to culture. In this religious group, women have been associated with bondage, suffering, and desire; female sexuality, then, is to be controlled by transcendence (or by motherhood).

Often the control of female sexuality and reproduction is linked to concerns about purity. The Aryan notion of purity was reflected throughout Hindu ritual and beliefs, but in particular it provided the impetus for early marriage and for *sati*. Colonial constraints upon Spanish women's behavior in the New World derived from the elite's desire to maintain "blood purity."

Expressed through virginity and chastity, in several cultural traditions a woman's purity had implications for her family. A Muslim woman's behavior affected her family's honor, for example, resulting in the ultimate penalty of death for adultery. Infibulation (briefly, the sewing together of the labia and one form of female genital surgery), found in both Muslim and non-Muslim areas, is commonly associated with virginity and the control of female sexuality. Although virginity was of little consequence in Inka society, adultery on the part of noblewomen was punishable by death. In seventeenth-century China, chastity was raised to a symbolic level not found in Japan or Korea. The 1646 Manchu rape law required women to resist rape to the point of death or serious injury; otherwise, they were considered to have participated in illicit intercourse.

The point here is not to list the multitude of ways in which women have been unfairly treated, but to understand the cultural construction of female sexuality. These examples, all drawn from religious traditions or the ideological systems of states, highlight the control of female sexuality. But the earlier African examples remind us that sexuality and sexual symbolism, like all cultural phenomena, are a terrain of struggle, to be manipulated by women as well as used against them. In their critique of Japanese society, the Bluestockings, a group of literary feminists in early twentieth-century Japan, saw sexual freedom as an integral aspect of women's rights.

Societies have sought to control men's sexual access to females through a combination of beliefs, laws, customs, and coercion. At times men enforced these sexual rules; at other times women policed themselves as individuals or curtailed the activities of other women—peers, younger women, daughters-in-law. Male control of sexual access to females has sometimes been a violent assault upon women, such as in enforced prostitution or rapes associated with wars. During the conquest of the Americas, for instance, Amerindian women were raped, branded, and viewed in general as the spoils of war. Also, enslaved women were often the sexual prey of their male owners, valued as both productive and reproductive laborers. Sexual tourism in the twentieth century, particularly in Asian and Pacific regions, exploits young girls primarily for the benefit of expatriate "tourists."

Concubinage, another institutionalized method of controlling female sexuality, existed in all the regions covered in this survey. Concubinage legitimated a man's sexual access to more than one woman outside of marriage. Although it clearly represented a double standard, concubinage as an institution offered certain protections or benefits to women. In the New World some Amerindian women gained substantial wealth and status as concubines; in addition, slave concubines might be manumitted at their owner's death and their children legitimized. Similarly, Islamic slave owners manumitted some concubines, encouraged by the belief that such action was rewarded by God. The protections offered by the institution of concubinage, albeit within a grossly unequal relationship, were lost with its abolition, and compensating institutions did not always replace concubinage. Hence, abolition in parts of Africa left poorer women, former concubines, without the legal rights of wives or concubines but still dependent financially. In contemporary Africa, women who in the past might have become concubines because of their economic or social vulnerability might today have children outside of formal marriage without the previous assurance that their children will be supported financially by the fathers.

Historically, prostitution has occurred under a variety of conditions that reflect different degrees of control of female sexuality. Prostitution may be seen as a strategy for a family's survival: impoverished Chinese families in the nineteenth century sold their daughters as prostitutes in the cities to earn money. Elsewhere in Asia, prostitutes functioned as part of larger institutions, or even imperial expansion. Hindu *devadasi,* or temple dancers, served as prostitutes tied to temples. In the nineteenth century the British, in an attempt to limit military expenditures, provided prostitutes rather than wives for non-commissioned British troops in India. During the period of imperial expansion in the 1930s, Japanese prostitutes were sent to service brothels in outposts of the empire, a process described in the film *Sandakan No. 8* (Brothel Number 9). Under these circumstances, prostitution did not mean increased autonomy for women, whether or not it provided subsistence.

In some places and times, however, prostitution has offered an alternative of increased autonomy. New colonial towns in Africa created spaces for women to escape from abusive or unwanted marriages. There, operating as entrepreneurs rather than under the supervision of pimps or other authorities, they supported themselves and their children by selling sexual and other domestic services to men, who frequently were migrant laborers. In addition, prostitutes were able to keep their children, an option that was not available to women in patrilineal marriages, where offspring belonged to the husband's patrilineage and were lost to a woman who divorced or absconded. Even under circumstances in which prostitutes had more control over their sexuality and their lives, it is important not to romanticize prostitution. It has been, and remains, an option for some women within a context of gender and class oppression.

The production of offspring (especially male offspring in strongly patrilineal societies) is often a measure of a woman's value. In some

African societies, this value is represented by bridewealth, the gifts that a groom must give to the bride's family in order to obtain rights to the offspring in a patrilineal society. The production of male offspring is essential for some religious rituals, for example, in Confucianism.

We have little historical information about control of reproduction. But even prior to the recent rise of reproductive technology, women found ways to limit birth. For example, in Congo in the late nineteenth century, slave women limited the number of children they had. In the complex conditions created by the internal African slave trade, slave women saw few advantages to producing children who belonged to their owners and who could not be expected to care for their mothers in old age. Advances in reproductive technology such as amniocentesis, which project the sex of an embryo or fetus, have sometimes been used to select male children and abort female children.

Recently, with the advent of population control programs adopted by nation-states and promoted by international agencies, control of reproduction has shifted away from individually initiated actions to highly bureaucratized operations. In that shift, the balance has slipped from birth control, which empowers women by giving them options, to population control, which regulates female reproduction in the interests of a nation-state or a donor country. Women may be encouraged or coerced to have babies for the nation, or the revolution, or conversely they may be manipulated or coerced into limiting childbirth. Stringent population policies were introduced in India, prompting protests by women's groups, and in China, where urban couples recently have been allowed to have only one child. In Puerto Rico one-third of the women of childbearing age were sterilized by the 1960s in one of the early attempts at widespread population control following policies initiated by the U.S. government. The white regime in South Africa promoted "birth control" among blacks as part of the larger plan of apartheid. In none of these population policies does birth control unambiguously empower women, since the elements of choice and safety have been compromised.

HOUSEHOLD RELATIONS

Household relationships are at the heart of most societies, since families act as the primary culture-bearing unit. In pre-industrial societies the family is also an important economic unit. Indeed, the way that families are organized is linked as much to the relations of production as to culture. Among other factors, a sedentary, nomadic, or hunting-and-gathering lifestyle, sex ratios, or the availability of land can affect family organization—and all of these factors also help determine the relations of production and culture. With few exceptions (Japan, for instance), the areas under discussion are still in the process of industrializing. Even while allowing for different levels of industrialization and cultural specificity, we can make some general observations.

In the Third World, historically and presently, domestic relationships have involved far more people than a nuclear family. The family most often functionally (not just emotionally) encompassed a wide range of relatives, including grandparents, parents, children, brothers and sisters, cousins, aunts and uncles, etc. Even when these people do not all inhabit the same household or compound, the sense of communal responsibility, obligation, and authority is wide-ranging and strongly felt and encouraged. The importance of the individual, as a general value, has been subordinated to that of the collective. Thus, domestic relationships and decision-making even between a husband and wife and their own children are often influenced by a wide variety of individuals and situations. Issues of polygyny, birth control, sexual conduct, education, allocation of economic resources, and so on are often group decisions, with elders frequently carrying more weight than younger members. The authority of a wide group of people who know about and sanction or approve behavior is accepted. Increasingly, however, factors such as class, personal mobility, and the proliferation of ideas about greater individual freedom are beginning to disrupt this pattern.

Historically, marriage was an important alliance that could not be viewed as a relationship between individuals, but between two kin groups, because the family was a primary unit for economic production and the concentration of wealth, for the allocation and legitimation of political power, and for conflict resolution. Consequently, marriages were often arranged for both women and men by other family members or by marriage brokers. Among the Aztecs, for instance, marriages were arranged by a go-between known as a *cihuatlanque*. Among the Spanish and Portuguese in Latin America, however (until 1776 when the Crown enacted new laws requiring parental consent for marriage), so long as a girl was twelve and a boy fourteen they could marry without such consent. Still, marriage was generally seen as an alliance between families by both the Spanish and the Portuguese, especially by those of the upper classes, where property was at stake and marriage between relatives was common. In the nineteenth-century Middle East, families exercised close control over marriage arrangements, and first-cousin marriage was commonly used as a method for ensuring political alliances and centralizing wealth. Arranged marriages seem to have held less importance for the poor, however, reflecting less wealth to protect and perhaps even the need to decrease the number of dependent kin. In Africa, also, arranged marriages were a prevalent means of ensuring the continuity of the transfer of resources. As men undertook wage labor their ability to pay their own bridewealth and hence arrange their own marriages increased, but rarely would this have been done over family objections to choice of a mate.

Gifts passed between families (and still do in many places) and between the bride and groom at the time of marriage. Dowry was brought by a bride to her marital home, and other transfers, such as bridewealth or brideservice, went from the groom (or his family) to the bride's family. The degree of access to and control over these gifts exercised by a bride varied greatly among the societies discussed here.

The institution of dowry served an important economic as well as social function. The dowry (or *dote*) was not a requirement for marriage among the Spanish and Portuguese in Latin America, but it served as a way of both compensating a husband for assuming the economic burden of a wife as well as providing a woman with some economic independence. Though it was administered by a husband, it remained the property of the wife and could not be alienated without her consent. If the husband mismanaged the dowry, a woman could petition in court to control it herself, and in the case of divorce, the dowry had to be repaid. In the case of the wife's death, however, the dowry was either divided among the children or returned to the wife's parents. In India, dowry encompassed both *stridhan*, which was usually jewelry and clothing belonging to the bride alone, and a broad array of household goods and other valuables that were gifts to the couple and to the groom's family, with whom they lived.

In various societies, wealth moved in the reverse direction, from the groom and his kin to the bride and hers. The system of bridewealth found in Africa was generally a gift from a man to the parents of his bride and signified their compensation for the loss of their daughter as well as his rights to the children of the marriage and, to varying extents, her labor. Among matrilineal peoples in Central Africa, a groom had to perform brideservice, (that is, labor in the bride's family's fields). Forms of bridewealth varied (including cloth, beads, cattle, and, after the introduction of wage labor during the colonial period, cash), and, in the case of divorce, it frequently had to be returned. In some places in Africa, women assumed control over a portion of their bridewealth. Some East Asian and Middle Eastern societies had both dowry and bridewealth. Under Islamic law, women retained rights to the personal ownership of their bridal gift, or *mahr*.

Polygyny, or the taking of more than one wife, was commonly practiced in a number of places. Sometimes, as noted above, it had an important political function in cementing alliances. In Islamic societies in the Middle East, Asia, and Africa, men could legally wed up to four wives. In non-Islamic areas of Africa and among some early Amerindian societies, such as the Inka in Latin America, polygyny also existed, but the number of wives was not limited. Judaism allowed polygyny by c.e. 70 in the Middle East. The economic obligations entailed by taking more than one wife could operate to curtail the degree to which polygyny was actually practiced; however, since women also produced wealth through trade, agricultural activities, and production of crafts, as well as by the exchange of bridewealth, it was often true that polygyny could be economically advantageous to men. Polygyny could sometimes be economically advantageous to women by allowing them to share household duties and obligations and by affording them more freedom to engage in trade and craft production.

Concubinage or the forging of sexual (and sometimes emotional) extramarital alliances was common in all four regions. Though concubines, as discussed above, were generally in a very vulnerable position, sometimes there were indigenous laws governing their treatment, and because these women often came from poor families, concubinage could represent a way of improving their economic position and even status. For example, Khaizuran, concubine of Caliph al-Mahdi during the Abbasid period in Iraq, saw two of her sons succeed their father as caliph, and she herself intervened in state affairs.

Since one of women's primary responsibilities was considered the production of heirs and the next generation, infertility could be a devastating circumstance and was the subject of many religious practices aimed at prevention or cure. Infertility was most often blamed on women until fairly recently. In Sumeria (3000–2000 b.c.e.) men could take another wife if their first did not bear children, historically a fairly common practice worldwide. Among the Aztecs a sterile woman could be rejected and divorced.

Some form of divorce or marital separation has existed for women nearly everywhere. (Among Zoroastrians, only men could divorce.) Although in general divorce was easier for men than women, there were exceptions to this rule. Extreme physical cruelty and neglect of economic duty were fairly common grounds by which women could petition for divorce. Adultery and a wife's inability to produce children, among a much wider range of other less consequential reasons, were common grounds on which men exercised their right to divorce women. In the early Spanish societies of Latin America, marriages could be annulled due to failure to produce children. Legal separation, known as *separación de cuerpos* (or separation of bodies) was also available on grounds of extreme physical cruelty, adultery, prostitution, or paganism, but such a separation forbade remarriage. From the sixteenth century onward, women were often the initiators of divorce in Spanish Latin America. In Southeast Asia women easily exercised their right to divorce, a situation some historians speculate was due to their economic autonomy. Prior to the twentieth century, however, divorce initiated by women was much harder in other parts of Asia, such as China and Japan. The ease with which divorce could be obtained was sometimes related to class. For instance, the divorce rate among the urban poor in nineteenth-century Egypt was higher than among the upper classes, for whom the economic components of marriage were more complicated. In Africa, because divorce often involved the return of bridewealth, women were sometimes discouraged from divorcing their husbands.

The treatment and rights of widows varied widely. During the Mauryan era in India (322–183 B.C.E.), widows could remarry, although they lost their rights to any property inherited from their deceased husbands. During the Gupta era (320–540), however, the Laws of Manu severely limited women's rights in marriage, including the banning of widow remarriage. Though its origins are unknown, the ritual suicide of widows among the Hindu known as *sati* is one of the most controversial treatments of widowhood. A complex practice, it appears to have economic as well as socioreligious foundations. Among the Aztecs widows not only retained the right to remarry but were encouraged to do so, especially if they were of childbearing age. In the colonial period in Spanish America, widows had the rights of single women who, after a certain age, were considered to have attained a legal majority. They could acquire control over their children or remarry. In parts of Africa, Asia, and the Middle East, widows were sometimes "inherited" by male kin of their deceased husbands. This practice, known as the levirate, could entail conjugal rights, but could also mean only the assumption of economic responsibility for a widow and her children. Women sometimes retained the right to refuse such a marriage. Among the Kikuyu of East Africa, for instance, women could opt instead to take a lover.

In many places women's activity in reform and nationalist movements, especially in the twentieth century, has been characterized by their struggle to liberalize laws governing marriage and family relationships. The Egyptian Feminist Union, led by Huda Sha'rawi, agitated for reform of laws governing divorce and polygyny in the 1920s and 1930s. Women (and men) of the May Fourth generation struggled in early twentieth-century China to make the reform of marriage and family law and practice central to their revolutionary effort. Even after the success of the Cuban revolution and the passage of a family code that explicitly gives women the same rights as men in economic and political arenas as well as in the family, women's organizations, with state support, continue to work to implement equality. In Africa women and men activists in liberation movements, such as the PAIGC in Guinea-Bissau in the 1960s and 1970s, clearly articulated the need to transform domestic relations as an important tenet of revolutionary ideology.

Women's roles, statuses, and power within the family have varied both through time within the same society and from one place to another. As reflections of material culture, they tell us more about societies than about women's place in them. For the regional areas under discussion, we can see the common threads, but we can also distinguish the wide variation.

WOMEN'S ECONOMIC ACTIVITY

In virtually all societies, the gender division of labor associates women with family maintenance. Overwhelmingly, gender segregation and domestic subsistence production have characterized the lives of women in the economic sphere, although before industrialization there was little distinction between the private and public economic spheres as most production took place in the family and in and around the home. In Nubian civilization in ancient Africa, for example, there is evidence that women were involved in the production of pottery for household use, while men specialized in producing wheel-turned pottery for trade. At times there were disincentives for women to be economic actors. In medieval Islamic society, elite urban men were cautioned not to marry women who engaged in economic activities in the public arena. But such observations should not be construed as an indication of lack of importance and variety in women's roles in agriculture, craft and textile production, the tending of livestock, trade, and other areas. In fact, many women engaged in economic activity that not only supplied subsistence but generated wealth, especially in agricultural and trade sectors of the economy.

In nearly all of sub-Saharan Africa, women historically played and continue to play important roles in agricultural production. In one of the few areas of sub-Saharan Africa where private property in land pre-dated European arrival, among the Amhara of Northeast Africa (present-day Ethiopia), women could control the entire agricultural production process. They owned, plowed, planted, and harvested their own fields. Amerindian women were important in agricultural production in Latin America before the arrival of the Spanish and Portuguese, who then sought to enlist men as agricultural laborers in cash crops. Although for the early centuries of the Atlantic slave trade the sex ratio was heavily imbalanced toward males, African women performed important agricultural labor, which was essential to the economies of colonial Latin America, the Caribbean, and what would become the United States. Women were cultivators in much of Asia, usually in family-centered production units. Even where women did not cultivate, they often performed other roles associated with agricultural production. For instance, in nineteenth-century Egypt, women did not plow land, but they worked at harvesting and in pest control activities.

Women undertook various kinds of manufacturing activities. In the Chewa-Malawi area of nineteenth-century East Africa, women were involved in producing salt and in other manufacture. In the eleventh-century Pagan Empire in Southeast Asia, women were important in the spinning of yarn and weaving of cloth. In eighteenth- and nineteenth-century Egypt, women were important in the textile crafts, though they were squeezed out by industrialization. In the nineteenth century, partially due to demand created by a European market, women became important to the growth of the silk industry in Lebanon and the carpet industry in Iran. Women were important weavers among the Inka, where they also worked in the mines. In the sixteenth and seventeenth centuries, women among the Shona of southern Africa worked in the gold mines.

Perhaps the most ubiquitous economic activity undertaken by women was that of trading. In Africa, Asia, Latin America and the Caribbean, and the Middle East and North Africa, women traded a number of items, including agricultural products, cooked food, cloth, beads, and handicrafts. Although women's trading activities were sometimes on a small scale, often referred to as "petty trading," that was not always the case. In Southeast Asia, women in twelfth- and thirteenth-century Burma were engaged in trade that included the large-scale buying and selling of rice and other commodities. They were also identified with the production and trade of a particular food-stuff, betel leaf, for which they made elaborate jewelled containers. Sometimes women engaged in long-distance trade that required their absence from home for extended periods of time. Among the nineteenth-century Kikuyu of East Africa, women engaged in long-distance trade and retained control over some of the wealth they accumulated. Even where women engaged in local, small-scale trade, they could be very important to the growth and development of long-distance trade and of port towns and urban centers. Such was the case with women traders along the west coast of Africa in the eighteenth and nineteenth centuries.

Residence in a harem and the practice of seclusion placed restraints on women's ability to engage directly in public-arena economic activity, thus forcing them to use intermediaries to conduct their business operations. This use of intermediaries, and the higher economic status that seclusion usually implied, meant women sometimes held considerable wealth and became significant economic actors. In the nineteenth century in parts of the Middle East (notably Cairo, Istanbul, Aleppo, and Nablus), upper-class women employed agents to conduct their business transactions in the public arena. They also invested capital as "silent partners" in other ventures and loaned money to men. Among the Hausa of northern Nigeria, Islamic women who were secluded used prepubescent girls to trade for them in public.

In some places, however, the strict gender segregation of Islamic societies in fact expanded women's economic alternatives, since only women could perform certain services for other women. In nineteenth-century Egypt women of lower economic status served as entertainers, cosmologists, and midwives to women of higher economic status who were in seclusion. Strict gender segregation opened up the professions (medicine, education, etc.) to women in the late twentieth century, especially in countries where economic resources are plentiful, such as Saudi Arabia.

The absence of male heirs, or the fact of widowhood, could also create economic opportunity for women. Under such circumstances women ran businesses and were important in trades. In sixteenth-century Mexico, Mencia Perez, a *mestiza*, married a rich merchant. When he died, she took over the business and became one of the wealthiest merchants in the province. In Syria, the *gedik*, a license that allowed one to practice a trade, was normally inherited by sons from their fathers. In the absence of a male heir, women could inherit the *gedik*, and although prevented from practicing the trade, they could sell, rent, or bequeath the license. In coastal West Africa creole women traders descended from African mothers and European fathers served as cultural intermediaries and often became very successful and wealthy businesswomen.

Yet women's tremendously varied and important roles in economic activity did not translate into economic, legal, or political equality with men. The more economic autonomy women had, however, the greater their freedoms. Whatever the origins of women's inequality, the complex processes through which it has been perpetuated will not fall in the face of economic parity alone.

POLITICAL POWER

In general histories of the Third World, political access is not normally discussed with gender as a factor of analysis, although frequently class, race, ethnicity, and other factors are considered. And being of a particular class, race, or ethnicity could influence women's power and status as much as gender. Still, the type and degree of women's political participation both as individuals and as a group have been underreported, and the present has frequently been mistaken for the past.

One of the most obvious ways women exercised direct power was by ruling. In the ancient African kingdom of Kush, women assumed power in their own right as well as sometimes co-ruling with their sons. There were women who ruled in early Austronesian societies from Polynesia to Madagascar, including the Philippines and Indonesia. In tenth-century Abyssinia in Northeast Africa, Gudit was a powerful queen of the Agao. Two African queens ruled in the sixteenth century, Queen Aminatu or Amina of Zaria and Queen Njinga of Matamba. The Mende of West Africa also had a tradition of women chiefs. Mwana Mwema and Fatuma ruled in Zanzibar in the late seventeenth and early eighteenth centuries, and Mwana Khadija ruled in Pate on the East African coast in the mid-eighteenth century. In India, several Hindu and Muslim women ruled small kingdoms during the late eighteenth century. In fifteenth- and sixteenth-century Burma and the Malay peninsula women also ruled.

What the existence of women rulers has to say about women's power qua women is a complex question. Most women who ruled were elite by birth, but then so were ruling men. However, Queen

Njinga certainly achieved rather than inherited her power, moving from the position of palace slave to that of a reigning monarch. Although the existence of women rulers indicates that women were not universally absent from the highest seats of power, having a woman ruler did not necessarily reflect the status of other women or empower them, any more than it does today.

Women also exercised direct power within arenas viewed as the female province; these varied based upon material culture. In Africa female networks seem to have arisen from the gender division of labor, and over many centuries women exercised considerable power and autonomy within society as a whole through all-female organizations. Women leaders of women such as the *iyalode* among the Yoruba and the *omu* among the Igbo are examples of such power. The *coya*, known as the "queen of women" among the Inka, is another example; she even had the power to rule in the absence of the male ruler. Women exercised considerable power within the royal harem in both Turkey and Iran.

Women exercised power as members of collectives of their own sex organized for particular purposes. Practices similar to the Nigerian institution of "sitting on a man" are found in various African societies. This phrase describes organized political activities of women who gathered as a group to protest policies or protect another woman by confronting a man and ridiculing him or making demands, sometimes even destroying his property as a punishment for some act against a woman or women as a whole. Women directed this practice against recalcitrant husbands and colonial officials alike. There is also evidence of the existence of this kind of activity in early twentieth-century China, where women forced husbands who had maltreated their wives to march through town wearing dunce caps.

Perhaps the most ubiquitous example of women's indirect and influential power is the existence of the queen mother, normally the progenitor of a male ruler although sometimes a woman appointed as his "mother." These women had power over women and men. Their power resulted not only from their access to the ruler, serving as his "ear," so to speak, but also because they often commanded formidable financial and personnel resources and/or had specific responsibilities over the governed. Queen mothers existed in ancient Kush, India, the Ottoman Empire, and West, East, and Northeast Africa, to name a few places. Some queen mothers, such as Shah Turkan of thirteenth-century Delhi, could be very instrumental in installing their sons on the throne, and consequently exercised considerable state power. Others, like Mihrisah, mother of the Ottoman ruler Selim II, who ruled in the early nineteenth century, exercised considerable power through largesse; she built a mosque and a medical school. Yaa Kyaa, mother of the West African Asante ruler Osei Yaw, also exercised considerable state power, even signing a peace treaty between the Asante and the British in the 1830s, and Yaa Asantewa led a large revolt against British rule. The *magajiya,* the title given to the queen mother in several of the Hausa states of the western Sudan in West Africa, even had the power to depose the ruler, or *sarki.* The queen mother, however, usually owed her power to her relationship to a male ruler and not to her relationship to other women. Even though she might be regarded as "queen of the women," she did not necessarily represent women's interests as a whole. Still, these women were often at the center of power, and many displayed formidable political acumen.

We also cannot discount the power and influence of women who were the wives, sisters, daughters, and consorts of powerful men. Precisely because of the intimate context in which such situations occurred, they are admittedly hard to document, but evidence exists. Women such as Inés Suárez, who accompanied Captain Pedro de Valdivia as his lover in his campaign to conquer Chile, played an important role as a spy and confidante and eventually took part in the conquest. Wives of emperors in the Byzantine empire wielded considerable political influence. Nineteenth-century Confucian reformers in China were influenced by increased contact with literate women at court and in elite families. The nineteenth-century Islamic reform movement led by Uthman dan Fodio in West Africa was certainly influenced in its ideas on greater education for women by the women in Fodio's own family, which produced five generations of women intellectuals who left bodies of written work in Fula, Arabic, and Hausa. In the West African kingdom of Dahomey, by the eighteenth century at least, no man could become king without the support of the powerful palace women. Royal women in nineteenth-century Iran also exercised considerable power and independence, even from inside the harem. There are many other examples which suggest to us that women's influential roles in politics were consequential.

Women's military participation as individuals and as organized corps of women fighters was also widespread. In many places women accompanied male troops, such as in Aksum and early Ethiopian kingdoms, in early Arabia, in Latin America, and elsewhere. But women were also actual combatants. The African Queen Amina of Zaria led troops into battle, as did the renowned Nguni warrior Nyamazana, of early nineteenth-century southern Africa, and Indian women in Delhi and Bhopal in the second half of the eighteenth century. In c.e. 40 two Trung sisters in Southeast Asia (in present-day Vietnam) led an army, including female officers. In eighteenth-century Jamaica, slave women played important roles as combatants in maroon societies composed of runaway slaves. One woman, Nanny, is still revered as a fighter and ruler of one of the most famous maroon communities, Nanny Town. Actual corps of trained women soldiers also existed, such as those in Java and in the West African kingdom of Dahomey, where they formed the king's bodyguard and were an elite unit of "shock troops." In eighteenth-century Egypt, women went into battle against Mamluks and the French. In the nineteenth century women fought in Japan, in the T'ai p'ing Rebellion in China, and in the Mexican Revolution. In early twentieth-century China, corps of women fought as the "Women's Suicide Brigade" and the "Women's National Army." Twentieth-century anti-colonial and liberation struggles are replete with examples of women as combatants, for example, in the 1950s "Mau Mau" rebellion in Kenya, the Frelimo liberation army in Mozambique, and the Cuban and Nicaraguan revolutions.

In addition to serving in military roles, women organized in other capacities with men and in women's groups against colonial policies that they viewed as inimical to their interests. In India at the turn of the twentieth century, women were active in the *swadeshi* movement, which sought to encourage the use of indigenously made products as opposed to European imports. In the 1930s Indian women participated in anti-colonial protest marches in Bombay and elsewhere. In 1929 the "Women's War" of the Igbo and Ibibio of eastern Nigeria was a massive uprising of women against the threat of female taxation by the colonial state. In 1945 the market women in Lagos, Nigeria were very instrumental in a general strike against economic and political policies of the British. Women in Egypt, Iran, and the Ottoman Empire worked with men in organizations promoting independence from European imperialism by participating in street demonstrations, public speaking, and writing. In the Algerian War of Independence against the French (1954–62), women were couriers of weapons, money, and messages, as well as actual combatants.

Women's participation in general strikes, major protest marches, economic boycotts, and armed rebellion was prevalent everywhere there was an anti-colonial struggle. As with any major societal upheaval resulting in challenges to existing authority, colonialism both created opportunities for and oppressed women. In the final analysis, however, the vast majority of women have opted to work for the independence of their societies and to pursue the issue of gender equality in the context of an independent and autonomous state.

Despite all of this, and despite the fact that improving women's status has often been a central point of anti-colonial ideology, women have usually not become the political and economic equals of men in newly evolving independent societies. In fact, the development of nationalist movements, at least in the nineteenth and twentieth centuries, has often operated to subordinate women. In nineteenth-century Japan the growth of nationalism and patriotism tended to subjugate women, requiring that they be good wives and mothers as their first "patriotic" duty. Although initially instituting reforms that served to empower women, within a few years the Kuomintang nationalist movement in early twentieth-century China began to repress a developing feminist movement that had supported its rise to power. The 1922 Egyptian constitution denied women the right to vote and barred them from the opening of Parliament, despite the active role they had played in the nationalist movement. After the success of the Algerian Revolution, women's roles in the war were viewed as validation of their "traditional" roles of wife and mother. After gaining independence, the Indonesian nationalist movement encouraged women to go back into the home to provide "social stability." In Nigeria, although the nationalist movements of the mid-twentieth century had courted women and counted them as strong supporters in the independence struggle, women remained generally excluded from political power after independence and especially under military rule. In many disparate places and cultures, nationalism left women unrewarded after independence was achieved.

There are exceptions, as some national liberation movements have challenged sexist ideologies regarding women. Frelimo in Mozambique criticized both the traditional initiation rites that included notions of female subordination as well as the colonial exploitation of women's labor. This kind of struggle was termed "fighting two colonialisms" by the PAIGC, a comparable liberation movement in Guinea-Bissau. In Cuba the government also sought to address the issue of women's equality in the post-independence period in a written family code that explicitly delineates women's equal status compared to that of men. The revolutionary Nicaraguan government of the 1980s also attempted to officially stipulate women as the equals of men. The positive difference in these countries, however, seems as related to women's continued organization as women (such as the Organization of Mozambican Women and the Cuban Federation of Women) as to state-supported revolutionary ideology.

CENTRALIZATION, BUREAUCRATIZATION, AND STATE FORMATION

Women's role in centralization, bureaucratization, and state formation poses some challenging questions. In the processes of state formation and centralization, women often have tremendous importance and potential for autonomy and power as marriage partners who centralize wealth, cement alliances, merge cultures, and produce heirs. In the Middle East the practice of first-cousin marriage helped establish the family as a base of centralized wealth and political solidarity. In the pre-colonial West African kingdom of Dahomey, the king took wives from wealthy and powerful families to cement political alliances. Among both the Hindus and the Muslims in India, marriages reinforced political bonds with the nobility and among rival states. In Latin America the Spanish sought unions with elite Amerindian women to legitimize and consolidate their control over indigenous societies. However, it appears that when the state begins to bureaucratize, making these relationships less important to state organization, women lose much of their potential for being central to state power. In the Middle East the growth of the state meant that the great family houses that had served as centers of societal organization and power lost much of that role. Similarly, in the West African kingdom of Dahomey, kinship ties became much less important in power relations as the state solidified and shifted to a merit system based more on service to the king than lineage connections.

Nationalist struggles in the nineteenth and twentieth centuries mobilized women nearly everywhere in the Third World. But once the state was established (or gained its independence from external conquerors), women often seemed to lose in the process. Particular and comparative research with gender as a central analytical factor can test this hypothesis and may open new windows on studies of state formation and the development of nationalism.

WOMEN'S CULTURE, NETWORKS, AND AUTONOMOUS SPACE

In male-dominant societies, women's activities, values, and interactions often form a "muted" subculture: their worldview is non-dominant and does not generally claim to represent that of the entire society of men and women. This subculture is reinforced by a strong gender division of labor that results in women and men spending most of their time in same-sex groupings and, occasionally, is augmented by ideological formulations or social rules (e.g., notions of pollution, or purdah).

At times, women demanded the separate space or take advantage of it as a refuge from oppressive features of their society. For example, the sisterhoods of silk workers in southern China, who pledged to resist marriage, provided an alternative to the patriarchal family. Buddhism allowed women to pursue the monastic life, albeit as less than equals to male monks. Still, Indian Buddhist nuns taught religion to other women and composed religious poetry. (Jainism accepted nuns as the equals of monks.) Women who joined Buddhist nunneries in China were criticized for ignoring female responsibilities of motherhood, although these nunneries, we might suspect, provided a space less controlled by male authority than the rest of Chinese society. Convents in colonial Latin America housed single women with various motives: some sought to escape marriage, others searched for religious fulfillment, and a few sought access to education. And not all who resided in a convent lived by vows of poverty and chastity.

Whatever its source or structural manifestation, this social space and the resulting female-controlled institutions offered women rich opportunities. Among the most important of these opportunities was the potential for female solidarity. Various African societies institutionalized female solidarity through activities such as "sitting on a man" (a Nigerian practice noted earlier). In Mende society in West Africa, the women's secret society known as Bundu (parallel to a men's secret society) provided a political base for female chiefs (it also perpetuated, as a central initiation ritual, the practice of clitoridectomy).

In addition to encouraging female solidarity, the separation of women and men had economic consequences at times. Islamic seclusion provided the impetus for the development of occupations serving the women of the harem or *zenana*, such as midwives, educators, entertainers, musicians, or cosmologists; for reasons of honor and modesty, these occupations were filled by women. The same rationale prompted the expansion of professions open to women: medicine, nursing, and teaching.

The physical separation of women contributed to a flowering of artistic, oral, and written culture from the female subculture. The world's first novel, *The Tale of Genji*, is only one example of the fine literary work of Japanese women writers in the eleventh century. Unlike men, who were restricted by gender norms to writing rather arid, but higher-status, poetry in Chinese characters, these women composed prose in *kana*, the language of indigenous expression of sentiment. Even where excluded from education and certain cultural outlets, women's networks produced a fine and rich tradition of oral expression, as in Bedouin communities in North Africa.

Women's networks and women's subculture, because they often derive from the marginalization of women from the centers of power, have been controversial in the scholarship. Even in extreme forms (perhaps more so there), the separating of women can provide a source of psychological support and connectedness and protection. In assessing the actions of women among themselves, the important issues of victimization and agency are played out and we must ask certain questions: On whose initiative are the women grouped? How do women respond to this grouping? How does the clustering of women, apart from men, empower and/or limit women? Is this a condition that encourages women's oppression of other women (since there are now distinctions of power drawn between women) as much as it encourages female solidarity?

WOMEN IN CROSS-CULTURAL CONTACT

Women are important intermediaries for cultural exchange. For several reasons, they are likely to end up marrying outside their community of birth. First, patrilineal societies outnumber matrilineal societies, and in patrilineal societies a woman marries into her husband's patrilineage and generally resides with her husband's kin (patrilocality).

Second, women have often been exchanged, as wives and as concubines, to cement alliances. In eighteenth-century Dahomey in West Africa, lineages were required to send their daughters to the king. During the same period in Java, the male ruler gave various women from his court to noblemen as wives. In sixteenth-century Japan, warrior families cemented alliances by the exchange of wives.

Third, in cases of European expansion into the Third World, the gender division of labor in Europe resulted in most explorers being male, which in turn created particular conditions for indigenous women to link with these men as sexual partners. Perhaps the best-known individual woman in this category was the slave Malinche (or Malintzin), who became the first Mexican mistress of Cortés. She served as translator in Maya, Nahuatl, and Spanish and apprised Cortés of the inland empire of Moctezuma. In the seventeenth century, the *signares* along the West African coast became wealthy traders and intermediaries through their relations with European men. Their mulatto children, familiar with two worlds, served as power brokers.

Similarly, initially in the seventeenth century, the Dutch administration encouraged the marriage of its junior officers to Indonesian women to provide a form of social order through mestizo culture on the frontiers of Dutch colonization. By the nineteenth century, the status of these mixed-race individuals had declined. The same gender division of labor, in which men were the agents of expansion, is also characteristic of societies outside of Europe. Most conquerors were male—for example, in the nineteenth-century Zulu expansion through southern and East-Central Africa, and among the Muslims who infiltrated Nubia from the sixteenth century on.

Women were thus well placed—as socializers of children, farmers, or traders—to transmit new ideas about social practices or mores, technology or techniques, religion, kinship, and so on to their new community. Female African slaves, valued for their horticultural labor and transported far from their natal villages, brought with them ways of planting or cultivating, thus encouraging agricultural innovation. Women, for the same reasons, were well placed to resist the cultural aspects of imperialism by perpetuating indigenous culture and customs. Amerindian women in Latin America, for example, continued indigenous religious practices in the face of Catholic proselytizing, as did African female slaves.

Women may become empowered by their intermediary position: it may give them pivotal control of information or material resources. On the other hand, as intermediaries they are sometimes marginal within their society of origin. They may lose the protections from their natal group accorded by custom without gaining those granted to indigenous women. As in-marrying strangers, they may suffer isolation. It is important to note, too, that the individuals and cultures resulting from these cross-racial liaisons were not valued everywhere: Anglo-Indians were shunned by both the English and the Indian communities during the Raj. The female intermediary risked being polluted by contact with outsiders and subsequently cast out or made a scapegoat when illness or other negative circumstances plagued a community. And some women who served as intermediaries—for example, Malintzin, or Eva in seventeenth-century southern Africa—have been labeled historically as traitors because they were seen as helping to facilitate conquest of their people by outsiders.

GENDER PLUS CONQUEST:
COLONIALISM AND IMPERIALISM

Contact resulting from conquest held vast implications for women as a group. Customs were transferred from one society to another. New practices that restricted women's physical mobility might be forced upon the indigenous groups or adopted by them in emulation. For example, although the *jihad* of Uthman dan Fodio improved conditions for Hausa women in numerous ways, such as providing greater access to Qur'anic education, it also led to the increased seclusion of elite women and a loss of their religious and political power.

Recent scholarship on women in European-dominated colonial societies presents evidence that there was no one colonial experience for all women, even within the same national boundaries. However, the position of most women declined under the aegis of colonialism both because of its sexist bias and because women were members of politically dominated and economically exploited territories. In general, women were dislocated economically and politically within a weakened indigenous order, and in those spheres at least, women were rarely compensated in the new order. Nevertheless, though women were often the victims of colonialism, they also took initiative both in resisting policies they viewed as harmful to them and in using new situations to their advantage. And sometimes the social fluidity created by the colonial experience allowed for the creation of alternative roles for women. As one scholar suggests, however, studies of gender need to be located as much in the changing relationships of production as in the political and social policies engendered by colonialism. Another scholar underscores this point in emphasizing that it was the integration of the Middle East into a global economic system which is the real canvas on which we must paint an analysis of women's changing economic roles.

Women were members of colonizing as well as colonized societies, and members of the former group eventually accompanied colonizers to conquered territories. For most of the regions under consideration here, these women were a small minority in colonial territories. In the initial phase of conquest, they were nearly absent; then a trickle came to join husbands; then more came, depending on the degree of expatriate settlement that the colonizers encouraged and the needs and size of the colonial bureaucracy.

In Latin America (and South Africa), however, the era of European conquest was marked by the rise of commercial capitalism rather than the industrial capitalism that would fuel the colonialist thrust of the nineteenth century, and it also pre-dated (by several hundred years) the colonization of other regions. After the initial phase of conquest, during which few women from the Iberian peninsula were in residence in Latin America, much larger numbers began to migrate there. The Amerindian population of Latin America was decimated due to European diseases and attempts at their enslavement (the Khoi Khoi of South Africa suffered a similar fate). Though the population of African slaves grew considerably from the sixteenth to the nineteenth centuries in Latin America, European immigration outstripped it. The region was effectively colonized centuries before widespread colonial penetration into other areas. Thus, by the nineteenth century, Latin American nations were gaining their independence, and the descendants of Europeans in Latin America were the predominant people in the population of the continent. In many regions Latin American culture became an amalgam of African, Amerindian, and European cultures, shaped on the anvil of a centuries-old slave mode of production and forced Amerindian labor. Therefore, the following discussion of women under European colonialism does not apply to Latin America after the early decades of the conquest.

Imperial and colonial expansion had economic, social, and cultural consequences for women. The greater development (or in some places the introduction) of wage labor that accompanied colonialism predominantly involved men, whom it drew away from work on the land, increasing women's subsistence agricultural labor. Among the Tonga of Zambia the absence of male laborers had a particularly deleterious effect on the agricultural labor of older women, who were no longer able to depend upon help from sons and sons-in-law. This situation was also common in West and West-Central Africa. Sometimes, however, women left alone on the land exercised greater power in the economic decision-making process. An example is late-nineteenth- and early twentieth-century western Kenya, where Luo women were able to experiment with new crops and agricultural techniques that improved their economic position.

In some places the existence of widespread wage labor among men eroded the importance of the family economy and women's role in it. In forcing male migration to wage labor in mining and other work among the Aztecs, Inkas, Mayas, and Arawaks, the Spanish eroded the significant role women performed in the pre-Columbian family economy. In Morocco during the French colonial era, women were only seasonal wage laborers but were still dislocated in the family economy.

The development of the cash-crop system created greater interest in establishing private property in areas where it had not previously existed. This change to private property often distorted land tenure arrangements and usufruct (usage) rights and seems to have operated overall against women's interests. In Morocco the French, pursuing a policy of consolidating landholdings, helped destroy a family-based economy in which women played an important agricultural role. The Swynnerton Plan, begun by the British in 1954 in Kenya, was a policy of consolidating and privatizing landholdings that severely disadvantaged women and set the stage for their loss of rights to land after independence. In West and West-Central Africa women also lost out in the privatization of land occasioned by the growth of wage labor and cash crops. In a few instances women were able to resist erosion in their economic viability; from the 1920s through the 1940s, women in the cotton-producing areas of Nyasaland (now Malawi) were able to utilize cash cropping to their advantage. There, remaining collectively organized, women delayed the privatization of land, participated in cotton production, and maintained their precolonial agricultural autonomy.

Competition from European imports often displaced women occupationally and pushed them to the margins of areas in the economy where they were formerly quite important. For instance, in the Middle East and North Africa, European cloth imports in the nineteenth century devastated local textile production in which women had been heavily involved. Among the Baule of the Ivory Coast, French monopolization of local cloth production, and its alienation to factories, displaced women's former predominance in producing cloth and related items, such as thread. Sometimes the colonial economy created jobs for women, and though they were often overworked and underpaid, this independent income still provided women with some autonomy. Often it was the situations fostered by the colonial economy, especially in the urban areas, that created room for women to establish their own occupations. These urban areas often had large populations of single adult men (or men separated from their families) and entrepreneurial women engaged in occupations that provided them with services normally provided by the family. Although sometimes these occupations were marginal (such as beer-brewing, selling cooked food, and doing laundry) or even dangerous and possibly degrading (such as prostitution) women seized whatever opportunity was available to stabilize themselves, and often their children, economically and to gain independence from men and other adult family members.

The colonial need to control the economy also marginalized women who had often exercised control over the production, pricing, and distribution of agricultural, textile, and household goods. In southwestern Nigeria, for instance, the British were constantly in disputes with Yoruba market women over the location of markets, their internal control, and the setting of prices for staple commodities—all areas women had formerly controlled and which the colonial state sought to regulate.

A small number of women in some places were able to benefit economically from an increase in market scale that accompanied European contact and colonial rule, such as Omu Okwei of Nigeria. This benefit came to few individuals and often at the expense of other women, since women's economic power had historically emanated from their operation in collectives.

Political independence in many countries did not eliminate economic dependence on former colonial powers and was often followed in the post–World War II period by the arrival of multinational corporations. Since colonialism situated women overall as an easily exploitable class of labor, this situation has had profound economic implications for women. On the one hand, a number of multinational industries, especially electronics and textiles, have shown a marked preference for female labor. This has meant women have been drawn into the formal wage-labor force and therefore have had independent income. On the other hand, it has also meant the severe exploitation of their labor at depressed wages in unskilled and low-skilled jobs with little stability or possibility of promotion, and under unhealthy conditions.

Yet colonialism was not merely an economic and political relationship; it was a social relationship as well. By the eighteenth and nineteenth centuries, European colonizers hailed from societies that had rejected prominent and public political roles for women and that empowered men to represent women's interests. Alternative colonialist definitions of femaleness reflected a European gender division of labor and sexist bias. Women's education was viewed as a vehicle for making them better wives and mothers, since women's role was to be domestic and dependent. The schools of colonial Latin America shared with those of colonial Africa, the Middle East, and India an emphasis on education for domestic roles. The provision of suitable wives for the male Christian elite and the importance of mothers as socializers of their children dominated the colonial agenda, as articulated by both the colonizers and the indigenous male elite. Colonialism sought to impose not only political dominance and economic control, but also Western culture.

Seeking to legitimate their presence, and based upon European views of women in society and their own notions of the value of human life, some colonizers and missionaries criticized polygyny and such indigenous women-oriented practices as clitoridectomy, *sati,* foot-binding, and seclusion. In the area of family law, especially relating to marriage and inheritance, Europeans did sometimes seek to provide women with increased individual rights. Among the indigenous Christianized elite in Nigeria, for instance, Christian marriage was initially popular with women for these very reasons; but because it also promoted women's economic dependence and reinforced a pre-existing sexual double standard without the historical protections provided by the extended family, women soon began to chafe under its restrictions. The arbitrariness with which European family law was often administered and its confinement primarily to urban centers combined with other factors to leave a number of states with more than one legal code—European, customary, Islamic, and so on—a situation still in the process of being reconciled in many places.

Gender—the roles, perceptions, ideologies, and rituals associated with sex—is constructed by society. All societies have broad experiences in common (everywhere people construct shelter, trade, procure food, resolve conflict, etc.), but they approach these tasks in vastly different ways. Similarly, with women, writ large, there is much that is the same in the construction of gender; writ small, there is much that is different.

Even accounting for the cultural and historical context, the commonalities in the construction of gender point to women as generally less privileged human beings than men. Women's sexuality has usually been more regulated than that of men. Women have been far more associated with household labor than are men. Women have been less likely to rise to the highest positions of political and/or religious power. Women as a group have exercised less control over wealth than men as a group. Even within the same space and time, gender has been constructed differently for certain women depending on class, race, ethnicity, religion, and other elements. Thus we must view constructions of gender related not only to sex, but to a number of other factors—mode of production, culture, religion, to name a few—that can sometimes operate to bond women and at other times operate to separate them. The fundamental construction of gender everywhere, however, has been to separate women from men—in role, status, privilege, access, and other ways.

Women in the Middle East and North Africa

INTRODUCTION

Guity Nashat and Judith E. Tucker

The history of women and gender in the Middle East and North Africa is a field in the process of transformation. In a previous version of this book, produced a decade ago in 1988, we lamented the paucity of scholarly studies, particularly prior to the twentieth century, and the marginality of women and gender issues to the field of Middle East history as a whole. While we cannot pretend that the situation has been totally rectified, the past decade has brought some very substantial advances in both knowledge of and interest in the history of women and gender in a variety of periods and locations in the Middle East. Studies of Islamic texts have greatly expanded our understanding of women and gender ideology in the early Islamic period. Work on women's economic activities in the Ottoman era has revolutionized our ideas about female participation in economy and society. Detailed histories of the role women and women's movements played in some of the nationalist struggles in the late nineteenth and twentieth centuries have reshaped the narrative of women's movements and nationalist movements alike. The programs of academic conferences in the field of Middle East studies and its various related disciplines (anthropology, history, Islamic law, political science, and so on) have also increasingly reflected the burgeoning interest in women and gender issues both past and present. It is very much our impression that many of the scholars most engaged with women and gender issues are relatively young, and therefore likely to have an even greater impact on our field in the future.

The synthetic essays below still suffer from an unevenness in scholarly research in the field of women and gender history. The twentieth century is much better served by the literature thanks in part to our ability to draw on the work of historically minded anthropologists, political scientists, and sociologists as well as historians proper. There is some exciting research being done on the Ottoman era, although in general we still know far more about later periods and urban areas than about the formative years and the majority of the population in the countryside. And for the pre-Ottoman Middle East, apart from a few recent signal monographs, our information is often spotty, gleaned from the stray article or source that covers gender issues in a piecemeal or even tangential fashion. Still, we have attempted here to pull together what we now know to construct a coherent narrative of the history of women in the region that raises significant questions about the role of gender in the history of Middle Eastern society, economy, and politics. Much is missing here, and we hope that others will be encouraged to make the study of women a priority in their own research.

"Middle East and North Africa" is, at best, a problematic unit of analysis, the definition of which owes more to Western geopolitical concerns than to indigenous rhythms. We have tried to exercise the utmost care in the face of the enormous varieties of language and culture, political and economic structures, and historical experience that can be found in this region. We have generally eschewed generalizations, and our narrative tends to shift geographical focus rather than attempt to provide a comprehensive picture of women and gender across the board. In the pre-Islamic era, we look primarily to the Tigris–Euphrates basin, the core area for many developments that shaped gender there and elsewhere. Then our narrative follows the rise and spread of Islam. We are not suggesting, however, that Islam was necessarily the decisive element in the definition of gender in the region, but rather that this religion encapsulated, reworked, and finally helped to diffuse many older cultural practices of the region, including those defining gender. We try to delineate how Islamic teachings were modified by the socio-economic and cultural traditions of the non-Arabian population so that the spread of Islam produced a discrete, although varied, culture with certain broad implications for women and gender issues. Our geographical coverage changes in the course of the narrative to reflect our sense of what constitutes a culturally coherent unit in different historical periods until, in the modern era, we adopt the standard geographical definition of the Middle East and North Africa. Certain parts of the region are far better served in our discussion than others, of course, and our understanding of modern history as well is uneven: we have a number of strong studies of woman and gender in lower Egypt or urban Iran, for example, but little to work with when it comes to the Gulf states or Anatolia.

We have not paid particular attention to non-Muslim women in the region. We have reason to believe that the lives of non-Muslims, including women, were not very different from those of Muslims. Goitein's work on the medieval Jewish community of Cairo, for example, describes gender roles that were very similar to what we think pertained among Muslims at the time. And although European influence in the nineteenth and twentieth centuries had an earlier and deeper impact on Christians than on Muslims, in the final analysis it was probably class rather than religion that was more significant as far as women's roles were concerned. A few parts of the region did witness the development of hybrid cultures that were the product of large-scale emigration from Europe: French Algeria and Israel are two examples of places where women's roles and gender relations took on distinct patterns as a result. We were not able, however, to include much discussion of such subcultures in a general history of this length focused on Middle Eastern and North African women.

We have retained much of the standard periodization in the field of Middle East history in the hope that both students and teachers will find this material relatively easy to integrate into existing courses and frameworks of analysis. We also hope, however, that these narratives might serve as a guide and encouragement for other scholars and students who may not only find useful information and ideas, but also employ this history as a springboard for their own research and rewriting of the history of the region.

Part I

WOMEN IN THE MIDDLE EAST
8,000 B.C.E.−C.E. 1800

Guity Nashat

WOMEN IN THE ANCIENT MIDDLE EAST

Introduction

The treatment of women in Middle Eastern societies is as diverse as these societies themselves. But women's traditional role, as it evolved in urban areas, is marked by their seclusion, the veil, and their subordination to men. Both the opponents of these practices (in the West) and their Muslim defenders generally attribute them to the teachings of Islam. A closer examination of the historical evidence, however, reveals that the practices in question pre-date Islam by many centuries. The misconception stems from the traditional periodization of Middle Eastern history, whereby the rise of Islam (C.E. 610) is treated as a new beginning. Whatever has occurred since the seventh century is treated as the domain of Middle Eastern or Islamic history, and whatever occurred prior to that period is relegated to the realm of ancient Near Eastern history. Scholars searching for antecedents for Islamic developments usually look to pre-Islamic Arabia, the birthplace of Islam, despite the awareness that the majority of those who embraced Islam even a few decades after its advent lived outside of Arabia, in regions with much older and highly developed civilizations. Yet few scholars have systematically looked for continuity between these cultures and post-Islamic developments.

Many Islamicists have followed the periodization of early Muslims, who believed their pre-Islamic traditions belonged to the time of ignorance and were thus worthless—an approach hardly suitable for the study of women, whose treatment and status in Islamic society is deeply influenced by cultural and economic conditions that preceded Islam. This fact is supported by recent scholarship, which indicates that a good portion of what Muslims have regarded as the teachings of Islam was already in place before the rise of Islam.

Most writings that deal with the history of women in early Islam—writings that generally use Arabia as their point of departure—do not adequately answer the question why Muslims adopted practices of the non-Arabians and how this process occurred. As for studies by Muslims, particularly modern Muslim apologists, much effort is spent justifying practices incorporated into Islamic law during the first three centuries of the Islamic era.

The treatment of women in the Middle East evolved over several thousand years and was shaped by the experiences of this region's inhabitants from neolithic times. To understand the history of women, then, we must look to the very beginning, when the first human settlements began in this region. Although the terms *Middle East* and *Near East* are of recent origin, the area to which they refer is one of the oldest centers of settled life, where the domestication of animals and cultivated agriculture began ten to twelve thousand years ago and a dependable food supply made the growth of human population possible. These material conditions were prerequisite to the emergence of civilization.

Settled agricultural life had become the predominant mode of existence in the Middle East by 6000 B.C.E.; villages emerged in the next stage. These developments stimulated the exchange of goods and the rise of trade. Cities appeared, and writing was invented sometime between 3500 and 3000 B.C.E.

Changes in social relations were as important as the new forms of material advance. Women made important contributions to each stage and were in turn deeply affected by it. In order to understand the cultural and economic milieu that eventually became associated with Islam, we must briefly examine the role of women in Mesopotamia, the core area of what is called the Middle East today. Many Middle Eastern cultural traditions, including those relating to women, developed in Mesopotamia first and then spread to the rest of the region. The veil, seclusion, and the general dependence of women were modified over time and adapted to local conditions, but they retained much of their Mesopotamian origin. Space does not allow a greater discussion of the regional variations in cultural and social patterns. Therefore, other cultural areas (such as Iran, Syria, or Anatolia and Egypt) will be brought in only if they bear directly on the main discussion. Little reference will be made to the role of women in Egypt before Islam; the development of women's role in pre-Islamic Egypt did not directly influence similar development in the rest of the Middle East. (Ancient Egypt is discussed in Iris Berger, "Women of East and Southern Africa," in Iris Berger and E. Frances White, *Women in Sub-Saharan Africa: Restoring Women to History* [Bloomington: Indiana University Press, 1999].)

Some of this discussion, then, focuses on the evolution of the role of women in the pre-literate Middle East. Because this is a period of over five millennia, we must reconstruct our story about women and their environment on the basis of sparse and fragmented archeological data from a few scattered sites. Archeology can at best offer a minimum outline of how these early humans lived. Therefore, I supplement the archeological evidence with materials from prehistoric legends, myths, epic poems, and religious beliefs.

Many of the ancient myths and legends from the preliterate period come from southern Mesopotamia. Despite their narrow geographical scope, these materials are highly relevant to understanding the situation of women in the Middle East as a whole because Mesopotamia became the center from which civilization radiated to the rest of the region. Furthermore, these myths reflect conditions and realities of the time. As Thorkild Jacobsen has noted, the mythmakers could not have "depicted a society quite outside their experience and unrelated to anything they or their listeners knew." In fact, he believes these sources have "preserved memories of greater antiquity than any other of our sources" (Jacobsen 1970: 137, 205).

Beginning with the Sumerian period, written data such as law codes, legal contracts, and religious materials provides additional sources for knowledge about women. However, several drawbacks reduce the usefulness of these records for the study of women's history. Many are written in languages not accessible to non-specialists, and the majority have not even been deciphered by specialists themselves. More material is available for some periods and localities than for others. Nonetheless, although these records were not designed specifically to record information about women, they can yield useful and even important information about how women of various social and economic groups lived.

Despite the great contribution women have made to the growth of Middle Eastern civilization, the course of women's experience, especially in the pre-Islamic period, is still largely uncharted. The dearth of primary data and secondary studies makes any attempt at an in-depth study truly daunting, but this ignorance is also the result of a lack of appreciation for the crucial contribution of women to the emergence of civilization in this region.

Because the state of our knowledge makes it difficult to offer a narrative recounting of women's experience, in what follows I will focus on women's activity in society. The nature of the sources will compel me to base some of the arguments on slim pieces of evidence. Despite their conjectural nature, I present such arguments in the hope of stimulating further interest and discussion on the subject. It should also be noted that the following discussion will place greater emphasis on the evolution of women's role in urban areas, even though women have continued to play a more active role in both pastoral and rural societies of the Middle East. This urban focus is partly mandated by the fact that early data provides much greater evidence about the urban population than about the nomadic or rural population. In addition, despite the presence of agricultural and pastoral communities in the region, the normative standards that regulated and affected women's role developed in the urban areas. These normative standards were eventually codified and imposed on women in the urban centers. Finally, because women of all social strata aspired to the norms developed in the urban centers, a better understanding of the role of urban women will provide greater insight about the evolution of women in the Middle East.

I will use the available data to delineate the gradual change in women's roles, from being active participants in communal life to becoming confined primarily to activities within the household, to child rearing and household duties, and to working at crafts that could be performed within the house. A better understanding of this important development will provide insight about other aspects of women's history in this region. The evolution of their various roles is a useful subject because it mirrors some of the other major changes that affected women: the division of labor along gender lines, the gradual seclusion of women, the emergence of the veil as a symbol of propriety, and women's eventual subordination to men.

In my study of these changes, I will apply a rational-choice model, which uses cost–benefit analysis to understand a wide range of individual and social actions. This method assumes that most humans, regardless of where and when they live, make choices that are intended to maximize their well-being. It shows that the choices made by individual and family members of a community—in the aggregate—affect the entire group and often result in consequences not intended by the individuals making these choices. The rational-choice approach, however, does not postulate that individual choice is motivated by selfishness, or is independent of culture, for it recognizes that most women and men are concerned about the well-being of their children, their spouses, and often the community in which they live (Becker 1985). The model explains how the decisions of individual women, who—for whatever reason—devote more of their energy to household activity and child rearing, in the long run may diminish the social power of women collectively.

When applied to the period under study in the Middle East, this line of thinking would suggest that as each woman became more involved in her particular family situation, she paid less attention to the making of vital decisions by the community. This reorientation eventually eroded the collective power of women as a group, because women's particular interests did not affect men as a group. The loss of collective power then made it possible for men as a group to demand more from women than they were giving them. In other words, it opened the door for the exploitation of women in the Middle East.

Most importantly, while the rational-choice approach recognizes that women as a group were widely exploited for millennia, it avoids treating women as passive and mindless victims who willingly cooperated with their oppressors without resistance. It also sheds powerful light on the frequent conflict between individual and group choices. Thus, when women made choices as individuals—as mothers and daughters—they contributed to strengthening a system that hurt women collectively. Similarly, it sheds light on how men contributed to furthering the exploitation of women as a whole, even though as fathers, brothers, and husbands they certainly cared about their female relatives' welfare. This approach also does not require the presence of a monolithic and immutable state and an oppressive ruling class—arguments that cannot be easily supported by the historical evidence for the Middle East—to explain how women were exploited.

Rational choice is consistent with commonsense observation of conditions that exist in various societies to this day as well as in the past. However, those interested in a different interpretation of the causes of the exploitation of women in the Middle East should consult Gerda Lerner's *The Creation of Patriarchy* (1986), which links the exploitation of women in the ancient Near East to the emergence of state and class. Another relevant discussion which offers some insight is Deniz Kandiyoti's "patriarchal bargain" (Kandiyoti 1991).*

Pre-Literate Society, ca. 10,000 b.c.e.–ca. 3000 b.c.e.

Sometime between 10,000 and 12,000 years ago, a group of humans roaming the plains and hills of the Middle East discovered how to domesticate animals and plants. This radical new step in human history made all subsequent developments of civilization possible. Prior to this point, humans supported themselves through hunting and gathering. They were able to adapt to their environment better than other creatures. They had discovered fire and could communicate through language. They were skilled tool-makers and crafty hunters. On the basis of cave paintings, some archaeologists speculate that these humans even had developed certain hunting rituals. In short, they created some culture and were able to transmit it to their descendants.

Yet like all other creatures, they depended on the balance of nature; their life-style was dictated by the availability of game and vegetation in the surrounding area. Since game was their major source of food, they followed the game herds and led a nomadic life in small groups of between twenty and sixty persons. Such trekking made it hard for women to have more than one child every three to four years. The social organization of these groups was simple. There was some division of labor, but many tasks were communally performed. What little inequality existed was related to strength and intelligence. The strong had better food, and the more intelligent led the group when trouble struck.

Why did grain-centered cultures emerge early in the Middle East? The answer may be found in the favorable combination of climate and geography. As the ice caps began to recede, the earth's climatic zones assumed their present condition. The Middle East had a tem-

---

*In addition to the works cited within this section, see Boserup 1970; Gelb 1967.

perate climate and a varied environment, and sufficient rainwater fell during the colder months. The foothills of the Zagros mountains and the northern parts of the region were covered with a variety of vegetation, wild grains, and trees to support the scattered small human communities (Flannery 1965).

Many of these early communities were small and lived mainly in caves for shelter. Some may have migrated seasonally. A simple gender division of labor existed at the start of this period. In search of ungulates, men roamed over a vast and hard terrain—steep, rugged rock-slide areas for wild goats, rolling hills for wild sheep, and flat valleys for gazelles and hare. These animals made up 90 percent of the meat consumed by early Middle Easterners. The less-mobile women, perhaps carrying a baby in one arm, collected edible seeds in the wild patches of wild wheat and barley (Flannery 1965). Women also harvested the wild grain by hand or with the help of primitive spades, and they may have learned to distinguish over time the useful seeds from the less useful. In the course of searching for seeds, they probably learned about seasonal planting and the best time for harvest. Gradually they may have discovered that they could help the growth of the more useful grains by pulling the less desirable grasses. In these ways, women may have observed that by scattering seeds on prepared ground, they could create grain fields where none had existed before.

The discovery of agriculture, however, ushered in a new period of human history, developed by the groups scattered over the varied geographies and altitudes of the Middle East over several centuries. The Neolithic Age is considered by cultural historians the most fundamental human revolution, though its onset is difficult to pinpoint. By 5000 B.C.E., it had spread across a wide area of the Middle East, from the Nile valley to Mesopotamia (Flannery 1965).

As agriculture developed and spread, it eventually replaced hunting as the primary source of nourishment. The increase in food supply gradually permitted a rise in the population of these early communities. By some estimates, the population of an early site in present-day Iran increased fiftyfold between 8000 and 4000 B.C.E. The change ushered in a different life-style; communities began to settle near their fields, and early villages appeared. A related development was the domestication of animals. As population increased and game became scarce, hunters began to protect their prey from rival hunters for future use. Eventually some of the protected prey, such as sheep, goats, pigs, and cattle, became additional sources of food and wealth by providing milk, wool, and meat.

However, not all groups turned to farming. Those in the low-lands, where grass was plentiful, gradually abandoned the hunting of wild game as their primary source of food, in favor of raising live-stock, a more dependable resource. These groups, even when they engaged in some agriculture, did not settle down but continued to roam the region in search of pasture for their livestock. The survival of nomadism was also dictated by the scarcity of arable land in the Middle East. Throughout Middle Eastern history, whenever the density of the population surpassed available resources, some groups in the marginal zones reverted to pastoral nomadism. Although during normal times the life-styles of herding and farming were complementary and interdependent, in bad times—such as serious drought, famine, or political upheaval—deadly conflict could erupt over the scarce resources. The pastoralists usually were better equipped for war than were their settled neighbors. The threat of attack from pastoralists, either living within the region or coming from the outside, undermined the security of those engaged in agriculture. Until recent times, the conflict between settled agriculturalists and nomadic pastoralists has been a perennial feature of life in the Middle East (Rowton 1967; Ibn Khaldun 1967; Malcolm 1845; Saunders 1965).

The most important advantage of settling was easier availability of food, and in the long run, the communities that settled down grew faster than the nomadic groups. By 6000 B.C.E., settled agriculture had gained ascendance in the Middle East. Numerous villages, containing anywhere from two hundred to five thousand individuals, appeared from Iran and Turkey in the north to Iraq and Syria in the south (Knapp 1988).

Settled life made possible a slow and corresponding change in material culture. Within a short time after communities settled down, a wide range of metal tools, household items, clay cooking pots, and types of cloth (made of flax, goat's hair, and wool) were used in daily life. Houses made of reeds and mud-brick became common. The growth of these early agricultural communities was accompanied by the slow development of social institutions. One of the earliest and most important of these was the family, which by this time had become a more permanent unit composed of parents and their offspring. Older fertility rites and rituals gave way to more elaborate cults of earth, sky, and sun. Later, these cults evolved into an extended pantheon of deities, with an elaborate network of temples.

As the population expanded, land per capita began to shrink, a problem that was alleviated when farmers developed the traction plow and discovered the value of leaving land fallow. Using the plow increased production by breaking up the surface and aerating the soil more effectively; it also allowed cultivation of hitherto unworkable land. On the other hand, leaving land fallow replenished the soil. It is impossible to say exactly when the plow was invented, but these closely connected techniques spread slowly. We know only that they were used in the Middle East sometime before 3000 B.C.E. Women heretofore had helped men dig and loosen the hard soil with sticks and sharp stones in preparation for planting, but the widespread use of the plow gradually shifted the burden of hard agricultural labor to men and left women with lighter agricultural work (Boserup 1970). The use of the plow coincided with the introduction of another equally important innovation: the transition from dry farming to irrigation agriculture, a practice which also enabled the early communities to expand the areas under cultivation (Adams 1962; Saggs 1965). It seems reasonable to conclude that the construction of irrigation canals and dams also increasingly became men's work.

These innovations must have been welcomed by most women, who were already burdened with many time-consuming responsibilities, including child care and such household activities as cooking, carrying water and firewood over some distance, and weaving baskets and textiles. At the same time, women had more time to devote to another important task facing their communities: caring for the children and ensuring their survival. Relief for men from arduous and prolonged labor under the harsh Middle Eastern sun came with the use of draft animals to pull the plow. The introduction of the plow with draft animals and development of irrigation techniques increased agricultural surplus enough to lay the foundation for the next stage in the evolution of Mesopotamian culture: the development of urban life.

The Role of Women in Pre-Literate Society

Women played a pivotal role in every stage of the developments just described. Although we cannot know with any certainty, the high status accorded to women in rites and the mythology of Mesopotamia suggests that women may have been the primary agents in the discovery of agriculture. Women's early contributions in agriculture were often recognized and rewarded. Their role as the major suppliers of food for the community and their association with agriculture sometimes even brought them greater prestige than men. Such status is suggested by the valuable offerings found in their early burial sites discovered in Asia Minor. Some of these sites appear to have been used as temples and dedicated to religious observance. No comparable burial sites have been found for men (Seibert 1974). Evidence from Mesopotamia reveals that the early deities associated with different aspects of agriculture and the harvest were also female. In the following passage, the Mesopotamian deity Damu alludes to some of the tasks associated with and, perhaps, performed by women. As he is being taken to the underworld, Damu enumerates his mother's various roles—including her role as protector:

> I am not one who can answer my mother, who cries for me in
>   the desert
> Who makes the cry for me echo in the desert,
> She will not be answered!
> I am not the grass—may not come up for her (again)
> I am not the waters—may not rise for her (again)
> I am not the grass, sprouting in the desert,
> I am not the new grass, coming up in the desert.
> (Jacobsen 1970: 42)

The above passage also associates women with water, the most valuable resource in this arid region. Indeed, water availability was a major concern of these early communities, and the preservation of water seems to have been women's responsibility. Men went hunting, so it was most likely the women who had to get water for the use of the household. Mesopotamian legends link women to this important task, and early Mesopotamian deities associated with water were women. In an account from Mesopotamia, Inanna, one of the most important goddesses of Sumer, laments the killing of her husband, Dumuzi, the shepherd, at the hand of the farmer Girgir, the son of Bilulu, a female deity and "Matriarch and her own mistress." Inanna avenges her husband's death by turning Bilulu into a "a water skin for cold water that [men carry] in the desert." Another significant point is that at an earlier stage of Mesopotamian mythology, Bilulu was the goddess associated with rain and thunder. However, in later Mesopotamian religious thought, the deity's gender changed to male (Jacobsen 1970: 57, 69). The change may mirror the demotion of women by that time and the important position men had attained as suppliers of water to the community by way of irrigation agriculture.

Women were also crucial in population growth. Once the early communities settled, individual women could bear children at closer intervals than when they had lived as nomads and could devote more effort to raising them. The importance of women's contribution to population growth is reflected in legends and myths from Mesopotamia and elsewhere. In the early stories of creation, the mother stood at the center of religious conceptions. (See discussion of creation, below.)

The value of children is suggested by the labor-intensive nature of agriculture, the rise of slavery, the increasing need for defense, and the institution of adoption. Adoption was practiced when urban life appeared, but its origins precede this period. In the village, a woman would raise children during most of her adult life because life expectancy for women in many pre-modern societies rarely exceeded the childbearing years. Demographic studies from a later period, the Middle East under the Romans, suggest that women's life expectancy at birth was twenty-one to twenty-four (Bagnall and Frier 1994). However, this highly important social role made women housebound. As long as communities remained small, women continued to participate in communal affairs. According to Thorkild Jacobsen, mythological evidence suggests that in pre-literate Mesopotamia, women took part in major community deliberations. He draws this conclusion from references to the participation of female goddesses in the assembly of gods (Jacobsen 1970). Although his conclusion sounds reasonable, it would be safe to assume that as women devoted more time to child care and other responsibilities, their participation in communal decision-making declined.

Although the invention of the plow released women from hard agricultural work, women often continued to perform much of the less physically demanding agricultural work. They still helped at harvest time, tended the vegetable plots, milked the cattle, ensured that fires did not die, cooked the meals, baked bread, cleaned their houses, and fetched water. Very likely, women and children became the first potters. Women made baskets and, later, wove wool, cotton, and flax. The association of women with weaving is suggested from the fact that Uttu, the deity of weaving, was a female (Jacobsen 1970).

The importance of the role women played in these early agricultural communities is confirmed by their strong presence in religious literature. Interestingly enough, the position of female deities in the hierarchy of gods mirrors their actual role in the various communities. For example, in the farming communities, female deities occupy the most important positions. The most important male god was Enlil, and his wife Ninlil was a goddess. In addition, she was the daughter of the goddess of grain and of ripening barley. Another important farming goddess was Nissaba, the goddess of cereal and grass. This goddess later became the "patroness of writing and the scribal arts, particularly of accounting" (Jacobsen 1970: 32). This last function may indicate the early importance of women in the administration of pre-literate temples.

In contrast, among the people who lived in the marshlands and raised stock, men were responsible for the important activity of administrating temples. Similarly, the important deities were males generally. Their major deity was Enki, a male god. His father was Enlil, also a god, but his mother was Enlil's housekeeper, not a goddess. Even among the herding communities, there was at least one important female deity; agriculture was represented by a female deity (Jacobsen 1970). This strongly suggests that before the introduction of the plow, women were playing a vital role.

Although ancient Mesopotamian communities and later city-states each had their own pantheon of gods, they also shared some deities. The most important of these deities was Inanna, a female, whose name was later changed to Ishtar, and who became a male god. According to Jacobsen, she was initially the deity who watched over the storehouse, where the community kept its most valuable resources: meat, grain, dairy products, and wool. Famine represented the worst calamity for the early human communities, and the association of Inanna with the storehouse, an insurance against famine, indicates the importance women played in providing and protecting foodstuffs (Jacobsen 1970).

What most reveals women's importance in these farming communities is the role of female deities in the earliest accounts of creation. Although these early communities lacked clear cosmogonic concepts, their myths tried to provide some answers to creation. No one knows when the first myths of creation were developed, but they originated before the invention of writing, and sometime before 3000 B.C.E. These early stories of creation reveal an important development in the Mesopotamian attitude toward women. In many of the myths, creation seems to have emerged from a female deity, a fact attested to by numerous statues of "the Great Mother" found throughout the Middle East (Seibert 1974). In Mesopotamian religious beliefs, goddesses shared the responsibility for creation with gods. In one story, the goddess Nammu—the goddess of the sea, according to Kramer, or "the watery deep," according to Jacobsen—conceived the first two deities, one male and one female, who created all others (Jacobsen 1970; Kramer 1976). The primeval source is the goddess Tiamat, "she who bore them all" (Roux 1980: 98). In another Sumerian tale, the great mother goddess, Ninhursag, was responsible for the birth of Ninti, who was born to heal the god Enki. This sets a sharp contrast to the familiar Biblical story of Adam and Eve, written some two thousand years later than the early Sumerian versions. In the Bible, the first woman is created out of the first man's rib. We are also told that Eve led Adam astray, that Eve's weakness led to their expulsion from Paradise and was the source of all of humanity's subsequent suffering. The association of women with the beginnings of life in Sumerian legends is also reflected in an early version of the story of the flood. The goddess Ishtar (still a woman), after agreeing with the decision of the assembly of gods to destroy humans by unleashing a flood, is beside herself when she realizes what is about to happen:

> Ishtar shrieks like a woman in birth pangs,
> The lovely voiced lady of the gods yells aloud:
> "The times before are indeed turned to earth,
> Because I myself in the gods' assembly
> Gave the ill counsel!
> How could I in the gods' assembly give such ill counsel,
> to decree the fight
> For the destruction of my mankind?
> I alone gave birth to my mankind." (Jacobsen 1970: 165)

The material above suggests that women were not only important contributors to the early communities but also received high recognition for their role in the advance of culture. Despite their likely pivotal role in the discovery of agriculture and the tremendous economic advances it generated, the agricultural revolution ultimately had mixed results for women.

To be sure, the new agricultural methods increased the food supply and made it more dependable. They also contributed to the expansion of the population and enhanced the possibility of forming permanent settlements. However, these same factors encouraged the fertility of women. Consequently, as women began to have additional children, they had less time to engage in heavier agricultural work, which required physical labor and long hours in the field. Contemporary evidence suggests that women in plow-using cultures prefer to devote themselves to work inside the house and lighter agricultural work in general (Boserup 1970). This has also been typical of the Middle Eastern women in areas where traditional agriculture is still practiced (Lambton 1953). We have no reason to believe that individual women in the pre-literate period would not have made a such a choice under similar circumstances.

While these developments and the changes that they helped bring about improved the material well-being of individual women, they contributed to the gradual loss of their social power and prestige, accelerating men's control over economic activity and social resources. They began to tip the scale of social power in favor of men, laying down the foundation on which women's subordination to men, as individuals and as a group, began to be erected. But despite the decline in social power and prestige, women continued to make important contributions to the evolution and progress of society. To see this, we must turn to the evolution of urban life and the emergence of Sumerian civilization.

The Sumerians and the Emergence of Agrarian-Urban Culture, 3500 B.C.E.–2000 B.C.E.

Although the agricultural revolution took place over a wide area, urban life emerged sometime between 3500 and 3000 B.C.E. in a limited territory—in the southern half of the delta between the Euphrates and Tigris rivers, the area known as Mesopotamia. The emergence of cities is in turn associated with the story of a remarkable people known as the Sumerians. Historians believe that climate and geography seem to have been the primary factors that eventually led to the rise of urban life in this dry area of the delta. It is thought that the decline in the rainfall in the northern part of the delta and the foothills of southwestern Iran may have forced some of the population from these areas to migrate to the delta region, where irrigation agriculture had already proved successful (Crawford 1991).

In the early part of the fourth millennium, large numbers of people seem to have migrated into southern Mesopotamia, which was already settled and relied on irrigation from rivers and their tributaries (Roux 1980). The absence of records of invasion or conquest by an outside force suggests that the newcomers arrived peacefully. As they entered the area, not as conquerors but in small bands, they had to settle land farther away from the river than that settled by earlier inhabitants. To convert their desert lots into fertile fields, they became more resourceful. Perhaps their need to feed the growing population spurred subsequent innovations, which increased food production and eventually increased other goods. Gradually these settlements began to attract more of the population and became the nucleus of the various city-states of Sumer.

The period 3500-2000 B.C.E. is marked by innumerable innovations. The Sumerians became the catalysts for many of the developments that make the third millennium one of the high points of human achievement (Roux 1980). The Sumerians may have developed bronze or borrowed this development from others; the discovery opened the way to the use of metallurgical technology and generated a wide range of cultural, economic, and socio-political developments. Cities had appeared in the preceding millennium, but it was in this period that urban life grew more complex and helped to change social organization. Urban life stimulated economic development, particularly the growth of long-distance trade, that generated new wealth, stimulated new crafts, and encouraged further specialization. These developments surely facilitated the invention of writing.

Cities had a diverse population and were characterized by considerable specialization by occupation. Although the cities relied on the products of their hinterland, farmers and agricultural laborers were no longer the majority of the population, which also now included merchants and artisans. The thriving urban center became a frequent target of plunder. The need for protection resulted in the emergence of a full-time military class (Adams 1962). The military and religious classes were at the top of the social pyramid. Maintained by other groups within the society, they in return provided protection from outside attack, kept internal order, and conciliated the gods with prayers.

Gradually a few of the leading families consolidated their control of political and economic institutions. Sumer's increased inequality in political and economic power eroded the closer ties that had existed in the earlier small communities and produced distinct social classes. Members of the privileged groups tried to perpetuate their economic and political power. Perhaps for this reason, the larger social units, such as the clan and extended family, gradually gave way to the smaller nuclear family, which became the most important social unit (Gelb 1972). The desire to perpetuate privilege may also explain why paternity acquired increasing importance in Sumerian society. The beginnings of the division of Middle Eastern society along gender lines can be traced to the greater specialization in crafts—as will be discussed below. As specialization created more wealth, families wanted to transfer some of this wealth to their own children. The easiest way for men to ensure their children's pure descent was to control women's sexuality by confining women to activities within the household.

Religion played an important role in urban life, and its power was represented by the temple. Each city-state had its own particular god, and these were sometimes female deities. Supreme authority in Sumerian society derived from gods, and all the temple officials were divine servants. In early Sumer, both religious and secular leaders were in the service of the gods, and the lines of demarcation between the two were not distinctly drawn. Later these two authorities were separated, but even after the emergence of strong secular leadership, the city god and his or her temple remained the most important expression of the city's identity. Initially, the temple was the focal point around which the city revolved. The temple elite in each city-state owned a sizable portion of the economic resources, both agricultural and manufacturing, and a large proportion of the working population also was employed by the temple (Knapp 1988).

The Sumerian era lasted nearly one-and-a-half millennia. Effective political power during the next two millennia b.c.e. passed to the various Semitic and Indo-European tribes that continued to infiltrate Mesopotamia, but the decline of Sumerian political power did not end Sumerian cultural influence. The urban institutions provided a model for succeeding populations within the immediate area and in the surrounding regions, as far as Western Europe. Even after their name was forgotten, many features of their civilization endured in a modified form in the cultures of the states that succeeded them, both before and after the advent of Islam in the Middle East (Kramer 1983).

The reason for the longevity of Sumerian cultural influence can be found in the fact that its civilization had emerged in response to the needs of urban life. Although over the next several thousand years social and political institutions grew more complex as the population expanded and wealth increased, the underlying economic conditions that gave rise to Sumerian civilization did not change radically. The economic base remained ultimately dependent on the surplus provided by agriculture until well into the nineteenth century. However, agricultural production in the Middle East depended on a precarious balance between human ingenuity and natural conditions, particularly the aridity of the land. Even in cities where long-distance trade played an important role, trade partly depended on what the peasant produced. The pastoralists, including desert nomads, also depended on the peasants for much of their food and other goods. Therefore, we may be justified in calling these economies agrarian urban societies (Hodgson 1974). Because the economic structure did not change markedly until the nineteenth century, the social and political conditions originally developed during the Sumerian period managed to survive. Urban life, with its concentration of population, gradually introduced elements of rank, status, and power within the population. The expansion of social organization, the development of religious and political institutions, and the increasingly complex specialization organized the population into different occupational and social categories. Those at the top made the major decisions. As time went on, the lines of social demarcation grew more rigid and became permanent divisions between the rulers and the ruled. What perhaps saved the Middle East from developing a caste system was its vulnerable geographic location, which constantly brought in new groups of people from the outside. Newcomers were absorbed by the existing social organization; hence, despite continual flux at the top of the social scale, the hierarchical nature of Middle Eastern society did not change perceptibly until the late nineteenth century, when the underlying economic base began to be shaken.

Women's Roles from 3000 B.C.E. to C.E. 600

Thanks to the invention of writing by the Sumerians, a wide variety of sources have survived—for example, economic and political records and correspondence, law codes, court proceedings, marriage and divorce contracts, literary and artistic works, religious writings, seals and artifacts, and burial remains. Although these diverse sources contain invaluable information about women, they have rarely been utilized for the study of women in the periods they cover, for a number of reasons. Most are in dead languages that can be read only by specialists, who until the last decade had little interest in the study of women's history. Nor is there consensus among scholars about what has been translated or studied. Much of the information contained in these sources deals mainly with women at the top of the social scale. Nevertheless, despite their narrow social base, they also shed light on women in other strata of society, since women at the lower reaches of society were employed by temples and in the households of the rich and engaged in diverse types of activities covered by these records (Van De Mieroop 1989).

Although neither the written records nor archeological evidence easily surrenders an accurate and detailed picture of women's history in the period under discussion, careful examination of the primary and secondary data provides some useful insight about the evolution of women's function in society. On the basis of the evidence, we can observe a slow but unmistakable deterioration in the legal, political, and to a lesser degree the economic position of women in this period (Kramer 1976). These changes seem to have been directly related to developments that were generated by the rise of urban life.

Before examining the various aspects of decline in the position of women, let us first explore why the emergence of urban life caused changes in their roles, a question that has not been adequately addressed in the context of the Middle East. It was suggested above that women's social power began to diminish following the agricultural revolution, which introduced the use of the plow, required the building of irrigation canals and dikes, and resulted in longer hours of work per day to increase the level of productivity. As the population increased, men had to devote more time to agriculture and women had to spend more time raising children and doing lighter agricultural work.

An important feature of urban life was specialization in many professions and crafts, which required the investment of much more time than women had available. For example goldsmiths, glass-makers, and masons had considerable expertise, and such activities were not compatible with child care and household duties. Furthermore, in the urban setting women's work was more time consuming than in the village, extended households divided the burden among several women, and food could be acquired more easily. (For a modern example of how this arrangement worked, see Fernea 1965.)

Poorer women did work outside the home some of the time. But if they were married, they had to take care of their children and also manage a household. Not surprisingly, this combination of duties would leave little time to worry about major decisions related to the outside world. So even when women worked outside the house, they generally could not work as long or earn as much as men. Evidence from the late third millennium B.C.E. shows a large gap between women's and men's wages in several professions. For example, skilled women oil pressers received 50 liters of barley per month, whereas the men received 300 liters (Van De Mieroop 1989). Even in the case of a profession like oil pressing, which requires physical strength, the discrepancy in wages cannot be explained by the differences in male and female productivity alone, but also probably reflects the discrimination against women in this period. Such wage differentials might well have discouraged many women from seeking jobs outside their homes. Considering the burden that working outside the home placed on women and the meager returns such work brought them, it is no wonder that marital life and motherhood appeared more attractive alternatives. In urban communities, as men began to earn a larger portion of a family's income, they exercised greater control over the use of these resources.

Another factor that may have encouraged women to devote more time to household activity was the greater demand for children throughout this period. Despite the dearth of information on Middle

Eastern demography, we know that the number of cities began to increase, as did the size of their populations, though not always at a steady pace. However, the population would not have increased without a rise in the fertility of women of child-bearing age, both in urban areas and in the countryside, where the food was being produced. Though uncertainty brought on by warfare or drought and famine would have temporarily put a stop to or reversed this trend, the population does seem to have slowly been on the rise in this period. It would also follow that such a trend would have made children more valuable and encouraged greater emphasis on child rearing as a worthwhile activity.

When we turn to the available evidence, even though it is sporadic and sparse, we observe the presence and spread of values that emphasized and extolled having more children. Evidence from the Neo-Babylonian period suggests that the age of first marriage in the ancient Middle East was mid- to late teens for the bride and around thirty for the bridegroom; these ages have been remarkably consistent for marriage until recent times (Roth 1987). The prevalence of this type of marriage also suggests the importance of and need for more children.

The legal code and religious teachings also encouraged marriage and, even more importantly, procreation. This emphasis is brought out by laws regulating marriage and divorce. In the Sumerian period, a husband could marry a second time only if his first wife did not bear children. This same rule applied to the husbands of *naditu* women, who were in the service of the temples. A *naditu* was allowed to marry but could not have children. Furthermore, after a man had children with his female slave he was not allowed to sell her. Causing a pregnant woman to miscarry was punished by a severe fine (Pritchard 1958). At the death of a father, the unmarried male and female children were entitled to use a share of his wealth to provide a dowry for the daughter and brideprice for the son. A late Sumerian law required a husband who divorced his wife to give her half his assets for the upkeep of their children. After they came of age, she was entitled to a dowry of the remaining assets to enable her to remarry. But if the wife was childless, the divorcing husband was still required to pay her a fine and return her original dowry.

The importance of children seems to have increased over time. By the seventh century C.E., Zoroastrian religious teachings condemned to eternal damnation those women who, in order to nurse the children of others, did not breast-feed their own children. The same punishment threatened women who aborted their fetuses (Haug and West 1872). The prevalence of adoption is another sign of the importance of children. Having children was so important in the late Sasanian period (c.e. 226–651) that a married man who died childless would be considered the father of the first child of his wife by another man, so that someone would pray for him.

The high rate of child mortality in pre-modern times and a less-healthy urban environment made child care more demanding; it is not surprising that women stayed home to bring up healthy children. By doing so, each woman may have contributed to the loss of power of women as a whole. This example illustrates the conflict of interest between what is beneficial for the individual woman and what is beneficial for women as a group.

As cities expanded, their population increased, their social and economic organization became more complex, and women tended to specialize more and more in child-rearing and activities that could be easily carried out in the house. In addition to food preparation and other household activities, these could also include spinning, weaving, pottery-making, and the processing of food. During the next two thousand years, women became less active outside the home. As women's access to the outside world became more limited, their role as wife began to assume greater importance and in turn highlighted women as sexual objects with a procreative role. Home-based activities began to be regarded as the most important activity for women (Glassner 1989). Side by side with these greater restrictions, certain attitudes and assumptions about women appeared. Men's work was valued more than women's work, and women received a much smaller ration for doing the same type of work as men (Van De Mieroop 1989). Eventually men's greater earning power began to be viewed as a sign of their superiority and greater intelligence.

As women became more isolated and limited to household activities, they grew more dependent on men for their subsistence. Consequently, men could more readily bring pressure to bear on women. Because men increasingly controlled the resources of society, they began to modify the moral code to further their needs and interests. Nowhere are these moral values more strikingly indicative of male bias than in the laws that regulate sexuality and the relationship between men and women. To protect the purity of the male line, virginity before marriage and continued fidelity afterward became mandatory for women. Those who deviated from the moral code were severely punished. Because these values were reinforced with religious teachings, women internalized these values and began to judge themselves by the standards set by men. The erosion of women's power was slow, but over the centuries, a gradual decline can be readily observed in their legal and political power, though not as clearly in their economic power. This decline affected women differently, depending on social rank. Women of the ruling and wealthier classes were not as affected by the loss of economic power, but their freedom of movement became restricted. A brief review of the changes that affected women will be useful.

WOMEN IN ECONOMIC LIFE

Most of the available economic information is about women of the ruling and the wealthier classes. These records show that women had the right to own property and to engage in different types of economic activity. However, as time went on, their roles in controlling and managing important economic enterprises for the state seem to have declined and perhaps even disappeared.

The historical records and building inscriptions show that during certain periods of Sumerian history, wives and daughters of rulers and high officials played an important role in the economy and possibly the administration of the various Sumerian city-states. These women generally managed and controlled vast households, which were the economic center of the city-state. The relationship between the household of the ruler and the main temple of the city has not been resolved, and some overlap can be observed between the temple and the royal (the queen's and or the king's) household in their function as the center of the city's administration. But there is little doubt that in certain periods royal wives played an active role in running the royal household. For example, records from the Sumerian city of Girsu in the twenty-fourth century B.C.E. show that Dimtur and Barannamtrara, wives of the city's successive rulers, controlled the e-Mi, the administrative center of the city. This center was later renamed e-Bau to indicate its additional function as a temple of the goddess Bau. The wives' household had under its jurisdiction vast agricultural lands, and they supervised and managed fruit orchards and vegetable gardens. The household owned cattle, sheep, and pigs and employed about one hundred fishermen. It also operated some industrial activities, such as textile workshops. The labor force consisted of male and female laborers, who were assigned rations of food, malt, and wool. The ration lists reveal that some of the female workers brought their children with them to work (Van De Mieroop 1989).

A question that cannot be answered with certainty is whether royal women were entrusted with these responsibilities as independent officials or in their capacity as relations of the ruler. Dimtur did not disappear from the administrative records immediately after her husband's death. Baranamtara was replaced by Shasha immediately when her husband was overthrown by Shasha's husband, Uru'inimgina. Women, however, ceased to appear in these administrative positions in later records.

In the Sumerian period (3500–2000 B.C.E.) wives of rulers and governors were able to use their wealth to engage "in production and sale of wool and textiles, lending, dealings in real estate and slaves" (Silver 1985). Some of these women also engaged in regional trade through their agents. Commercial activity was not limited to women in the royal households, however. Women of the wealthy and the merchant classes also engaged in these activities. They continued to be active in the second millennium, and evidence from seals used for validation of a variety of contracts shows that women played entrepreneurial roles and were active in international trade. During Hammurabi's period women served as witnesses to contracts and as scribes, an indication of their high place in business activities.

What were the sources of women's wealth? Usually it came from inheritance or was given to them by their husbands. Marriage contracts contained clauses in which the husband promised to give his wife a share of his wealth. However, some women seem to have acquired their wealth through their own work. Typically, what the wife inherited or earned was hers alone, and the husband had no right to interfere with it. When husbands or other members of the family did, the women sought redress in the courts (Batto 1974; Silver 1985).

Women of the lower classes also engaged in a wide variety of economic activities, the most important being the manufacture of textiles, which women apparently dominated. A late third millennium text indicates that textile factories were large and staffed mainly by women (Silver 1988). Women were employed in breweries, and frequently worked as tavern keepers or bakers; they were even prophets and interpreters of dreams. The menial tasks in the households of the rich and in temples were generally performed by slaves (Batto 1974), but temples also employed women in their workshops. The temples, in fact, provided women with employment and opportunities to develop managerial skills. Women held the highest positions, such as *en*-priestesses, to lesser ones, including the *naditu*s, or workers in many of the activities run by the temples. In the third and second millennia, women also worked as scribes. Even prostitution was an acceptable option. Apparently, it was not regarded as socially degrading, undoubtedly due to its early association with the cult of Inanna (later Ishtar), the goddess of love and fertility (Seibert 1974).

The ability of well-to-do women to own property and other assets, and the presence of lower-class women in some occupations outside the house, did not diminish over time. In the seventh century C.E., women were as visible in economic life as they had been at the beginning of this period.

POLITICAL RIGHTS

Evidence of women's involvement in political activity is meager and sporadic, since in much of the period under discussion political power was controlled by a small group of men at the top. However, women seem to have exercised a greater degree of political power in the third millennium B.C.E. than is generally recognized. Gradually their political power waned, and by the first millennium B.C.E. political power seems to have passed completely to men. Though the evidence for the women's involvement in political activity is circumstantial, it is nevertheless persuasive. In his discussion of primitive democracy in Sumer, Jacobsen has suggested that initially women may have participated more actively in political deliberations than they were later allowed to do. In his view, Sumerian women were considered citizens though they may not have participated in major decisions by the city-states (Jacobsen 1970).

In addition, archaeological finds from the Heroic Age of Sumer (2700–2500 B.C.E.) reveal that queens had their own seals and "occupied an important role beside the charismatic warriors who ruled Sumerian city states" (Hallo 1976: 27). During the next stage, the Dynastic State (2500–2300 B.C.E.), women's names appear on the dynastic tables, and women themselves formed a link of legitimacy in succession. The Sumerian king list for this period mentions the name of a woman, Ku-Bau, "who consolidated the foundation of Kish, became 'king' and reigned a hundred years" (Harris 1989: 147). But in later traditions, Ku-Bau is described in an unflattering way as an "alewife" and her reign is mentioned as the cause of the conquest of Kish by Sargon (2350-2294 B.C.E.). The reasons for these derogatory references are not hard to detect. By the time her tradition was being recorded, women's active role in society was frowned upon. Therefore, while the male kings were being turned into legendary heroes, her reign was described as an aberration and cause of misfortune—even though Kish was taken by Sargon not during her time but in the reign of her grandson, Ur-Zababa. Her long reign, however, indicates that her contemporaries did not consider her rule abnormal, but rather viewed it positively. Furthermore, in Ku-Bau's period women participated in all spheres of life, as attested to above. The political role played by women in the early period of Sumerian history thus lends credence to Jacobsen's view.

In his discussion of the extensive economic activities of royal women in Girsu, Van De Mieroop has suggested that these women were also empowered with some independent authority to exchange letters and gifts with royal wives in other city states. The fact that these women administrators would be removed from their posts should not detract from the importance of the position these women held. Obviously, the administration of such vast economic units, even if managed in the king's name, must have carried enormous authority and political weight (Van De Mieroop 1989). It is also an indication that the wielding of such power by women was accepted at this early stage of Sumerian history.

But gradually women began to lose the independence and authority they had as managers of the royal households. According to Batto, when women acquired political positions, as they did in Mari and other Mesopotamian cities in the second millennium, the queen's authority depended on the prerogative of the individual king. In Batto's opinion, the ascendance of women in Mari was no longer representative of the times but reflected the dynasty's pastoral background and culture, which allowed women greater participation in public life than did urban culture. This particular dynasty had not yet been acculturated to the ways of Mesopotamia (Batto 1974).

Another position of great influence open to women was that of high priestess, or *en*, of a temple. According to Sumerian religious practices, each city had a temple dedicated to the service of its god. If the god was female, the *en* would be male; if the god was male god, the *en* would be female. One of the earliest recorded priestesses is Enheduanna, daughter of the above-mentioned Sargon. She was appointed by her father as the head of the main temple at Ur, one of Sumer's largest temples. According to Kramer, Enheduanna was also a distinguished poet and writer (Kramer 1976). The position from this time on was occupied by daughters of rulers, but an incumbent high priestess of Ur would not lose her position because of her father's death or the dynasty's downfall (Hallo 1989).

Initially *en* designated both secular and religious authority, but gradually the title was applied only to those in the religious sphere (Knapp 1988). The use of the term *en* (lord, used in reference to a deity) to designate the highest priestess in the temple offers an intriguing possibility. It would be worth exploring whether any woman in the pre-literate period enjoyed both secular and religious authority. Though temples had lost their secular function by the end of the third millennium, they still played an important role in the social and economic structure of each city. Therefore, the significance of this role as a barometer of women's political power should not be overlooked.

A new development that paralleled women's loss of political power was the prevalence of dynastic marriage to cement alliances between quarreling city states. This trend, an indication that even the royal princesses were beginning to lose control over their destiny, continued during the second millennium even after the rise of more stable national states in Mesopotamia. No doubt it reflected some of the other developments in the role of women.

The first millennium, known as the Age of Empire, witnessed the rise of states that brought under control much of what is known as the Middle East. Women became increasingly less visible in public office during this period. The exclusion of women from public life is demonstrated by the dearth of documentary evidence about them. The decline in the public role of women and their political influence is also confirmed by their absence from important positions within the temple. Although women could not hold cultic offices that required performance of any functions within the temple, they were still able to inherit or receive shares of temple property. Such a restriction seems to have been motivated by a desire to minimize women's contact with the outside world (Kuhrt 1989).

During the first half of the first millennium C.E., women faced further restrictions on assuming public positions. The rule of two women, Buran (or Purandukht) and Azarmidukht, in the late Sasanian period (C.E. 226–651) indicates that there were no institutional barriers to prevent women from gaining the highest political office. But these rulers were chosen during a critical period of civil war, when competing factions had run out of suitable male contenders. The same applied to the Byzantine empire. Wives of emperors wielded a great deal of political power because of the favor they curried with their husbands. A large body of evidence reveals that there was no lack of able women to assume public office. Rather, women stayed out of politics because of prevailing attitudes toward a woman's place in society. This awareness is amply revealed in a speech by Theodora, the wife of Emperor Justinian (C.E. 527–565). She personally averted one of the most serious crises of his reign by going out and meeting with a hostile mob. In her address, she apologized to the men for appearing among them and for showing daring, since such behavior was improper for women (Bullough 1973; Herrin 1993).

LEGAL STATUS

The change in women's legal position is striking evidence of the decline of their power and is illustrated in the evolution of the laws of marriage and divorce. Marriage was an important institution, and procreation was considered its main aim. As noted earlier, this aspect of marriage was encouraged by the provisions of the various codes of law. In early Sumer, marriage was treated seriously and required a written contract between the husband and the wife's guardians. Furthermore, a man had to ask the permission of both father and mother for their daughter's hand (Pritchard 1958: I, 135). The need for the mother's permission was later dropped from the codes of law; the man was required to pay bridewealth to the girl's father. This payment has been interpreted by some historians as a purchase price for the wife, indicating that she became the absolute property of the husband (Bullough 1973; Seibert 1974). But this argument neglects to take into account other evidence showing that women continued to have civil rights after marriage, although fewer rights than men. For example, the father was required to provide a dowry for his daughter, a sum usually at least equal to the bridewealth. This interpretation is supported by the laws of inheritance, under which the father was obligated to provide his male and female children with sufficient dowry and bridewealth. Women retained their economic rights, including rights to what they earned.

Throughout most of the period (3500 B.C.E.–C.E. 600), marriage was generally monogamous, and the position of the wife was relatively secure. A man was allowed to take a second wife, however, if the first wife did not bear children. According to the Law of Eshnunna, of the early second millennium B.C.E., the second wife had to be of a lower status—slave or concubine—so as not to challenge the primacy of the first wife. But the laws of marriage gradually changed and made it easier for men to have more than one wife. By the time of the Assyrians, about a thousand years later, the rulers had more than one wife and many concubines. In the seventh century C.E., both Judaism and Zoroastrianism allowed polygamy. Even Christianity, despite its hostility to sexuality, compromised with the current trends and sanctioned concubinage. In practice, however, only the wealthy and the rulers took advantage of this privilege (Bullough 1973; Parsay 1977; Pigulevskaja 1963).

The idea of the husband as absolute and undisputed master of the household arose in Sumer. In theory, neither the wife nor the children had the right to disagree with him, although a new bride had the right to refuse having intercourse with her husband without incurring punishment. Nonetheless, by 2500 B.C.E., a law empowered the husband to break his wife's teeth with burnt brick if she disagreed with him (Seibert 1974). After monotheism appeared in the Middle East, religious teachings further pressured women by attempting to instill in women total subordination to their husbands. For example, a religious work written in the ninth century C.E. (but believed to be of late-Sasanian origin) stated, "Those [women] who practiced acquiescence and conformity, reverence and obedience to their husband and lord" would be rewarded with eternal salvation. Defiant wives were threatened with eternal hellfire (Haug and West 1872). Although religious norms demanded total obedience to husband and devotion to children, they did not reward women for compliance. Women were thought to be inferior to men, and their judgment was deemed untrustworthy: men were advised not to confide in their wives. Women's right to refuse sex with the husband also vanished by the time of the Code of Hammurabi (1792–1750 B.C.E.). A woman who refused to consummate her marriage could be killed by drowning, and a late Sasanian Zoroastrian text warned that women who refused their husband's sexual demands would suffer dire punishment in hell (Haug and West 1872).

Women's position also deteriorated with regard to divorce. In the third millennium, a Sumerian woman had the right to dissolve her marriage. According to the Law of Eshnunna (early second millennium), a man could not divorce his wife and take another if he had children by her. If he did so, he would be penalized: "He shall be driven from his house and from whatever he owns" (Pritchard 1958: I, 138). The Code of Hammurabi, perhaps two hundred years later, placed restrictions on the wife's ability to divorce, but the husband was now able to divorce his wife. (As noted earlier, he did, however, have to support her and the children.) A childless wife could be divorced more easily (Pritchard 1958). Women could seek divorce, but they had to petition the city council. If a woman had not humiliated her husband publicly, she would be allowed to divorce him: "That woman without incurring any blame at all, may take her dowry and go off to her father's house." However, if she had caused her husband public humiliation, "then they shall throw that woman into the water" (Pritchard 1958: I, 153-154). However, the right of the husband

to divorce his wife without obligation to her was further strengthened over time. A few centuries later, the law provided that "[w]hen
a husband leaves his wife, he will give her something if his heart
desires; if he does not desire it, he will not give her anything; she will
leave empty handed" (Seibert 1974: 15). Finally, by the seventh century c.e., although Christian men could divorce their wives, divorce
was much harder for the women. Among Zoroastrians divorce was
limited to men, and the woman was not allowed to remarry while
the husband lived (Bullough 1973; Parsay 1977).

Another measure of women's status is the type of punishment
meted out for the murder of a free woman. In the Law of Eshnunna,
causing death to a woman—no matter what her status—was considered a capital offense, and the person would be put to death. By the
time of the Code of Hammurabi, however, if a person caused a noble-
woman's death, his punishment would be to put his own daughter to
death. The death of a female commoner, on the other hand, would
incur only a fine.

One law that did not change much over the period under discussion was the punishment for adultery, defined as intercourse between
a married woman and any man other than her husband. In the Law
of Eshnunna, the punishment for adultery was death for both partners. The major aim of the adultery law was to bolster the husband's
right to ensure the purity of his descent. Thus the code distinguished
between the rape of an unmarried virgin and the rape of a virgin who
was engaged to be married. In the first case, the man was required to
marry his victim. In the second case, the rape was treated as one-sided
adultery, and the man was put to death (Finkelstein 1966). The same
attitude prevailed toward adultery in the seventh century c.e. Among
the Jews, the guilty were stoned. In Zoroastrian teachings, eternal
damnation awaited the guilty. Christianity adopted a double standard toward adultery: it overlooked men's extramarital relations while
treating women's transgressions more strictly. The husband who did
not divorce an adulterous wife was charged with the crime of pan-
dering (Bullough 1973).

The Veil and Seclusion

It is difficult to state with certainty why the veil was introduced. Most
likely it was part of the attempt to isolate women and minimize their
contact with men. According to earlier studies, the purpose of the
veil was to protect upper-class women from the gaze of common men,
but the reasons are ultimately not clear. More recent studies, however, view the veil as an indication of the marital status of woman.

Evidence from Sumerian sources reveals that it was the husband who, during the wedding ceremony, covered his spouse's head with the veil (Glassner 1989). This practice would suggest that some sort of veiling was already in force almost three millennia before the rise of Islam. In addition, recent findings from Sumerian graves indicate that court ladies seem to have worn a fine veil, or head covering (Crawford 1991). While Mesopotamian society sanctioned prostitution, it also required heavy protection of those who were to be future wives. It distinguished between woman as "prostitute," who embodies sexual pleasure, and woman as "spouse," who embodies domesticity. The former is a woman of the outside, who offers her services at the door of the temple, the tavern, and the square. The latter stays indoors to protect her purity and shield it from evil influences that could defile her husband's honor. This sharp distinction emphasized virginity of women before marriage and probably prompted parents to keep their unmarried daughters indoors. A provision of the Law of Eshnunna puts some of the responsibility for ensuring a girl's virginity on the parents, lest she be raped. Evidence from the Assyrian period indicates that by the mid-second millennium, free married women were required to comply with a dress code when they left their houses. The Assyrian code stated, "Wives or [daughters as well as concubines] when [they go out] on the street, are to have their heads [covered]. The daughters . . . whether in [street] costume . . . or in garments of [the house] . . . are to be veiled [and] their heads [covered]. . . . If she goes out into the street during the day, she is to be veiled" (Jastrow 1921: 211). This same law forbids prostitutes from veiling themselves and even threatens them with punishment for veiling, since this would be an act of deception. Contrary to what Jastrow suggests, the veil does not seem to indicate that the woman was the property of the father or husband, but rather that she is chaste. The fact that brides in recent times also wear a veil may be derived from this earlier practice.

Perhaps seclusion of women was developed for a similar reason. The Assyrian kings of the fourteenth to the eleventh centuries B.C.E. were the first rulers to develop extensive rules regulating life within the royal household and the duties of the palace officials. The women of the royal household lived in secluded quarters within the palace (Seibert 1974). This practice seems to have become standard in following dynasties. The women of Achamenid dynasty (559–331 B.C.E.) were also secluded. By the seventh century C.E., respectable women in the Byzantine and Sasanian empires were secluded, and they appeared in public veiled (Bullough 1973).

Ruling-class and wealthy women were freed from domestic drudgery by using slaves. These wealthy women had the economic resources, access to education, and ability to qualify for any position. As a rule, however, they spent their life in the harem. The only proper activity for them outside the household was charitable work. Side by side with the seclusion of women, an attitude had developed that a proper woman's place was within the house (Girshman 1978).

Conclusion

In sum, the long-term trends that affected the role of women in the Middle East had evolved in response to social and economic conditions in the region prior to the rise of Islam in the seventh century C.E. Many of the major factors that influenced women's role in the Middle East developed in Mesopotamia, and they did not change much until the conditions that gave rise to them were altered. By the seventh century, many of the basic features associated with women in the Middle East—the veil, the harem, the seclusion of women and their subordination to men—were already present. A moral code of conduct that sanctioned the status and treatment of women was also in place. While some of these, such as severe punishment for adultery, were universally accepted and practiced, others, such as seclusion and the veil, were limited to women of the ruling class and wealthy families. Within four centuries after the advent of Islam in C.E. 610, as the majority of the population converted, many of the older beliefs and practices regarding women were institutionalized in the religious law of Islam. In the next part we will examine how this development occurred.

WOMEN IN THE ISLAMIC PERIOD

Introduction

Islam was revealed in C.E. 610 in Arabia. Muhammad, the founder of this religion, witnessed the submission of Arabia to Islam before he died in 632. A decade after the Prophet's death large parts of the Middle East were conquered by the newly founded Muslim state. Within four centuries, the majority of the population in this region converted to Islam. However, many aspects of the older cultures were preserved under an Islamic veneer (Hodgson 1974).

One area where the older Middle Eastern cultural traditions began to exert strong influence was in the treatment of women. Arabian/Muslim women during Muhammad's time were active in many areas of public life. By the end of the first century of Islam, they had become less visible and their contact with the outside world had become increasingly restricted. The change in the role of women is reflected in the difference between the general Qur'anic teachings and Muhammad's treatment of women in contrast to their position in the *Shari'ah*. This change in women's role resulted from the triumph of the cultural norms of the agrarian-urban Middle East over Arabian and early Islamic attitudes toward women. The regulations of the *Shari'ah* legitimized the transformation.

While change in women's role has been noted by many scholars (Rahman, Abbott, and others), the reasons for such development have not received sufficient attention. The dearth of studies that account for the transformation of women's place in Islamic life reflects the radically differing evaluations of the condition of Middle Eastern women in recent scholarship. Detractors have blamed all of women's ills on the teachings of Islam. Apologists have tried to defend the treatment of women by justifying everything, even some clearly reprehensible practices such as child marriage. What both sides have missed is that the position of women in the *Shari'ah* represents an amalgam of two opposing cultural traditions. The Arabian attitude toward women, reflected in the Qur'anic teachings, comprises one component. The other derives from cultural norms governing the treatment of women in the societies that embraced Islam following the conquest of the Middle East.

It is much easier to study women in the first century of Islam, when they were highly visible and active in their own right. The abundant mention of women in the official chronicles reflects their visibility. However, as women became secluded, they gradually disappeared from direct sources, and we must turn to such indirect sources as literary and artistic works and court records for details.

Information on women comes from various sources. One category consists of chronicles and biographical materials about Muhammad and the few decades after his death. These biographies offer information on women who had personal contact with the Prophet and his major companions. Because the Muslim community in these decades was small and women were active in social life, a wide range of Arabian women appear in these sources. For example, the ninth-century biographer Ibn Sa'd devotes the eighth volume of his biographical dictionary to women.

Another major source is the voluminous legal and theological literature. Despite their seemingly limited scope, these works offer important insights about the changes in women's role. Some of the arguments that appear in these works were used in support of the laws of the *Shariʿah*, which had crucial effects for women.

Literary and artistic works (prose, poetry, popular romance, manuals of government, painting, and ceramics) supplement information on how women lived. For example, details on women's clothing, mannerisms, houses, daily activities, and interaction emerge from these sources. Some, such as the twenty-volume *Kitab al-Aghani* (*The Book of Songs*), by Abuʾl-Faraj al-Isfahani (d. 967), offer a panorama of women's life from the pre-Islamic to the early Islamic period. Few of these works are available in Western languages.

During the second Islamic century, mention of women became less frequent in the chronicles, a dearth of information offset by other sources. The most important of these are correspondence and court records (wills, commercial contracts, marriage contracts, judicial litigations), especially from the Ottoman period. These records are particularly valuable for information on women during the tenth to nineteenth centuries c.e., when mention of women became less common in the official chronicles.

The evolution of women's role in the first two centuries of Islam is the focus here. The role of women in Arabia before Islam, the early teachings of Islam on women, and the gradual changes that these teachings underwent are described briefly. This part ends with a review of the various aspects of the role of women up to the eighteenth century. In the discussion that follows, the term *Arabian* is used instead of *Arab* to distinguish the early Muslims from Arabia from present-day Arabs, which include all the Arabic-speaking population of the Middle East.

Women in Pre-Islamic Arabia

The Arabian Peninsula was situated on the southern periphery of the Byzantine and Sasanian empires that controlled the Middle East. The majority of its people lived in numerous settlements in oases across much of Arabia and led settled or semi-settled ways of life. However, the camel-herding nomads, the Bedouins, rose to the challenge of the desert and set norms for behavior. Living in small tenting groups, they supported themselves with their flocks. Bedouins tended to roam with their camels nine months of the year in the territory where their wells were situated. In the summer, they camped near the wells. They supplemented their meager income through occasional raids on the settled or semi-settled groups, or even the agricultural population, on the fringes of the two empires (Hodgson 1974, I; Dickson 1951).

The individual's survival depended on group solidarity and protection by the tribe. Consequently, the tribe would become the focus of the person's loyalty, rather than the clan or the immediate family. Because of the high premium placed on belonging to the tribe, new members would not be readily accepted.

Nomads did not produce much surplus or amass wealth; hence Bedouin life was fairly democratic. The nomadic life-style also influenced the division of labor. When men were away, women looked after the tribe, even if some older men were left behind to supervise. Women also contributed to such vital activities as milking, spinning, and weaving in addition to child care and food preparation. Despite their active contributions to the tribal economy, women did not enjoy equality with men, and they were deemed less useful to the survival of the tribe. The problem of overpopulation was solved by burying infant girls alive. Nevertheless, Arabian women had more social power than women in the northern empires. Women were thought trustworthy and intelligent. Their opinion was sought on important communal issues, and their judgment on poetry, the favorite pastime of the tribes, was valued. Women composed some of the best poems. When the tribe needed to be rallied, women accompanied the men on campaigns and encouraged the men to do their best fighting. Women also played useful roles behind the battle lines. Women's and men's relative positions were not delineated by law; rather, custom prescribed the roles of every individual within the tribe, and women's status depended ultimately on the men in their lives (Lichtenstadter 1935).

The sexual mores of Arabia also differed radically from what prevailed in the northern empires. Both polyandry and polygyny were practiced. In one type of marriage, later sanctioned by Islam, a man needed the permission of the woman's father and payment of bride-wealth. In other types of marriage, a woman could have as many as ten sexual partners or cohabit with two brothers at the same time. Presumably, these practices were exercised by women within their own tribe, since marrying outside the tribe was not common. Tribal members considered themselves descendants of the same ancestor, and tribal membership was ascertained through the mother. These various types of matrilineal relations acquired importance without necessarily a predominant matriarchal social organization (Watt 1956). Women who married outsiders usually kept the children of such a marriage in their own tribe. There were women who charged money for sex, but they were not considered social outcasts (Smith 1903).

Islam, however, was revealed in the city of Mecca, where conditions had been changing throughout the sixth century. These changing circumstances are clearly reflected in the teachings of Muhammad, who was born in Mecca in 570. He came from a lesser clan of the Quraysh tribe, which had settled in Mecca about two centuries earlier. During this interval, the city had become the most important center of trade in Arabia. The fact that the Kaʿbah, one of the important Arabian shrines, was located in Mecca enhanced the prestige of the Quraysh, who were its guardians (Peters 1994).

Wealth brought by trade increased the social and political power of the Quraysh. It also undermined their customary social organization and code of behavior, which had been formed by their earlier pastoral way of life. As wealth became concentrated in the hands of a number of merchants, inequality grew among its inhabitants. Although kin-based bonds were still extolled, in practice, personal considerations began to motivate behavior.

These changes in Mecca's social and economic circumstances also began to affect the position of women and the mores governing their relationships with men. Though more research must be done before the nature of these changes is fully delineated, it is possible to offer some tentative suggestions.

Increased wealth and the urbanization of Mecca improved the quality of life for its women. Some well-connected women, such as Khadijah, Muhammad's first wife, took advantage of the increased commercial opportunities to engage in trade. The availability of female slaves may have freed some women from housework, but the weakening of tribal values and the rise in wealth began to erode women's social power. Descent from the father gained importance. For example, in this period, the guardianship of the Kaʿbah passed exclusively through the male line, but a few generations earlier, the Quraysh had acquired the guardianship of the shrine through the female line (Ibn Ishaq 1955). The nuclear family's growing importance, which accompanied urbanization, imposed stricter sexual mores on women. While men practiced polygyny, respectable Meccan women were monogamous. But in Medina, which was poorer and more tribal than Mecca, women could have relations with more than one man (Tabari, 1954–68, vol. 28).

Despite growing restrictions, the change in social structure of Mecca was slow, and many of the Bedouin customs survived. A woman could choose a husband—as did Khadijah, who proposed to Muhammad. Other women also engaged in trade and, presumably, other occupations. Meccan women were neither veiled nor barred from contact with men.

Women after the Advent of Islam

Submission to Islam for both women and men involved belief in a single God, the Day of Judgment, and the prophethood of Muhammad. It also required refraining from adultery and female infanticide. In addition, the individual had to perform certain rituals—such as daily prayer and the payment of alms tax. These beliefs were new to most Arabians, who until this time had been polytheists.

For a minority of women and men, the message of the Qur'an involved moral commitment, and they devoted their time to creating a society in which its teachings could be implemented. One early example was Khadijah, whose role in the success of Islam has not been adequately examined. She was the first convert in Islam, and her support of the Prophet during a critical period was crucial to him. Other women also played an important role in propagating Islam. For example, two were responsible for the conversion of 'Umar and 'Uthman, major companions of the Prophet and the second and third caliphs. Such women showed as much courage as men in facing hostility and hardship for their belief. Their loyalty is exemplified by Sumayyah bint Khubbat, a newly converted slave woman, whose death under persecution made her the first martyr of the new faith. Ramlah, the daughter of the wealthy Abu-Sufyan, led the Meccan opposition to Muhammad. She converted early and chose the hardship of exile over giving up her belief. After her husband's death, she married the Prophet and became known as Umm Habibah (Abbott 1942a).

For other women, becoming Muslim did not require radical changes in how they lived; it involved merely modifying some of their ways. The life of Hind bint 'Utbah, a prominent woman of Quraysh and a contemporary of the Prophet, is typical of this latter group. Sometime before Islam, she was divorced by one of her husbands on a charge of adultery. The accusation was embarrassing for her but not life threatening. As was the custom of the day, her father referred the matter to a soothsayer, who proclaimed Hind innocent of wrongdoing. Following this incident, she was pursued by many admirers. At first, she became involved with a minor poet, who celebrated their involvement in poetry. After losing interest in him, she married Abu-Sufyan, one of Mecca's richest merchants; she had a son with him, Mu'awiyah, the fifth caliph of the Islamic state (661–680). Hind joined her husband in opposing Muhammad, who was forced to leave Mecca for Medina in 622, and she participated in some of the wars waged between the Meccans and the newly established Muslim community in Medina. During the Battle of Uhud in 625, when Hamza, the Prophet's uncle, was killed, she rushed over to him, tore open his chest, pulled out his liver, and bit into it to avenge her father's death at his hand. Hind did not convert until Mecca surrendered in 628. After the conquest of Syria, she became actively involved in the Syrian trade. Though she was chided as the "liver-eater," her amorous involvements were never brought up and did not create problems for her son, Mu'awiyah (Ibn Ishaq 1955).

Hind's life sheds light on the sexual mores of Mecca before Islam. It also reveals the continuity between the pre-Islamic and Islamic lifestyles of women. During the first few decades of Islam, although becoming a Muslim involved an inner commitment, it did not require many outer changes. This understanding of the religion also fell within the parameters of Qur'anic teachings. As recorded in the Qur'an, Muhammad saw his role as a that of a man sent to correct existing abuses rather than overhaul the system. This approach is suggested by many statements in the Qur'an—including "Thou art a warner only, and for every community a Guide" (XIII, 7)—and it is also conveyed by Muhammad's perception of himself as one in a long line of prophets. Even more illustrative of this point is Muhammad's perception of his relationship with Ibrahim, the biblical Abraham. This perception explains why the Prophet retained some pre-Islamic rituals and practices, such as those related to the Hajj pilgrimage: he believed they had been introduced by Ibrahim. Hence the Prophet only prohibited those practices that in his view were in conflict with the central messages of the Qur'an. Central to the Qur'anic teachings is the effort to help the individual to lead a moral life. Such a life can be accomplished when the person turns to God, by showing gratitude to the Creator and concern for fellow-beings (Hodgson 1974).

The Qur'an also contains some legal injunctions, but it is important to bear in mind that the main thrusts of the Qur'anic teachings were religious and moral. The legal provisions were revealed in response to specific situations faced by the newly established sovereign community following the Prophet's emigration to Medina in 622. Although his departure was the result of an imminent threat to his life, it proved a blessing in disguise. The event—*Hijra*, or emigration—was so important to the fate of the new community that it was used by the next generation as the beginning of the Muslim calendar. Whereas in Mecca the Muslims were a tiny minority (perhaps not exceeding two hundred), in Medina, the majority of the population submitted to Islam and accepted Muhammad's leadership. This circumstance made it possible for the practical implications of the new faith to unfold gradually. Beginning in this period, the members of the community turned to the Prophet for temporal as well as spiritual guidance. Generally the legal ordinances aimed to solve an ambiguous situation or meet an urgent need of the community, and they were the by-products of day-to-day needs. While they ensured the end of existing abuses, they did not turn the situation upside down (Rahman 1983).

This is true of the Qur'an's legal pronouncements on women. Most of the injunctions affecting women were revealed in connection with specific situations faced by Muhammad or the community. For example, according to Tabari, the Qur'anic revelation prohibiting men from marrying women who engaged in adultery was meant to prevent the marriage of poor Muslim men in Medina to *baghiyah*s, women who engaged in sex for money. Another example is the Qur'anic sanction of polygamy, revealed in Medina following the Battle of Uhud in 625 when Muslims suffered many casualties. This revelation was intended to resolve the problem created by the wives and children of men killed in battle.

The teachings of the Qur'an also reflect the social and economic changes of Mecca and Medina during Muhammad's time and the new needs that these changes had created. The Qur'an forbids anything that can leave paternity in doubt. In line with this tendency, it prohibits polyandry. Many of the laws, such as equal treatment of wives in polygynous marriages or allocating specific shares in bequests to wives and children, reflect the Qur'anic effort to strengthen family bonds. The banning of adultery is another example. In pre-Islamic Arabia, including in Mecca, adultery was not considered a crime; the Qur'an bans adultery and ordains that the offenders be whipped one hundred lashes (XXIV, 2,3). This punishment is mild compared to what the *Shari'ah* prescribed: death by stoning for married offenders. But concubinage, which neither undermined patrilineal family formation nor led to children of uncertain paternity, was not banned, even though believers were encouraged to lead a chaste life.

The Qur'an's primary religious and moral stance is reflected in its strong reaction to the excesses caused by the growing commercialization of Mecca. The effort to alleviate the economic and moral hardship on women, particularly slave women, can be discerned in provisions concerning marriage and divorce. The Qur'an highly recommends marriage for everyone, and individuals are informed that God "created for you mates from yourselves that you might find rest in them, and ordained between you love and mercy" (XXX, 21). Men are enjoined to marry free women in the first instance, but if they cannot afford the bridewealth for free women, they are told to marry slave women rather than engage in wrongful acts (IV, 25). The Qur'an sanctions polygyny, and men are allowed to marry up to four wives. But it also stipulates that a man should marry only one wife if he cannot treat all wives with fairness (IV, 2-3). Men are repeatedly urged to treat their wives with kindness. Finally, men are made responsible for the support of their wives, while wives are not obligated to share their wealth with their husbands. This provision somewhat offsets the inequality in women's share of inheritance, discussed below.

The Qur'anic injunctions on divorce continued this effort to improve prevailing practices. In pre-Islamic Arabia, divorce was informal and easy; men could walk away from their wives anytime they wished. To some extent, these provisions reflect the growing power of Meccan men, and the Qur'anic provision seems to allow men the unconditional ability to divorce their wives while restricting women's ability to divorce their husbands. Yet while men appear to have unconditional power to divorce their wives, a closer examination of the restrictions imposed by the Qur'an reveals that men's ability to divorce is not as easy as has been claimed. Husbands are forbidden to take back gifts they have given to the wives (IV, 20). In addition, the Qur'an recommends reconciliation. Finally, the Qur'anic ordinance makes it hard for men to take divorce lightly. If the husband pronounces the divorce formula three times, he is not able to remarry the same wife unless she has married another man, is divorced by him, and has observed 'iddah, the waiting period of three months and ten days between each divorce and remarriage (II, 228). If he divorces the wife, he is required to give her the full bridal gift and any dowry she may have brought to his house. The husband is responsible for her maintenance if she is pregnant, and he must also support her and their children while they live with her.

The Qur'anic law of inheritance provides women with a share of their parents', husbands', siblings', and children's estates. It stipulates that "a male child shall have the equivalent of two female children" (IV, 11). The same proportion applies to the widow's share of her husband's estate, which is one-eighth compared to his one-fourth share of her estate, if there are children. In the absence of children, she gets one-fourth and he one-half of the estate, respectively (IV, 13). In pre-Islamic Arabia some women, Khadijah for example, were wealthy, but the source of their wealth is obscure (Watt 1953). As far as it is known, women were financially dependent on their husband's or father's favor. The Qurʾanic provisions became an important asset to women in the later periods when many of their other rights were circumvented (see below).

With respect to religious duties and obligations, women and men are treated equally in the Qurʾan. The phrases "believing men" and "believing women" and "Muslim men and Muslim women" appear repeatedly. Men and women are reminded that they will be judged by God only for their piety, regardless of race, wealth, or sex (II, 414). Given that the religious aspect, not legal considerations, was the main concern of the Qurʾan, this equality was a major departure from the prevailing attitudes. The Qurʾan's concern with individual worth also accounts for the banning of female infanticide. The references to female infanticide in the Qurʾan indicate that it was current practice both in Mecca and in the rest of Arabia. The Qurʾan banned it categorically and equated female infanticide with idolatry, which the Qurʾan considers the highest sin.

Women's role in the Qurʾanic story of creation contrasts sharply with the biblical version. While in the Qurʾan Eve also succumbs to Satan's enticement, the consequence of the act for her descendants is not original sin but acquisition of knowledge. In addition, humans in the Qurʾan do not fall from grace as a result of this act but are made God's trustees in creation. However, knowledge is a double-edged sword; it sets humans apart from all other creatures and endows them with the ability to distinguish right from wrong. It also puts the burden of choice and responsibility on the individual. In this respect, women are placed on the same platform as men in rising to God's challenge. Undoubtedly, this revised role for Eve was also a reflection of the basic Bedouin attitude toward women.

While in the Qurʾanic teachings women's religious obligations, duties, and spiritual rewards are equal to those of men, the Qurʾan leaves no doubt that in the affairs of this world "men are a degree higher than women" (II, 228). The Qurʾanic rationale for this point is interesting since it states that "they [men] spend of their property [for the support of women]." The remaining passage of this verse reveals the attitude of the Qurʾan toward women's sexuality, in which the good wife is defined as one "who obeys her husband and guards his secrets" (IV, 32, 34). In return for financial support of her, the husband is empowered to punish a disobedient wife by admonishing her, sleeping in a separate bed, or beating her. While the first and third punishments have been universally used against women, the second punishment seems unique to Islam. It suggests withholding sex as punishment; in other words, it is a recognition of women as sexual beings. The acceptance of women's sexuality and their sexual needs sets the early teachings of Islam apart from other religions, particularly Christianity. The Islamic attitude toward human sexuality has been until recently one of the major sources of Western criticism of Islam.

As this brief review indicates, the Qurʾanic teachings delineated many aspects of women's rights and responsibilities: women's legal right to inheritance from parents, spouse, children, and siblings was spelled out, and the right of women to own and dispose of their own property was established. The Qurʾan did not call for dramatic changes in women's position, but by defining their rights and responsibilities it established important guarantees for women that would become more important to them in the future.

The positive Qurʾanic attitude was reinforced by Muhammad's treatment of women. The Prophet's personal experience as father of several girls could only have deepened his awareness of the insecurity of women's position in Arabian society. He sought the consent of his daughters before their marriage. For the first time he also required that the *mahr*, or bridal gift, be given to the bride instead of to the father or male guardian. Muhammad forbade the exchange of two female relatives by men, since this practice deprived each woman of getting her *mahr*. He ruled that a woman did not need her husband's permission to manage her own property, while the husband needed her permission to use her assets (Abbott 1942a; Rahman 1983).

During Muhammad's lifetime, women participated in communal religious activities. Their participation is attested to by the large number of women who transmitted *hadiths* (statements relating the Prophet's actions and sayings). Women also played a major role in collecting the Qurʾan. Some memorized and acquired their own collections of the Qurʾan. Muhammad's wives played the major role in these two activities, but they were not the only women to do so. Women attended the mosque and participated in religious festivals; they listened to Muhammad's public preachings. Like men, they prayed over the dead and went on pilgrimage. However, information on women occupying positions of authority, such as leadership of prayer, is scanty. According to a single *hadith*, one woman, Umm Waraqah bint ʿAbd-Allah, was appointed the leader of prayer in a group that also included a man. It is possible that as women in later Islamic society became more confined to their houses, gradually their active religious role began to be omitted from the sources (Abbott 1942a).

Many pre-Islamic women's activities survived. For example, Muslim women accompanied men on military campaigns. Women from both sides were present at the Battle of Uhud in 625. Muhammad's aunt, Safiyyah, chided her fellow Muslims for abandoning the Prophet when he was injured. Safiyyah, in the manner of the women of her time, recited an elegy on the death of her brother, who was killed during this war (Ibn Ishaq 1955). Another pre-Islamic Arabian attitude that survived was the ability of divorced and older women to marry again. Muhammad's practice may have contributed to the survival of this custom. His first wife, Khadijah, was a widow and fifteen years older than he (some of the other women he later married were also widows older than he). Marrying three or four men consecutively was quite common. Umm Kulthum, ʿUthman's stepsister, was a typical example of this trend. As her name (mother of Kulthum) indicates, she may have been married before her conversion to Islam. Then in 628, she fled to Medina to be with other Muslims. She settled in the city and married four major companions in succession: Muhammad's adopted son, Zaid b. Harithah, Zubair ibn ʿAwwam, and the wealthy ʿAbd al-Rahman ibn ʿAwf. After ʿAbd al-Rahman's death in 653, she married ʿAmr ibn al-ʿAs, the conqueror of Egypt (Abbott 1942a).

The practice of seclusion was introduced during Muhammad's time in the form of a revelation addressed to his wives (XXXIII, 32). There is no indication that the community regarded this to be a general ordinance, and it may have been originally viewed as the revelation that banned the remarriage of the Prophet's wives after his death. The circumstances surrounding this revelation confirm its private nature. The Prophet lived in a few rooms off the main mosque in Medina. The revelation concerning the seclusion of the Prophet's wives came to correct the behavior of some of his unruly followers who entered his private rooms at all times. Contemporary women do not seem to have followed the example of his wives. Furthermore, the participation of Sukaynah, his own great granddaughter, and other high-born women in social and religious functions suggests that seclusion and the veil were not mandatory for Muslim women during the first Islamic century.

Women in Early Islam (632–750)

Muhammad died in 632. Within the next few decades, in a succession of swift campaigns, his followers defeated the Sasanian empire and wrested control of the eastern Mediterranean from the Byzantine empire. During the Umayyad caliphate (661–750), the Muslim state continued to expand into North Africa and Spain. These conquests had a profound impact on the development of Islam and many aspects of the life of those Arabian Muslims who settled in the newly conquered regions. The Arabian newcomers constituted a military ruling class. Since they lacked the necessary knowledge to run the complex administration and economy of the conquered territories, it was decided to leave the existing Byzantine and Persian officials in charge of running the empire. Consequently, as Lewis has noted, "the Umayyad Caliphate was not so much an Arab state as a Persian and Byzantine succession state." Mu'awiyah (661–680), the founder of the dynasty, moved the capital form Medina to Damascus, the capital of Byzantine Syria. Steeped in Byzantine and Christian tradition, Damascus became the earliest channel for transmission of the habits and tastes of the conquered empires to the new rulers (Lewis 1966).

Exposure to older cultures and contact with the population of the conquered territories produced profound changes in Arabian culture, many of which had serious implications for Arabian Muslim women. But the changes occurred slowly, and their impact was not felt until a century later when the Abbasids came to power in 750. However, the remaining decades of the seventh century turned into a golden age for Arabian Muslim women. They retained the active social role they had before Islam. In addition, the regulations that the Qur'an had spelled out for women enabled them to reap fully the results of the sudden enrichment of their society—witness the long list of women who were on the registry of the Muslim treasury, which divided the enormous tax revenue from all over the empire among the Arabian conquerors.

Although we do not as yet know how average women were affected by this sudden transformation of Arabian fortune, the life-style of women in the leading families of Quraysh indicates that they took advantage of their position fully. A woman who stands out in the early sources is Muhammad's youngest and favorite wife, 'A'ishah. She was eighteen when the Prophet died, so she witnessed many of the changes that Arabian society underwent in its adoption of what she viewed as foreign cultural practices. Her recollections about life with the Prophet reveal his human side and what went on in his household. For example, we learn from her that Muhammad helped his wives with their housework (Ali 1983). We also learn about the rivalries of his wives and other details. 'A'ishah's sardonic comments vividly contrast the simple earlier Arabian life with the opulence after the conquest (for example, she notes the straw-mat beds of the Prophet's time as opposed to the sable-covered beds of some of her relatives).

The episodes narrated by ʿAʾishah and the Prophet's other wives became one of the major sources of *hadiths*, statements about a saying or action of the Prophet and hence his tradition. The *hadith* acquired increasing importance in various fields, such as theology and law, because it was used for elucidating difficult Qurʾanic passages and for setting proper norms of conduct for the pious. The role of ʿAʾishah and the other wives in transmitting material with such religious significance indicates the high esteem in which they were held. ʿAʾishah's involvement in the first civil war, a conflict that erupted after the death of the third caliph, ʿUthman, in 655, on the other hand, shows that women's involvement in the political life of the community was also accepted. ʿAʾishah was instrumental in organizing the opposition to ʿAli, the Prophet's son-in-law, who had succeeded ʿUthman. But the side she supported lost in the conflict, and ʿAli forced her to return to Medina. This incident, known as the Battle of the Camel, resulted in the death of many major companions and left deep scars in the Muslim consciousness. Those opposed to women's involvement in politics undoubtedly used ʿAʾishah's pivotal role in beginning the cycle of violence as ammunition in the argument against women's active involvement in politics.

Muhammad's family produced other remarkable women. Perhaps the distinction for exceptional courage should go to Zaynab, whose mother, Fatimah, was the Prophet's daughter. Zaynab's father was the caliph ʿAli. She accompanied her brother Husayn on his fateful journey in 680 to Kufah, from which he intended to lead the opposition to the newly installed caliph, Yazid. Before reaching Kufah, Husain's party of seventy men, women, and children was intercepted by four thousand fighting men of Yazid's governor. For one week Husain and his supporters were surrounded and denied access to water. Finally, according to the historian Tabari, when Husain tried to break through the enemy lines, a number of men from Yazid's troops fell upon him en masse. They stabbed and slashed him repeatedly and cut off his head while the women and children watched. Eighteen of his close male relatives—including two of Zaynab's sons—were also killed. The only male survivor of Husain's party was his teen-age son, who was sick and could not fight; Zaynab saved him. When the soldiers came to drag him away, she shielded him with her body and told them they would have to kill her first. She showed the same courage when she was brought with her relatives before Yazid in Damascus. It is worth noting that—since the 1970s—Zaynab has become the role model for diverse revolutionary women's groups in Iran.

Two of Zaynab's nieces, Fatimah and Sukaynah, also attained fame. While the first was known for her piety, the second set the fashion trends for women of her time. The many extant descriptions of her beauty, charm, wit, and brilliance indicate that she associated with men outside of her family circle. These accounts also show that seclusion and the veil were not mandatory for women in this period. Many men pursued her, and she married some of the most distinguished men of her time. Other female descendants of the Prophet and his major companions were sought in marriage by powerful and wealthy men to enhance their own prestige. But these women were hardly pawns, and in fact many exercised their freedom to choose a husband. Sometimes even a caliph could not win the hand of the woman he desired (Abbott 1942b).

From the time of the caliph Walid (705–715), the picture began to worsen for women. Walid was perhaps the first Arabian Muslim ruler to attempt to seclude the women in his household. He showed a preference for non-Arabian women and the culture of his non-Arabian subjects, and his effort to keep his wives secluded may have been influenced by his contacts with foreign subjects. In addition to his four legal wives, he began to fill his household with numerous women of non-Arabian origin. Sixteen of his nineteen sons were born to non-Arabian wives, and the other three resulted from an early marriage to Umm al-Banin, his cousin. But, ironically, only his son from an enslaved Persian princess attained the throne, as Yazid III: with his ascension to the throne, the tradition of the pure-Arabian caliph was shattered for good. For the Abbasids (750–1258), having a free-born Arabian mother for the caliphs was more the exception than the rule.

From the time of Walid I, women of the royal household also began to lose their freer, easy-going Arabian way of life. Walid I ordered harem women not to mingle with outsiders, especially court poets who competed for the patronage of royal women. His leading wife, Umm al-Banin, disregarded Walid's command and continued to receive poets, particularly her favorite, Wadda, in her private chamber. One day when the poet was visiting, she heard the caliph approaching, unannounced. She hid Wadda in a large chest—to which Walid took great liking. He had the chest sent to his quarters, and thereafter no one saw the poet or sang the praise of Umm al-Banin again. On her next public appearance, Umm al-Banin was veiled (Abbott 1942b).

Women, including those of the royal harem, were not pushed out of the public domain overnight. But the trend had been set. The

Umayyads after Walid made greater efforts to establish a Sasanian-style imperial tradition. Hisham (724–743), for example, had many manuals of government translated from Pahlavi (the language of the Sasanians) into Arabic. These older traditions became so widely accepted that Umayyad caliph Yazid III (743–744) could boast, "I am the son of a Chosroes [title of the Sasanian emperors], and my father is Marwan" (Sprengling 1938–1939: 215). These words were uttered when the dynasty was on the verge of collapse. Following another civil war, the Abbasids became leaders of the Islamic state.

Women in the Abbasid Period (750–1250)

After the rise of the Abbasids, the center of the caliphate and Islam moved to the heartland of the former Sasanian domain, in Iraq (the earlier Mesopotamia). The new Abbasid capital, Baghdad, was near the ruins of the old Sasanian capital, Ctesiphon. The members of the dynasty paid lip service to their Arabian origin and their relationship to the Prophet (they descended from his uncle, Abbas), but they revived much of the pre-Islamic imperial Sasanian tradition and many aspects of the older cultural practices under an Islamic guise (Hodgson 1974, I).

Arabian Muslim women were similarly affected by the triumph of agrarian-urban cultural traditions. As noted earlier, women's role in that tradition was limited mainly to home-based activities and child care. Once Arabian women settled in the conquered territories their lives were also gradually transformed. The veil and seclusion had become the norm for royal women from the time of Walid. But with the coming of the Abbasids, the seclusion of women and the veil became official policy. This change was signaled when the caliph Mansour (754–775) ordered the building of a separate bridge for women over the Euphrates in his new capital, Baghdad (Lassner 1965).

The shift from the freer life-style of the Prophet's days to greater seclusion and veiling can be better understood in the context of the overall adoption of the cultural traditions of the conquered population by the Arabian newcomers. Although we lack precise demographic information about the number of Arabians who settled in the conquered territories, we know they moved into inhabited areas and constituted a small minority in these regions. In addition, the conquered territories included some of the oldest centers of culture in the Middle East. The existing cultural traditions had evolved in response to the demands of social and economic conditions that had prevailed in these regions since the rise of urban life. Although the Arabians constituted a ruling class in the conquered territories, they did not create new conditions. Their presence merely modified and sometimes accelerated some of the existing trends, in agriculture, urban life, and so on. Furthermore, the former Arabian ways neither suited the life-style of rulers of a prosperous and mighty empire nor could they be easily adapted to the complex and vastly different conditions of the conquered regions: Arabian culture and institutions had developed in response to the needs of the desert and semi-pastoral conditions. Therefore, in the course of the first century, as Arabian men and women settled into their new environment, like earlier conquerors they gradually absorbed the culture and values of their subjects. The indigenous population from Egypt to Khurasan, however, began to adopt the language and religion of their Arab masters, while preserving many aspects of their way of life under a veneer of Islam.

What eventually legitimized many of these older cultural traditions was their infiltration into the *Shari'ah* (literally "path"), which was developing simultaneously. Two reasons prompted the need for development of the *Shari'ah* to guide Muslims along the path of the proper Islamic life. The first was the speed with which the early Muslims, many of whom had only recently converted, had scattered over a large area so soon after Islam's inception. The second was the conversion of growing numbers of the non-Arabian population following the conquest of the Middle East.

The Qur'an, considered by Muslims the word of God, played a central role in the ongoing effort to define the proper way of life for Muslims. As noted earlier, the Qur'anic injunctions are primarily moral, and the Qur'an's legal and practical injunctions form only a small part of its teachings. During his life, the Prophet supplemented the Qur'anic teachings in a manner he believed to be in agreement with God's will. After his death in 632, the Qur'an became the guide for pious Muslims, who sought to pattern their behavior according to its teachings. The judgment of the Prophet's close companions, particularly his first four successors (known as the righteous caliphs), was also sought, since everyone assumed these men best understood the Qur'an and the Prophet's teachings. Not surprisingly, interest in the Prophet's life and his actions also became increasingly popular among the growing Muslim community. Therefore, *hadiths*, which conveyed his sayings and actions, began to circulate and were transmitted widely because they could inform the pious about his *sunnah* (tradition). For a while these sources provided the more pious with the guidance they needed to lead a life they thought would please God. The decisions of the major companions and the early community were deferred to, since it was assumed that they also conformed to the Prophet's behavior and intentions (Gibb 1970; Schacht 1984). Finally, those practices of the pre-Islamic Arabians that did not contradict the teachings of Islam were also sanctioned.

The conquest of the Middle East (634–655), however, created new needs for the community. As Muslims from Arabia grew accustomed to their new environment, the teachings of the Qur'an and the Prophet's *sunnah* could no longer provide the necessary guidelines for the totally different conditions that existed outside of Arabia. This problem was resolved by following the Prophet's precedent. He had retained pre-Islamic Arabian practices that he believed were in keeping with the teachings of the Qur'an. Before a given practice could be sanctioned, it had to prove compatible with the Qur'anic teachings and the Prophet's *sunnah*. In an effort to integrate newly conquered territories into an Islamic empire, practices from those regions were sanctioned that had little or nothing to do with the Prophet's *sunnah*, the Qur'anic teachings, or pre-Islamic Arabian norms and traditions.

Sometime during the third century, Muslim jurists and theologians were alarmed by the haphazard dissemination of many practices that seemed contrary to the teachings of the Qur'an and the Prophet's *sunnah*: they demanded that only these two sources should provide the basic guidelines for Muslim behavior. It was already too late for orthodoxy, however, since some foreign practices in the conquered territories had been sanctioned already. Furthermore, much of what circulated as the Prophet's tradition seemed obviously embellished, and even fabricated. In this manner, older non-Arabian cultural practices became accepted norms for Islamic behavior and were sanctioned through the *Shariʿah*. This process also explains why different interpretations, or various schools of law, evolved in different regions. Iraq, the home of the oldest cultural tradition in the Middle East, became one of the earliest and most influential centers of the development of the *Shariʿah*. By the end of the third Islamic century, a systematized body of laws and regulations governing the daily life of individual Muslims had been devised. Gradually the entire *Shariʿah* began to be considered by Muslims of later periods as inspired by God and, some would argue, therefore unalterable (Schacht 1984; but Wael Hallaq, Babir Johansen, Rudolph Peters, and others publishing in the *Journal of Islamic Law and Society* have questioned the assertion that from the ninth century C.E. the *Shariʿah* was seen as unalterable and unquestionable).

These two radically different origins of the *Shariʿah*—the Qur'an and the teachings of Muhammad on the one hand, and the cultural traditions encountered in conquered areas on the other—explain why, despite the freedoms they enjoyed initially, women became restricted in Islamic society. The triumph of the pre-Islamic non-Arabian traditions is demonstrated by the adoption of the veil (*hejab*) and seclusion, at least among the upper- and middle-class women in urban areas, despite the absence of an ordinance in the Qur'an or precedents in the Prophet's *sunnah*. Although the extent of seclusion and the veil were debated by various theologians, the need for some covering of most, if not all, of the female body, was never doubted. However, the ambiguous nature of the term allowed for some regional variations and interpretations of the form it came to take (Stowasser 1994).

The general Qur'anic dictum that women dress modestly and "not reveal their sexual parts, except those naturally exposed and to draw their covers over their bosoms" (XXIV, 31), has been one of the verses used to argue for the necessity of the veil. This verse, however, is not sufficient as argument, because the previous verse recommends modesty of dress and gaze to men as well. Furthermore, many anecdotes from the Prophet's time clearly show that women in Mecca and Medina were not veiled. This problem was resolved by using another verse, which was addressed to the Prophet's wives, "to cover themselves with their outer garments when they go out at night . . . so that they can be recognized as Muslim women and not be molested" (XXXIII, 50-60). The rationale was that what was good for the Prophet's wives was good for other Muslim women (see, e.g., Ghazali 1968).

The tremendous economic expansion following the Islamic conquest of the Middle East made possible the acceptance and further development of the confinement of women. Although the full extent of this development has not been studied, we know that the impressive economic expansion stimulated the growth of many medieval Islamic cities. As mentioned earlier, the seclusion of women in the Middle East is linked to the development of urban culture. Similarly, this trend, beginning with the Abbasids, played a part in making seclusion of women a fact of life in medieval Islamic society (Mazaheri 1951).

Economic growth made possible the abundance of domestic female slaves in medieval Islamic society. The availability of female slaves, in turn, undoubtedly made it easier for middle- and upper-middle-class women to become increasingly confined to their homes. They went out only to visit friends and relatives, the shrines of saints, or the bath, and occasionally the bazaars. Respectable married women did not go out on foot, but in a litter or on a mule. They were fully veiled when they left the house. Female slaves, however, did not have to be veiled (Mazaheri 1951).

The new wealth, which affected all segments of society, also enabled most of the urban population to build their homes in a way that ensured the seclusion of the women living within. The women in the households of the ruler and the wealthy class lived in elaborate establishments consisting of various apartments for each wife, courtyards, gardens, baths, and separate quarters for servants. The harem was separated from the outside world by high walls, courtyards, and corridors. The houses of the less wealthy also contained an outer courtyard and an inner courtyard (Mazaheri 1951). Even in the houses of the poor, the inner part of the house was separated from the outside by an entrance hallway. The only male strangers allowed access to the inner courtyard were delivery men and vendors, who rarely encountered the mistress of the house.

It was also during the Abbasid period that the harem organization appeared. For Westerners, the term *harem* conjures up two conflicting images. One, created mainly by nineteenth-century Western travelers, is of myriad women languishing under the watchful eyes of eunuchs; the other, created by Hollywood, is that of numerous merry women frolicking in revealing and sensuous clothes in a Garden of Eden setting. The *raison d'être* of the harem, however, was to ensure complete separation of women from male strangers. This function of the harem is borne out by the etymology of the term. Literally "sanctuary" or "forbidden place," it referred to that part of the house set aside for the women and children. As mentioned earlier, the origins of the seclusion of women may go back to Assyrian times. Before Islam only the ruler and very rich men could seclude their women. But by medieval Islamic times, seclusion had become standard practice in cities throughout the Middle East and even survived in some parts until recently.

Similar misconception colors the view of Westerners of the prevalence of polygyny in Islamic society. Despite the absence of adequate studies of this practice, it seems fairly certain that only rulers, princes, and some high government officials had more than one wife, and some men of this class had concubines. In the average household, however, polygyny seems to have been more the exception than the rule. This impression is conveyed by such diverse sources as biographical dictionaries, works of popular fiction, manuals of ethics, and modern ethnographic studies.

In addition to the wife or wives and children, a large number of female slaves, who did the domestic work, also lived in the harems of the ruler and the rich. Slaves played an important role in the social life of medieval Islam. During the first century, female slaves came from the women captured during the conquest of the Middle East. This source dried up, however, after the submission of all of the Middle East to Arabian Muslims, since non-Muslims living within *dar-al-Islam* (the abode of Islam) were in theory protected and could not be enslaved. Similarly, Muslims could not sell their children into slavery. Hence, slaves brought from neighboring lands became an important commodity. Slave markets were standard features of medieval Muslim cities, and slaves came from Central Europe, Russia, the Byzantine Empire, Italy, and Africa.

Slave prices depended on national origin, age, and physical attributes. The youngest and most beautiful slave women fetched premium prices, and they were given the best education and training in music, singing, and literature. According to the essayist Jahiz (d. 868), some female slaves became accomplished poets and learned philosophy. Such slave women could match the best of men in philosophic discourse. Men competed for the love of these women slaves and treated them almost as legal wives (Pellat 1969).

Islamic law permitted men to have sexual relations with their female slaves. The birth of a child to a female slave secured her eventual freedom, either during the master's lifetime or on his death. For a small minority of slave women, winning the master's affection opened unlimited opportunities. Khayzuran was the most celebrated example of this group. She became the wife of the caliph al-Mahdi (775–785), and two of her sons, al-Hadi (785–786) and the more illustrious Harun al-Rashid (786–809), became caliph successively. According to Tabari (d. 923), the great theologian and historian of early Islam, during the first few months of her son's reign, Khayzuran played an active role in affairs of state, as she had in her husband's period.

Tabari's account indicates that some women could wield power, at least indirectly, in Islamic society. The impression the historian conveys, however, is that the exercise of power by Khayzuran was a subversion of normalcy and did not bode well for the young caliph. When Hadi tried to end "women's interference in the affairs of men," his mother became so indignant that she brought about his downfall— he died of poisoning at the age of twenty-six. Another lesson Tabari tries to impart, though it is not spelled out, is a link between the predominance of Khayzuran and the decline of the state. Her ascendance ended in the reign of her second son, Harun al-Rashid. Tabari counts on the familiarity of his readers with al-Rashid's reign to imply a relationship between the greatness of his period and Khayzuran's withdrawal from interference (al-Tabari 1964: Ser. 3, I, 546–99).

Tabari reserves his unqualified approval for Zubaydah, al-Rashid's wife, and Buran (or Puran), the wife of his son, al-Ma'mun (813–833). We learn from Tabari that neither woman meddled in the affairs of the state but, like Byzantine queens, engaged in philanthropic and charitable work. The details that made 'A'ishah (or Umm al-Banin) so familiar are no longer provided in the chronicles. We learn how much Buran's father spent on the wedding celebration—the equivalent of the annual revenue of a province. However, the account leaves out any information that can bring her to life for the reader: her idiosyncrasies, her looks, her sense of humor, or why Ma'mun, the most erudite Abbasid caliph, became so captivated by her.

Growing stereotyped treatment of women in the chronicles was accompanied by their increasing seclusion and the spread of the veil. Only slave women went out unveiled. Although the veil and seclusion were at first urban phenomena, they gradually spread to the countryside. It is difficult to determine when these practices reached rural areas and how extensively they were observed there. Evidence suggests that Muslim men were not accustomed to seeing unveiled women anywhere except in the privacy of their homes. A ninth-century Muslim traveler who went among the Slavs was surprised by the sight of their unveiled women. During the Crusades, Muslims were shocked by the freedom of Frankish women. By the fourteenth century, when Ibn-Battuta (d. 1377) traveled from one corner of the Islamic world (Morocco) to the other (China), the only unveiled women he encountered were the Tuareg women in the Western Sudan* and in the Maldives. He expressed indignation at the sight. He was also surprised to see women earning their livelihoods as servants and spinners (Ibn Battuta 1977: I, II).

Ibn Battuta's disapproval reveals that the arrival of the Turkic and Mongol pastoral groups into the Middle East during the previous three centuries had not left much of a mark on the society's perception of the role and status of women.

The Turkish Influence: Mid-Thirteenth to Sixteenth Centuries

The Turks were a pastoral people who began to arrive in the Middle East in the ninth century. As mentioned earlier, pastoral nomadism had existed in the Middle East before Islamic times. The nomads rep-

---

*The "Western Sudan" refers to the region of West Africa between the forest to the south and the desert to the north. It is not to be confused with the present-day country of Sudan.

resented the shepherds and fighters, and the sedentary population was composed of the settled agriculturalists. Before the arrival of the Turks, two types of nomads inhabited the deserts and steppes of the Middle East. The first were the desert nomads of Arabia, called Arabs or Bedouins, and of North Africa, known as Berbers or the Tuareg. The second were the steppe and mountain nomads of southwestern Iran, known as the Kurds, and some smaller nomadic remnants of earlier Indo-European migrations, such as the Bakhtiyaris, in northeastern and northwestern Iran. In this arid region of the world, the nomadic and sedentary life-styles coexisted peacefully most of the time. Sometimes, however, when the balance between the two populations was upset, the sedentary population suffered. Arable land in the Middle East is scarce, so agriculture also depended on marginal lands, and maintenance of irrigation works is crucial to the survival of agricultural activity. Pastoralist pressure undermined these important resources. The same disruption happened when new nomadic groups came from the outside. The last wave of nomadic invasion in the Middle East followed the rise of Islam when Arabian nomads overran this region. The size of the Arabian population was much smaller than the indigenous population, so the coming of Arabians did not disrupt sedentary life as had the invasion of Western Europe by the Franks and Goths, which had occurred slightly earlier. Gradually a group of Arabians settled in the Middle East and were absorbed into the larger indigenous population. The rest either withdrew to the fringes of the desert or returned to Arabia.

The Turks consisted of numerous tribes who spoke many different Turkic dialects, had inhabited the plains of Eurasia for at least two millennia, and had interacted with the people of the Middle East during that interval. However, their social and economic structure was not deeply influenced by this interaction. Tribes relied on the exchange of the products of their large herds—milk by-products, meat, wool, and leather—as their major source of livelihood. They supplemented their income by guiding caravans along the Silk Road, which carried merchandise between China and the Middle East. Endemic skirmishes and occasional warfare with these tribes were facts of life for Middle Easterners who lived in areas adjacent to Turkish territories.

Women played a vital role in pastoral Turkish society. They tended and milked the cattle, made cheese, cooked, spun wool, and wove fabric for tents, rugs, and clothing in addition to raising children. During the annual migration of the tribes, women shared the responsibility for moving cattle and children. Turkish women were excellent horsewomen and occasionally participated in combat. These various roles gave the women corresponding political power, demonstrated by the importance of women in the tribal councils. Their high status astonished Ibn Battuta (d. 1377), who traveled among non-Muslim Turkish tribes living on the fringes of the Muslim world (Bayani 1973b).

The Turks, who began to arrive in the ninth century, did not initially make much of an impact; later, however, larger immigrating groups began to alter the ethnic composition of the Middle East. At first the Turks, brought in as slaves from the northeastern borders of the Islamic world and the Eurasian plains as mercenaries, served mainly as soldiers and mercenaries in the caliphal and various local armies. Turkish female slaves were favored as concubines by the members of the ruling and aristocratic families. By the end of the ninth century, Turkish commanders were using their positions as heads of military units to seize power. Within a few decades, Turkish military leaders were added to the list of numerous local dynasties that characterized the political development of Islam by the mid-tenth century, when the Baghdad caliphate was on the wane. The Ghaznavids in northeastern Iran and the Tulunids in Egypt were two of these dynasties. During this early phase, Turks came singly or in small groups and converted to Islam, assimilating the Islamic culture. Beginning in the eleventh century, Turkish tribes began to enter the Middle East in large numbers. (For example, the Saljuq confederation of tribes, which came in the early twelfth century, numbered about a hundred thousand tents.) The Turkish influx was followed by the arrival of the Mongols, another pastoral group from Eurasia. The Mongol conquest occurred in two phases. It began in 1225 under Genghiz Khan and ended in 1258 with the capture of Baghdad by his grandson, Hulagu, and the downfall of the Abbasids. Hulagu became the founder of the Ilkhanid state, which until 1355 controlled the area comprised of the present-day states of Iran, Iraq, parts of Afghanistan, and Central Asia.

Before these new groups were fully integrated into the societies they had conquered, the life-style of the Turko-Mongol ruling-class women reflected the status women enjoyed in the Turko-Mongolian society. In the eighth-century Central Asian city of Bukhara, where Turkish presence had become pronounced following the death of their ruler Tughshada, Tughshada's wife, Khatun, ascended the throne because her son was a minor. "She had the custom every day of coming out of the gate of the fortress of Bukhara on a horse. . . . She used to sit on a throne, while before her stood slaves, masters of the seraglio, i.e., the eunuchs, and the nobles. . . . When Khatun came out all made obeisance to her and stood in two rows while she inquired into the affairs of the state" (al-Nashkhi 1954: 9). This account is also supported by the reports of the two historians Juvaini (d. 1283) and Rashid al-Din (d. 1318). Initially Turkish and Mongolian women exerted direct influence over major decisions and could ascend the throne as regents. Royal wives played an active role in the internal politics of the Ilkhanid state and participated in the deliberations of the highest Mongol council, the Kuriltay, in the choice of the ruler. This lively participation was especially characteristic of the wives of the great Mongol Ilkhans, whose exploits are recounted in Rashid al-Din's *Jami* *al-Tavarikh* (*The Universal History*). He justified his departure from the contemporary norms of Islamic society, which left women unmentioned, by explaining that the Mongols accord their women equal treatment.

Another group of Turkish mercenaries in Egypt became founders of the Mamluk dynasty, which began in 1249; Egypt, however, protected by distance and the absence of geographical conditions attractive to steppe nomads, was saved from being overrun by unruly Turkic invaders. Turks and Mongols who were mainly brought as mercenaries to join Egypt's military were collectively known as Mamluks. They constituted a caste that controlled Egypt's political and economic resources. The first-generation Mamluks generally preferred not to mix with the indigenous population but instead married women of Central Asian origin. These women also controlled vast estates and acted as their children's guardians. Many became patrons of charitable institutions and one, Shajar al-Durr, took power after the death of her husband and minted a coin in her own name.

However, these new waves of Turkish and Mongolian pastoralists did not alter the basic condition of women in the Islamic Middle East. Since the *Shari'ah* was fully developed and considered indirect divine revelation by the ninth century, it was not subject to alteration. Therefore, the Turko-Mongol ways and norms left even less of a mark on Islamic culture than had pre-Islamic Arabian traditions a few centuries earlier. On the contrary, it was the customs of the Turks and Mongols that were gradually changed. After converting to Islam, they began to adopt the sedentary population's life-style, a life-style still characterized in the late medieval and early modern periods by the seclusion of women and the veil. But among the Turkish and Mongol pastoralists (Turcomans) who remained nomadic and roamed the vast hilly plains, the mountainous regions, and the dry deserts of the Middle East, women continued to be active in communal life even after their conversion to Islam (Lambton 1988).

Women in the towns and cities of the Islamic world, however, became increasingly confined to activities within the household. Women's withdrawal from public life led to their disappearance from the chronicles. In contrast to the early chronicles, by the fourteenth century even the mention of women was considered improper. Rashid al-Din (1318), the great historian and minister to two Mongol rulers, apologized to his readers for including an account of ʿawrat (women) in his history of the Mongols. The term, used in reference to women, was a euphemism for genitals—in other words, the unmentionable part of the human anatomy. By this time even the mention of a wife's name had become tantamount to dishonoring her. *Manzil* (home) and *zaʿifa* (weak female) were also used in reference to women. Rashid al-Din justified his discussion of women by explaining that the Mongols accorded their women equal treatment (Bayani 1973b).

Despite the absence of direct discussion of individual women by historians, we can glean information on how women lived and the values that governed their lives from a rich body of medieval literary and artistic works. These sources do not offer exact information on specific women, but they provide detail on many aspects of medieval Muslim life. A typical example of this genre, accessible in translation, is *The Thousand and One Nights*, better known in the West as *The Arabian Nights*. The earliest extant versions of this work come from the fifteenth century, compiled in Egypt during the Mamluk period. Some of the stories suggest Baghdad in the early Abbasid period and thinly disguised accounts drawn from the lives of actual characters, including members of the Abbasid dynasty. Although some aspects of the tales are pure fantasy, the details mirror how people lived, what they thought about many issues, and what values society inculcated. The descriptions confirm the rare information that appears in drawings, or references to women in popular sermons and treatises, and provide a rich tapestry of how women actually lived in many cities throughout the Islamic Middle East, including Mamluk Cairo.

Women are the protagonists of many of these tales and range from selfless, loving wives and daughters to selfish, destructive sisters and promiscuous, evil wives. Women of the leisure classes predominate, but we also get a glimpse of women engaged in various professions, from international trade to spinning and menial tasks. The stories unfold in a setting in which respectable urban women were veiled, with limited access to the outside world. Direct contact between men and women was generally limited to those types of contact allowed in the *Shariʿah*. Despite their confinement, however, women appear anything but helpless victims of their circumstances. Many are active participants in the events that unfold around them, and it is they who control events. Some women manage to circumvent the social barriers, usually by posing as slaves, but those who break the rules, despite momentary gain, meet unhappy endings.

Some of the women prove themselves superior to men in intelligence, resourcefulness, and courage. The embodiment of this type is Shahrzad, the teller of the tales and the main female character. She "had perused the books, annals and legends of preceding kings, and the stories and examples of bygone men and things. She had perused the works of poets and knew them by heart; she had studied philosophy and the sciences, arts and accomplishments; and she was pleasant and polite, wise and witty, well read and well-bred" (Lane n.d.). Against the advice of her father, she marries King Shahriyar, who is in the habit of marrying a virgin every night and putting her to death in the morning, to punish all women for the unfaithfulness of his first wife. Shahrzad averts the threat that hangs over her head by telling the king amusing stories every night until he falls asleep. By the thousand-and-first night, she succeeds in changing the king's view of women and is amply rewarded for her efforts by becoming the queen and bearing three sons.

Shahrzad is not the only good woman of these tales; there are many others. The good women manage themselves and their households efficiently in their husbands' absence. Their highest virtue, however, is preserving their chastity and resisting temptation when their husbands are away. Such women become the objects of their husbands' eternal love and devotion.

The bad woman represents the other side of the spectrum; her fatal failing is the sexual betrayal of her husband. By so doing, she goes outside the bounds set for a married woman by society, which demands that a wife remain sexually faithful to her husband, even in his very long absence. A woman's violation of these rules constitutes the worst calamity for a man. Typically these women bring harm to themselves and others, the innocent bystanders, as did the first queen of King Shahriyar. These tales offer many examples of such women and act as a reminder to all women not to transgress these limits.

Although these tales are meant to entertain, they are also intended to teach. The lesson they impart is that ultimately the forces of good overcome the forces of evil. It is the good woman Shahrzad who ends the cycle of violence unleashed by the evil deed—unfaithfulness—of the first queen. Shahrzad and her counterpart, the evil queen, represent two views of women: the good, wise healer and the dangerous, irresistible enchantress, who can seduce any man and bring about his ruin.

These conflicting views of women also reveal cultural norms that were alien to pre-Islamic Arabia and absent from the teachings of early Islam. The Qur'an neither exalts women nor treats them as inferior; it treats them as secondary in society to men. For the origins of the view of women as both protectors and seducers of men, we must go back to the non-Arabian cultures that embraced Islam after it left Arabia. It is to be recalled that both these images have Sumerian and Babylonian precedents.

These conflicting images of women and many other aspects of the older cultures were brought into Islam by the millions of Christians, Jews, and Zoroastrians who converted to Islam gradually. While free spirits like ʿAʾishah, Muhammad's wife, and Sukaynah, his great-granddaughter, could not be wiped out of the pages of early Muslim history, various statements denigrating women began to circulate. The fourth caliph, Imam ʿAli (d. 661), was quoted as saying, "Woman is wholly evil; and the worst thing about her is that she's necessary evil." In another statement attributed to him, ʿAli advises men to avoid women because "they are without religion. The most virtuous among them are libertines. But the most corrupted among them are whores" (Bouhdiba 1975: 117–18). The commentators seized upon these statements, allegedly from ʿAli and other close companions such as ʿUmar (d. 644), for development of misogynist views on women. They referred to women as *fitnah* (temptation or revolt against God) and Satan's agents, among other epithets. Thus the fear of women prevalent in the older cultures began to influence Islamic views. Such statements were used to justify developing stringent laws to gradually restrict women and thereby neutralize their so-called harmful influence and power over men. It would be useful to bear in mind that none of the compilers of the six canonical *hadith* works were of Arabian origin.

At the heart of this view of women was their allegedly insatiable sexual appetite. This point is brought out in many of the tales of evil women in *The Arabian Nights*. When not under the control of social limits, lust can get the better of women. To satisfy their unlimited lust, women can become conniving and dangerous; they use their beauty and charm to ensnare men. Interestingly enough, this theory also suggests that men are too weak to resist women's charms. In other words, a woman is much more powerful than a man, and nothing can keep her from getting what she wants: "Women are very devils, made to work us dole and death. . . . Prime source are they of all ills that fall upon mankind" (Lane n.d.).

The fear of women's sexuality provided additional incentive for the greater restrictions that began to be placed on women's freedom of movement and their contact with men after the first Islamic century. The idea of women's seclusion was advocated by a wide spectrum of philosophers, theologians, essayists, and authors of popular literature. A typical example was the influential philosopher and theologian Imam Abu-Hamid al-Ghazali (d. 1111). In a famous manual, *Nasihat Al-Muluk (Advice to Kings)*, written for the edification of the official class, he advised the reader against permitting women to have contact with male strangers. Embellishing his views with appropriate parables, he warned of the dire consequences of allowing women contact with outsiders. In his opinion, "A women's piety and seclusion are favors from God." He explained the distance needed to protect a woman from the harm that could come to her from male strangers: "It is not permissible for a [male] stranger to hear the sound of a pestle being pounded by a woman he does not know. If he knocks at the door, it is not proper for the woman to answer him softly and easily because men's hearts can be drawn to [women] for the most trifling [reason] and the greatest number of them. However, if the woman has to answer the knock, she should stick her finger in her mouth so that her voice sounds like the voice of an old woman." The author then advises women not to come in contact with a man even if he is blind (Ghazali 1968: 130–31).

Ghazali's comments reveal that underlying the discussions of the need to seclude women was the fear of men's inability to resist women's lure. The commentators' call for the need to seclude women also reveals a fear of competition with other men. The following passage by the philosopher Nasir al-Din Tusi (d. 1274) amply reveals both fears. He advises a husband to keep his wife busy within the house lest idle time lead to her desire "to see the sights, and with looking at strange men, so that not only are the affairs of the household disordered, but her husband even comes to enjoy no esteem or awe in her eyes. Indeed, when she sees other men, she despises him and holds him of little account, she is emboldened to embark on abominable courses, and even to provoke admirers to quest for her" (Tusi 1964: 163-64).

Theologians' and political philosophers' discussions of the need to seclude and shelter women, however, represents one side of the social effort to convince women to stay indoors and to confine them.

These appeals represent the normative values that society hoped to inculcate. At the same time, the repeated appeals to both women and their menfolk also suggest that women were not as obliging as men would have liked them to be. The evidence that reality was somewhat different and that women did not fully comply with the rules of propriety developed by men comes indirectly through many sources. One of the most revealing is a treatise called *al-Madkhal*, by Ibn al-Hajj (d. in 1336–1337), a religious scholar. He laments what he calls the evil ways of Cairene women. In his elaborate condemnation of their ways, he inadvertently provides the modern reader with a vivid picture of how women lived at that time. At least in Cairo of the fourteenth century, women engaged in many activities that shocked the religious scholar, from mixing with male strangers in bazaars and other public places, to attending mosques to listen to sermons, to selling their goods. To the chagrin of Ibn al-Hajj, women were lax in veiling themselves. His discussion deals with the ways of lower- and lower-middle-class women. But, as Hoda Lutfi suggests, it also shows clearly that, contrary to the prevailing stereotypes, the women of Cairo "were strong willed and defiant of male authority" (Lutfi 1991: 99–121).

Although al-Ghazali, Tusi, Ibn al-Hajj, and others blamed men for their own weaknesses, the remedy they suggested was the seclusion of women. Before the nineteenth century, the poet-theologian Ibn Hazm (d. 1064) lamented this practice; other thinkers advocated the absolute separation of the worlds of men from women to guarantee that men did not fall prey to women. In addition, they supported their arguments in favor of seclusion of women in religious terms. The teachings of orthodox Islam, in order to ensure that men did not give in to their weaknesses and stray from its guidelines, put the burden or women by keeping them indoors. The development of laws to contain and control women was only one reaction of a society that recognized the sexual nature of human beings. The other response was the recognition of women as sexual beings and the development of a positive attitude toward sexuality in general. The acceptance of sexuality, so long as it occurred within boundaries sanctioned by the religious law, was perhaps the only course open to the medieval theorists who could not disregard the teachings of the Qur'an, Muhammad's example, and his attitude toward marriage. Therefore, many theologians met this problem head-on and devoted lengthy treatises to various aspects of conjugal relations and responsibilities.

The eminent theologian al-Ghazali discusses at length women's need for sexual satisfaction. Al-Ghazali considers marriage the most important solution for containing the sexuality of women. However, procreation is only one of the important aims of marriage; the other is the individual's need for sexual fulfillment. Men's need for pleasure takes precedence in theological discussions of sexuality—men can take four wives and an unlimited number of concubines, and, in some schools of law, they are permitted temporary wives (*mut'ah*).

However, the theory also recognizes women's right to sexual pleasure. Many theologians have argued that women are entitled to sexual fulfillment apart from their desire to have children. Since the religion accepted pleasure as one of the aims of women's sexuality, the law sanctioned the use of contraceptive devices. Such theologians as al-Ghazali argued that too many children would impoverish the man and imperil the beauty of the woman. In addition, according to some schools of law, a man cannot practice coitus interruptus without his wife's permission, on the grounds that this would deprive his wife of her rightful pleasure. Ibn al-Hajj, a severe critic of Cairene women's ways, even advises husbands to sleep with their wives in the nude in order to give the wives greater pleasure (Lutfi 1991). Finally, some schools allow a woman to appeal to the court for divorce on the basis of the husband's impotence (Bowen 1981; Musallam 1983). Although we have only limited evidence, it would be safe to assert that women took advantage of this right.

The effort to seclude women and to restrict them to household and child-rearing activities made it harder for urban women to utilize fully the economic rights spelled out for them in the Qur'an, even though these became embedded in Islamic law. The Qur'anic provisions regarding inheritance and those governing marriage and divorce were too straightforward to allow any tampering and continued to provide women with a measure of power over their destiny. Inheritance was the most important source of wealth for women, and medieval *waqf* (religious endowment) documents and judicial records indicate that women of the ruling and upper classes controlled considerable wealth. They also had the right to pass their possessions to their heirs (Sourdel-Thomine and Sourdel 1973). Women entrepreneurs generally invested their wealth in real estate; but commerce, the most effective source of expanding wealth, did not attract many women. Occasionally, of course, we learn of wealthy women who invested their capital in commercial activities, joint ventures, and international trade (Goitein 1967: I; Marcus 1973). Interestingly enough, *The Arabian Nights* recounts the adventures of fictional women who engage in international trade and manage to do extremely well.

The fear of women's sexuality in itself, however, created an attitude that regarded the single woman as an anomaly and a threat to the established social order. These norms set marriage as the ideal state for a woman. Since a girl attained legal puberty at the age of nine, or first menstruation, at which time she was at least betrothed if not married already, few young women's vision was set beyond marriage and motherhood.* Furthermore, society developed positive incentives that rewarded women for marrying and raising children. Increasingly, marriage represented a female rite of passage, and improved a woman's position. An unmarried woman was under the authority of her father or a close male relative, but after marriage she came into her own. Although she was not equal to her husband, the rights and obligations of a married couple were more clearly drawn. The arrival of children—especially sons—further enhanced a woman's status. Even in the absence of sons, motherhood was insurance for old age. If a woman became a widow, she often acquired additional prestige and power by becoming the guardian of her husband's estate while her children were minors (Dengler 1978). Even in poorer households, if the husband predeceased his wife without leaving her an estate, his widow could find some charitable endowment to provide for her and the children (Lutfi 1983–1984). These factors made marriage the standard path for most women in the Middle East.

Marriage as a social force limited women to household activities; other social pressures mitigated against women's public pursuit of wealth or even simple independent support. For example, seclusion made it hard for women to invest seriously in commerce because such activity would have required contact with male strangers or appearance in court. No provision in the *Shariʿah* barred women from participating in court proceedings, and a minority of women did appear in court to present their cases. But the impropriety of dealing with male strangers forced women to cope with such problems through male agents, usually a family member. Court records indicate that often women were forced to turn over the management of their wealth to male relatives. This situation was fraught with danger and often led to the de facto loss of power by many women. Records also show that some male relatives tried to rob women of their assets (Lutfi 1983–1984).

For women the most important source of wealth was inheritance. Often the reluctance of the kin group to share its wealth and capital with those outside the familial group made it hard for women

*Evidence of actual marriage age and age at consummation is hard to find for this period. In later periods in various Muslim societies, there is evidence that young women did not routinely marry at such an early age and that if they did so, the marriage was not consummated until menstruation was well established.

to do as they pleased with their inheritance. Families resorted to different methods to get around the Qur'anic injunction on inheritance. The effort of the paternal family to control the woman's share of the estate or buy it at a fraction of its real value was one method of dealing with this disruption of the traditional system. Another solution was the prevalence of cousin marriage in Islamic society. Occasionally a brave woman might appeal to the courts, but most women went along with the system.

These negative pressures were felt by respectable married women from the lower-middle class and above and discouraged women from contemplating any serious interest outside of caring for their children and families. Social norms further undermined the desire of those who may have seriously contemplated such a prospect. For example, the philosopher Tusi (d. 1274) warns against marrying a woman who trades: "The wife trading on her wealth places her husband under an obligation." He also discourages men from marrying wealthy wives, because "when women own property it invites their domination and authority, a tendency to use others and to assume superiority" (Tusi 1964: 162, 166). Whereas middle- and lower-class women had many tasks to perform within the house even if they had some domestic help, wealthy women had few domestic responsibilities since they had many servants and slaves. Therefore, wealthy women became major consumers of the luxury products for which medieval Islamic society was renowned. Some women used their wealth to become patrons of religious foundations, mosques, *madrasah* (religious schools), and orphanages.

Lower-class women had greater freedom of movement, as demonstrated by the concern of Ibn al-Hajj about the unorthodox ways of Cairo women. These women also worked as peddlers, midwives, undertakers, bath attendants, and domestic servants; thus they could defy the strict rules of propriety along gender lines (Lutfi 1991). Nevertheless, prevailing attitudes toward working outside the home influenced even the poorer urban women. Although our information is still elementary on this important subject, evidence from sixteenth-century Bursa suggests that poorer girls worked as domestic servants in order to provide themselves with trousseau, as a prelude to marriage (Dengler 1978). Spinning provided a source of income for many poorer, especially widowed, women; for example, in *The Arabian Nights*, the widowed mother of Aladdin supports herself with spinning. This activity could be done at home because weaving workshops commissioned the work on a putting-out basis. ("Putting out" refers to a system in which workers are paid on the basis of the number of pieces they complete rather than the hours they spend on the job.) But women did not play an important role in the mass production of textiles, which was usually based in large workshops in Damiatta and Tinnis in Egypt and in Iranian and Syrian cities (Mazaheri 1951).

Rural women, however, played a more active role outside the home than did urban women. Agriculture and maintenance of irrigation networks were primarily men's work, but women made important contributions to economic life outside the home in addition to their role within the household. Men and draft animals prepared the ground for cultivation because this activity required the use of the plow and was physically demanding. But women took part in planting seeds and in the harvest. They grew vegetable gardens. In areas where rice was grown, particularly in the Caspian region, Khuzistan, and Iraq, women and children did as much work in the field as men. Women also took care of the domestic animals and milked the cows, sheep, goats, or camels. What spare time they had left they spent spinning wool. Sericulture and production of silk textiles were important to the medieval Islamic economy. The raising of silkworms, which required long months of care, was primarily the task of rural women (Mazaheri 1951).

The making of rugs was one of the important cottage industries of the Middle East in Islamic times. Many of the rugs produced were either made by rural women or woven by women and children in workshops set up by entrepreneurs in villages in many regions in Anatolia, Iran, and Central Asia. The entrepreneurs supplied the wool and the design to workshops; workers were paid by the day or by the piece.

A question that cannot be answered with any certainty is the extent of the veil and the seclusion of women in rural areas. In the absence of adequate studies, we can only offer tentative suggestions. Medieval Muslim travelers such as Ibn Battuta (d. 1377) rarely encountered unveiled women in the course of their travels, even in rural areas. In small and distant villages where the majority of the population was related or well acquainted, these practices were not observed fully. In the larger villages and those closer to towns, where the likelihood of encounter with male strangers was greater, women would have been required to veil themselves in the presence of these outside males. Lower-class women, however, especially those who worked outside the home, probably did not observe the veil as strictly as those women who could afford to spend more of their time within the house (Lutfi 1991).

In contrast to orthodox Islam, which ensured men's proper conduct by requiring women to stay indoors, Sufism, another important form of Islamic piety, sanctioned for women a much greater role in spiritual and religious life. Sufism, the generally accepted term for mysticism in Islam, can be defined as the attempt to attain intimate knowledge of "Divine Reality" through a process of purification, in which the seeker tries to rid the soul of all worldly trappings imposed upon it by the "self." Although this personal and spiritual quest remained the aim of a small number, it became one of the most important forces in the culture of Islam by the end of the eighth century C.E. The favorable attitude of Sufism toward women came from the Prophet's sympathy for women, the veneration of his daughter, Fatimah, by Muslims (particularly those of Shiʿi persuasion), and the fact that the first saint in Islam was a woman, the renowned Sufi Rabiʿah al-ʿAdadawiyyah (d. 801).

A small number of male Sufis were antagonistic to women. They saw marriage as a horrifying experience that would purify the soul through "the afflictions that wait for you will certainly lead you on the way toward God" (Schimmel 1975: 428). But the majority accepted women as equal participants in religious life and honored them for their endurance in the hardship that they suffered on the path to God. Some Sufi masters also revered their mothers for their initiation into their choice of the Sufi path. One of the greatest Sufis, Ibn al-ʿArabi (d. 1240), discovered "Divine Beauty" in the form of a woman he met on his first pilgrimage to Mecca, and in his mystical poetry, he sang the praises of "Divine Beauty" as perceived through the beauty of women.

Sufism offered women a greater chance to participate actively in religious and social life. Some Sufi orders, such as the Bektashi order in Ottoman Anatolia, accepted women as full members, an action that sometimes brought the charge of immorality against the order. Women could have their own Sufi organizations where they could congregate and conduct their religious services undisturbed. Some of these organizations opened their doors to women who had nowhere else to go. From the earliest times, wealthy women became great patrons of charity organizations and hospices for Sufis, using their wealth as endowment for the support of what they established (Schimmel 1975).

While the social rights Muslim women had enjoyed in the first Islamic century were gradually eroded, women, like their male counterparts, did gain in the area of education. Vast numbers of theological and literary writings and letters indicate that women who had an interest in learning could pursue this interest rather freely. Ruling-, upper-, and middle-class women and those from scholarly families could receive an education. A fifteenth-century biographical dictionary by al-Sakhawi contained 1,075 entries on women, of whom 411 had received some amount of education. Women were encouraged to study subjects deemed suitable for their spiritual well-being: the study of the Qur'an and *Shari'ah*, particularly *hadith*. However, women could also study philosophical, literary, economic, or artistic subjects (Berkey 1991). Women were taught calligraphy, and a well-known teacher of *hadith*, Fatimah bint 'Ali from Baghdad, was reputedly an excellent calligrapher. In order not to transgress the gender boundaries, women studied not in the *madrasah*, which became the favorite venue for education of boys beginning in the twelfth century, but informally within the homes of religious scholars or family members.

Education was a feature essential to the practice of Islam. Devotion—required equally of men and women—was guided by the study of the Qur'an and other spiritual sources, a practice possible only for a literate people. Therefore, many women of ability were able to take up religious studies, and some, like the Sufis mentioned above, devoted themselves entirely to seeking salvation. One of the earliest persons to initiate mystical worship in Islam was Rabi'ah al-'Adawiyyah (d. 801), from Basrah. The biographical dictionary of Ibn Khallikan (d. 1282) includes the names of eighty women out of the total of about fourteen hundred eminent individuals. A minority of women attained a high degree of expertise in the study of *hadiths* and received *ijazah* (diplomas). Some of these learned women had received licenses to teach and attracted seekers of knowledge and disciples from all over the Muslim world (M. Smith 1928). Occasionally, a woman became so renowned for her knowledge that scholars mentioned attending her lectures with pride; one such scholar was Ibn Khallikan, the famous biographer. A field in which women's expertise was readily acknowledged and accepted was the transmission of *hadith*, the prophetic tradition, which forms an important branch of Islamic law. A fourteenth-century scholar mentioned the names of 19 women from a total of 172 scholars with whom he had studied the subject. The fact that some of the important early transmitters of *hadith* had been women—the wives of the Prophet and his other female associates—facilitated the acceptance of women in this field. However, women's exclusion from positions in which they could pass judgment on men may well have discouraged them from pursuing fields such as *fiqh* (jurisprudence). For example, as judges, women would have been able to reveal their analytical skills and use them to judge men—something the prevailing value system could not allow or acknowledge for women (Berkey 1991).

To be sure, seclusion, the low marriage-age for women, and the emphasis on marriage and child rearing kept many women from exploiting the opportunity to pursue a scholarly career. But equally important were the prevailing attitudes about women's inferiority that hampered exceptional women who had the ability to learn and the desire for knowledge from taking advantage of their training and expertise.

The Ottomans and Safavids

Although in c.e. 1500 the Middle East was ruled by three independent dynasties, by 1517 the Ottomans ended the rule of independent Mamluk rulers of Egypt. The increased presence of the pastoralists was also one of the reasons for the pressure of the newly converted Turkish tribes on the Byzantine borders. Eventually this resulted in the emergence of the Ottoman state in 1300, which by 1453 had conquered Constantinople (renamed Istanbul) and sprawled over Eastern Europe, Egypt and North Africa, Anatolia, and most of the present-day Arab states. Despite the Ottomans' great military successes—they almost conquered Vienna in 1683—and administrative skills, their state resembled earlier Middle Eastern empires. It lacked the growing technical skills and expanding economic base of rapidly industrializing Western Europe. Therefore, the Ottomans were not able to stop the European advance when the balance of power shifted against non-industrialized states by the end of the seventeenth century.

After the decline of the Ilkhanids, their territories became the battleground for many other Mongol leaders, who carved out smaller principalities for themselves and continued fighting until the rise of the Safavids (1500–1725) in Iran. The Safavids reunited much of the central lands under one rule, restored political stability, and revived agriculture and commerce, but they were not able to restore fully the pre-Mongol prosperity. The rise of the industrial age in Western Europe made full economic recovery even more difficult (Petrushevsky 1968).

Both in the Ottoman state, which had been initially pastoral, and the Safavid state, which relied heavily on pastoralist support, royal women retained some of the social power women had enjoyed in pastoral society. This tradition may account for the involvement of Ottoman and Safavid women in court politics, particularly in the sixteenth and seventeenth centuries (Nashat 1983). For example, when a long line of inexperienced Ottoman rulers ascended the throne

(1574–1676), the queen mother (the *valide sultan*) emerged as the most important figure in political life. She "became the glue that held the empire together" (Peirce 1989).

An important outcome of the rise of the Ottomans was the preservation of millions of documents that deal with many aspects of social and economic development of the territories that the Ottomans controlled. These documents offer an opportunity for scholars interested in the condition of women during Ottoman rule. Thanks to Ottoman records, which have been used in a few studies, we are beginning to learn more about Muslim women in the early modern period: sixteenth-century Konia and Bursa, both in Anatolia; seventeenth-century Kayseri and Bursa, in Anatolia, and Aleppo in Syria; and eighteenth-century Palestine and Lebanon. These studies show that seclusion and the veil were still practiced and that they limited the ability of women to become active outside the household. But opportunity for women who were determined to break the conventional mold was not totally absent. Some women managed to circumvent the limitations imposed on them by engaging in activities that promoted their financial well-being. The picture that is beginning to emerge from these recent studies suggests that women in general were not helpless, submissive victims of tyrannical fathers and husbands, but could indeed exercise some control over their lives. In short, women felt a sense of self-worth and were aware of their rights.

Within marriage, women were treated with dignity. They were full partners in the marriage contract. Women's marital rights were defined according to one of the four major Sunni schools of law, each of which differed in details. Women took recourse in the judicial system when their rights were threatened. Court protection was sought not only by well-to-do women but also by rural women living in villages in the proximity of towns. The records show that no one, including husbands or even fathers, could make use of women's property without their consent, and women appealed to the courts when anyone tampered with their assets. The judges consistently upheld women's property rights (Jennings 1975).

Many women made use of available resources to protect and promote their welfare. Most women still relied on male relatives to represent them in court, but a minority appeared in court in person. Some women acted as legal agents, usually for female relatives, and occasionally for close male relatives. Women were appointed guardians of their minor children, and this position earned them social prestige. Overall, the records concerning marriage and divorce suggest that, while the parents arranged their daughter's marriage, the woman entered marriage voluntarily. In addition, women were the recipients of the *mahr*, or bridal gift, and their absolute right to this settlement, which was sometimes considerable, could not be challenged or removed by anyone, including their fathers. The court records also show instances of women appealing to the judges for divorce on the basis of *khulʿ*, a pre-nuptial agreement which empowers the woman to seek divorce. Some of the reasons mentioned in the petitions as grounds for divorce were physical abuse, inadequate financial support, or desertion (Jennings 1975).

These records show that many women were active in the buying and selling of urban and rural real estate. Some women accumulated considerable wealth and created religious endowments. As before, only a small number participated in trade and financial activities (Jennings 1975). In seventeenth-century Aleppo, a few women even engaged in money lending, an activity banned by Islamic teachings but highly popular with men (Marcus 1973).

These studies support a wide body of evidence that contradicts the stereotyped image of the submissive and victimized Muslim woman. In fact, by contemporary standards, they compared favorably with European women. It is not surprising that European women who visited Istanbul in the eighteenth century sent envious letters home about the status of Turkish women. One of these, Lady Elizabeth Craven, observed, "I think I never saw a country where women may enjoy so much liberty, and free from all reproach, as in Turkey." She added, "The Turks in their conduct towards our sex are an example to all other nations" (Jennings 1975: 57). At the dawn of the modern age in the eighteenth century, many of the patterns that regulated Middle Eastern women's behavior remained; they had been set by the *Shariʿah* in the first three centuries of the Islamic era and had been declared immutable. Of course change had affected these patterns, but only unobtrusively, since all the provisions of the *Shariʿah* had acquired the same weight of authority as God's direct words in the Qurʾan, but within the next century many of the provisions that controlled women's daily life began to be examined in a new light. This re-evaluation was undertaken because developments within the Middle East and changes in its relationship with Western Europe began to undermine faith in how things had been done for centuries. The re-evaluation also affected the destiny of women of the Middle East, because the old answers no longer provided remedies for what seemed to have gone wrong.

Part II

WOMEN IN THE MIDDLE EAST AND NORTH AFRICA: THE NINETEENTH AND TWENTIETH CENTURIES

Judith E. Tucker

In the nineteenth and twentieth centuries, or roughly the period from the middle part of the eighteenth century up to the present, the history of women in the Middle East and North Africa has been inextricably bound up with the changes wrought by an encroaching world economy as well as various forms of European imperialism, including settler colonialism. The history of the period in general, and of women in particular, is not reducible, however, to the effects of such integration of the Middle East into a world economy. Rather, the patterns of economic development and political pressures arising from the growing European presence intersected with a pre-existing economic system and state and cultural formation to forge a new context for both women and men. As we follow the history of women in the

modern period, we need to be sensitive to the fact that there is neither pure "tradition" nor pure "modernity"; we are dealing with a
complex process in which outside pressures interact with internal
developments.

One is also struck by the unevenness of change in the region.
Certain areas, such as Egypt and the Eastern Mediterranean littoral,
as well as Maghribi countries like Tunisia, felt the impact of Europe
early on and saw accelerated change beginning in the eighteenth
century. Elsewhere, especially in the desert redoubts of the Arabian
peninsula, rapid transformation began fairly recently. Everywhere,
however, women—their participation and power as well as the social
definition of gender—were part of this change in the ways they experienced it and shaped it. We are only beginning to come to terms with
the complexity of women's economic contributions, political participation, and social life in the early modern and modern period.

THE NINETEENTH CENTURY

Economic Transformation

The sweeping economic transformations of the nineteenth century—
including the commercialization of agriculture, rise of monoculture,
and erosion of indigenous craft industry as a result of European competition or outright control of local economies—held special implications for women and the family. Much of the historical literature on
the period, however, insofar as it alludes to women at all, emphasizes
one of two points about the impact of the economic transformation.
First, many authors simply have assumed that women and the family
were largely untouched by the economic changes of the period: wom-
en remained in the inviolate world of the harem or in the "traditional" confines of the peasant family, pursuing an existence on the
margins of economic life, making few contributions outside of the
admittedly often strenuous work performed in the home. Secondly,
this pattern of female marginality was disrupted by modernization
and Westernization: women began to undertake broader economic
activities, to enter the professions or the working class, for example,
only in the context of the Westernization and industrialization of the
late-nineteenth and twentieth centuries. Both of these points have
come under close scrutiny recently, and studies of women's economic
activities in the nineteenth century now suggest the complexity of
women's roles in the pre-capitalist era and contest the idea that nineteenth-century developments brought automatic improvements.

Clearly the backdrop to women's economic roles was the entire process of the integration of the Middle East into a global economic system, an integration that gradually transformed patterns of trade and production in the region. The unevenness of this integration meant, however, that different areas in the region underwent change at different times and to varying degrees. Although the number of specific studies of women's economic life is still limited, information on peasant women on the one hand, and upper-class women on the other, highlights the complex impact of economic change.

Some of the most detailed information on peasant women in the nineteenth century is available for Egypt. Prior to the Muhammad 'Ali period (beginning in 1805), subsistence farming along with limited production for a market dominated Egyptian agriculture, and the individual peasant family formed the basic unit of agricultural production. Although the peasant family certainly practiced a division of labor based on age and gender—women, for example, did not plow but did work in the fields at harvest and pest-control time—women were very much part of a family productive unit. In addition to their work in agriculture, rural women also practiced a number of handicrafts and were particularly active in spinning. Many worked on their own account, using domestically produced or purchased wool, cotton, and flax, and then selling the finished yarn to weavers or middlemen. Thus women, as agricultural laborers on the family plot or as craftswomen, played a critical and central role in the rural economy. Not surprisingly, they sometimes owned agricultural implements and animals and, upon occasion, even managed to assert rights to the usufruct (use of, as opposed to ownership of) of agricultural land, as the records of the Islamic court testify (Tucker 1985).

Research on the rural areas of northern Syria in the early nineteenth century suggests that similar patterns held there. Women were active members of village society, and their tasks included fetching water, gathering firewood, tending animals, gleaning, and, upon occasion, laboring in the fields. As in Egypt, women not only worked but also enjoyed legal rights to farm implements and to the land. Although most of the land in Syria, as in Egypt, was owned by the state or was part of a religious endowment (waqf), peasants held rights of usufruct that could be bought, sold, and passed on to heirs. Of forty-five sales of usufruct rights to agricultural land recorded in the Aleppo courts between 1770 and 1830, twenty-four involved women (Meriwether 1993). An examination of the Tunisian state fiscal registers (Dafatir al-maqbudh wa al-masruf) shows that along the Mediterranean coastal regions of nineteenth-century Tunisia, peasant women owned between 10 percent and 13.6 percent of the region's olive trees, the principal source of wealth (Largueche and Largueche 1992).

In Egypt, events of the Muhammad 'Ali period (1805–1849), especially from the 1820s on, had significant implications for rural women. As the demands of the European economy and the ambitions of the Egyptian state fostered increased commercialization of agriculture and consolidation of land, the state drafted peasant families for work on agricultural infrastructure (canals and dams) and for the cultivation of large estates. Although the corvée, or system of forced labor on public works, might recruit an entire family for a certain project, males were far more likely than females to be drafted. In addition, Muhammad 'Ali's military reforms, which included the institution of the first peasant conscription, siphoned off still more men. This disruption of the family labor unit had a number of effects on women. First, women whose husbands, brothers, or sons had been drafted, either for the army or for regular labor, had to take on a crushing burden of work—even, at times, substituting their labor for that of requisitioned animals. For many women, the tasks were too formidable, so they followed their menfolk, camping close to the military barracks or corvée site. Even after the heavy labor demands abated with the reversal of Muhammad 'Ali's development projects, certain patterns had been set: men continued to be recruited for agricultural labor on the large estates while women were relegated to the shrinking family plot (Tucker 1985).

Syria experienced a similar pattern, although at a slower rate of change. In northern Syria during the Egyptian occupation, Egyptian recruitment policies instituted in 1825 had many of the same effects on peasant families: some peasants fled their villages into Ottoman-held territories to avoid conscription, and the women left behind took on additional responsibilities. The Egyptian presence was short-lived, however, and by 1839 the Egyptians had retreated. The commercialization of agriculture at the time had more long-term effects on peasant labor: as cotton, silk, grain, pistachio, and gallnut crops increasingly were grown for cash, the labor of both men and women might be utilized, but women were called upon less and paid lower wages. As in Egypt, a heightened sexual division of labor emerged, with men employed in cash crops and women left behind in household production. In general, however, this process proceeded more slowly in Syria than in Egypt because of the limited area in cash crops. Outside of the areas near Ayntab, Antioch, Kilis, and Latakiyyah, the rural areas of northern Syria were still, throughout the nineteenth century, dominated by the peasant economy in which all family members labored primarily for subsistence (Meriwether 1993). Although we have less information on peasant women in other parts of the region, we may assume that the more commercialized areas, such as the Anatolian coast, saw similar changes in the apportionment of family labor, while the more remote areas, particularly Iran and much of the Gulf, were little transformed in this period. In northern Algeria after 1830, two decades of French military conquest, massive land expropriations of Algerian peasant families, and the influx of tens of thousands of European migrants who settled the seized lands created an indigenous rural proletariat. The consequences for women were often disastrous, since they were reduced to casual laborers on European-owned estates; others were forced into prostitution in the coastal cities (Clancy-Smith 1991, 1996).

Integration into a world market also changed the rural craft sector. Textile crafts were particularly hard hit by European exports of cloth that, over the course of the nineteenth century, decimated indigenous textile production in most regions of the Middle East and North Africa. In Egypt, the industrialization strategy of Muhammad ʿAli accelerated the erosion of local textile crafts: many rural women, who had worked as own-account spinners at home, were squeezed out of the textile sector. Although some of them were recruited to work in newly established factories, they were invariably restricted to the less-skilled support jobs in the factory, and their wages were appreciably lower than those of the men. Although most of the factories closed in the 1840s, textile crafts never recovered their former vitality, and, indeed, most cotton and linen cloth of daily wear came to be imported. Nonetheless, a precedent had been set for the use of female labor in factories: when ginning mills and cigarette factories were established in the later part of the century, women were an important, albeit still lower-paid, part of the labor force (Tucker 1985). In the region around Aleppo, women faced many of the same problems. First, the decline of textile production (from between 16,000 and 20,000 weavers in Aleppo in the early nineteenth century to some 2,000 by mid-century) deprived many women of their work of producing yarn at home for the weavers. Even when the textile industry stabilized, and perhaps rallied, at mid-century, it was restructured in ways that permanently excluded women: cotton cloth came to be spun from imported twists and dyes. Local looms, operated by men and children, managed to secure a place in the local economy, but women lost their productive role in textiles altogether (Meriwether 1993).

One of the first countries in the region to experience profound transformations in its weaving and handicraft industries was Algeria after 1830. The demise of the pastoral-nomadic economy (which had provided many of the raw materials for these economic activities), together with the dislocation of the peasant household, brought ruin to artisan-producers, both male and female. Dramatic shifts in local or regional market structures, in commercial networks, and in patron-client relations, as well as the progressive impoverishment of the middle to upper ranks of Algerian Muslim society, deprived many female producers of outlets and customers. In some regions, such as Tlemcen in western Algeria, unmarried women and girls were employed in European-owned carpet factories or workshops. These factories catered to European tastes and particularly to the growing demand for cheap tourist souvenirs as tourism to North Africa expanded precipitously in the late nineteenth century (Clancy-Smith 1999).

Occasionally, certain European demands expanded the rural woman's productive role. In the mountains of Lebanon, the growth of the silk industry, particularly in the second half of the nineteenth century, increased the demand for female labor: women were the mainstay of the labor force in workshops where silk cocoons were processed (Meriwether 1993). European demand also stimulated the carpet industry in Iran, greatly raising the demand for female knotters who worked at home or in factory settings (Helfgott 1994). In Anatolia, the three most rapidly expanding export industries—silk-reeling, lace-making, and carpet-making—employed predominantly female labor, both at home and in factories (Quataert 1993). In areas where the growth of such specialized crafts expanded women's opportunities to earn an additional monetary income, some women might have been able to improve their position within the family. But as long as the bulk of household work and child-rearing remained the woman's responsibility, and her ability to dispose of her earnings was undoubtedly circumscribed by the prevailing power relations within the family, the expansion of productive roles did not necessarily empower rural women. There is also ample evidence to suggest that women were very poorly paid relative to male workers and that in fact low female wages allowed Ottoman industry to remain competitive (Quataert 1993).

As the pace of land consolidation and population growth quickened in the course of the nineteenth century, many rural women, along with their families, migrated to urban areas. The productive activities open to poorer women in cities were limited, in part by the restrictions on female membership in most craft, trade, and service corporations that regulated entry into the majority of urban occupations. Corporate control was particularly strong among the better-organized and more highly remunerated crafts, which thus remained, for all intents and purposes, closed to women. There is evidence to suggest, however, that women frequently worked on the margins of certain crafts: in textiles urban women, like their rural counterparts, often spun yarn at home for the weavers (Tucker 1985). In nineteenth-century Tunis, female workers were integrated into many of the productive stages of the important proto-capitalist *shashiya* industry that produced men's red woolen caps for local sale as well as for export to other Muslim countries. The earlier phases of wool preparation and the spinning of the treated wool were exclusively female activities organized in a sort of "putting out" system (Clancy-Smith 1999). Women also might, in some cities, gain some control over entry into male corporations or guilds. In Aleppo, for example, the *gedik*, a license of sorts that allowed its holder to practice a trade, was normally passed from father to son. In the absence of a male heir, however, the *gedik* might be inherited by a woman who could not practice the trade but could sell, rent, or bequeath the *gedik*, thus gaining an important say over entry into the trade (Meriwether 1993).

There were, of course, certain trades strongly identified with women. In Cairo, sellers of milk and pancakes, soothsayers, women's bath attendants, and musicians were women who might, by virtue of their activities, earn a not-inconsiderable independent income. In many cases, the society's gender segregation promoted women's activities: upper-class women, secluded in the harem, required the services of lower-class women as entertainers, peddlers, cosmologists, and midwives, who provided not only services but crucial links to the world outside the elite household. Still, these women's relationship to the corporative structure remained a tenuous one. Although lists of guilds included guilds of female milk sellers or female prostitutes, for instance, there is no evidence to suggest that these "guilds" were anything more than collection units delineated for the convenience of government officials. The protections and social welfare benefits available to members of bona fide corporations did not accrue to these women (Tucker 1985).

During the course of the nineteenth century, then, changes in the number and nature of corporations probably had only a minor impact on women. Women migrants to urban areas were far more likely to gravitate toward the unorganized sector of the economy— petty trade and domestic service in particular. The demand for servants accelerated as the wealthier households lost access to slave domestics with the outlawing of the slave trade in much of the region in the late nineteenth century and began to employ free women in greater numbers. In the European-dominated cities of Mediterranean Algeria, impoverished Algerian women, who had migrated to urban areas from the countryside, sometimes found work in domestic service for European families. Untrained peasant women newly arrived in the city found, however, that domestic service placed them in a vulnerable social position; outside of the harem quarters of the very wealthy, domestic service involved contact with unrelated men in the intimate surroundings of the household. Kurdish peasant women in Iraq, who found work as servants in urban areas, invariably resorted to a more "conservative" life-style, including the wearing of the veil, as part of their adjustment to the social strains of their new environment (Hansen 1961). In general, although poorer urban women did continue to work in a number of different trades in the nineteenth century, their economic activities remained confined to the poorly paid and little-respected spheres of casual trade or domestic service.

Upper-class women held a more central position in the urban economy of the region, at least from the sixteenth into the nineteenth centuries. As members of wealthy and powerful families, women were important holders of urban land. All the available studies of sales and purchases of urban land, *waqf* (pl. *awqaf*, property endowed ostensibly for some religious or charitable purpose) transactions, estate partitions, and merchant activities, as they were recorded in the various *shari'ah* courts, arrive at similar conclusions: upper-class women owned considerable property, controlled large amounts of money, and managed some businesses themselves. The rights under Islamic law that women enjoyed to inheritance and the personal ownership of their *mahr* (bridal gift) were clearly more than a legal fiction (Baer 1983; Fay 1997; Jennings 1975; Marcus 1983; Meriwether 1993; Peirce 1993; Quataert 1991; Tucker 1985).

Although the women of the upper classes (wives and daughters of the ruling group and wealthier merchants) remained sheltered in the harem quarters of the great households, they still might participate in the economy. Using agents to conduct their business outside the confines of the harem, women were especially active in business connected with immovable property: speculation in, and management of, urban properties were common features of women's activities in Cairo, Istanbul, and Aleppo. Women were less likely, however, to own productive property such as workshops and the tools of a trade, and when they invested in important business ventures, such as the lucrative long-distance trade, they often provided capital as the "silent partner" in a trading partnership. The estates of wealthy women in the town of Nablus (Palestine) in the eighteenth and early nineteenth centuries commonly contained large amounts of capital and outstanding loans to men, reflecting their ability to amass capital and the uses to which they put it (Tucker 1993).

The women of the Ottoman imperial harem demonstrated their prestige and piety by using their considerable personal resources to build monumental public works, most often in the form of a building complex housing an array of social services. This practice dates back to the sixteenth century, when Hurrem Sultan, the *haseki* (principal concubine) and dearly beloved of Sultan Suleyman, endowed a major mosque complex and a public bath in Istanbul. She also built a complex in Jerusalem devoted to serving the poor. The scope of her activities was exceptional for a consort, but the mother of the reigning Sultan, the *valide sultan*, typically enjoyed enormous wealth, much of which she used to endow institutions and public services. Such activities on the part of the women of the imperial harem served to provide important public services while, at the same time, promoting the power and image of the reigning dynasty (Peirce 1993).

Other elite women also used the *waqf* institution to their advantage. The *waqf* was critical to the organization of urban property, often serving as a way to consolidate family property by evading Islamic inheritance law and as a means of securing property against state encroachments. Anywhere from one-third to one-half of urban *awqaf* were founded by women in the cities (Aleppo, Cairo, Istanbul), which have been examined in detail (Baer 1983; Fay 1997; Marcus 1983). Female founders were likely to appoint themselves administrators of the *waqf* property during their lifetimes and to name female as well as male descendants as the future administrators. Women founders were also far more apt than men to designate other women—daughters, sisters, mothers, or their manumitted female slaves—as the beneficiaries of *waqf* property. Women were employing the *waqf* to secure their own hold—and that of their female descendants—over property.

As the economic activities of the official and merchant elites altered significantly in the course of the nineteenth century, the women of these classes shared in the shrinking fortunes of their menfolk. The decline in long-distance trade controlled by indigenous merchants, as a result of growing European control of the import-export sector and the erosion of the *waqf* (at least in Egypt and the Ottoman Empire) as the state grew more powerful, narrowed the field of economic opportunity for wealthy women. Still, the harem remained a place where elite women acquired skills of household and money management, laying the foundations for a smooth transition to expanded economic activities in the twentieth century (Marsot 1978).

In the nineteenth century, the ground was also sown for the later entry of women into the liberal professions. In Egypt, as early as the Muhammad ʿAli era, the government sponsored a school to train women health officers and a separate palace school to educate women of the harem in reading, writing, geography, and drawing (Tucker 1985; Kuhnke 1990). Foreign missionaries also established schools for girls as early as the 1830s, and the Coptic community followed suit in the 1850s. The history of the government school for health officers (*hakima*s) illustrates the ambitions, and the limits, of these forays into female education. This school sought to educate women at a sophisticated level. The six years of training included instruction in basic literacy skills, obstetrics, and postpartum hygiene, as well as techniques of cauterization, vaccination, the preparation of medicines, etc. Kuhnke points out that the Egyptian government's extreme concern about underpopulation prompted the establishment of the school as part of an effort to upgrade traditional medical practitioners. It thus represents an interesting departure from the European model of institutional development in health care that sought to enforce the "single standard" by discrediting traditional female practitioners. In Egypt, on the other hand, women were recognized as the appropriate health-care providers for their sex, and the state deployed resources as early as 1832 to draw them into a regulated health service. Graduates of the school played an active role in various state-sponsored programs of immunization and collection of information on female mortality, as well as in infant and maternal health care. Over the course of the nineteenth century, however, the Western disdain for paramedical personnel and the promotion of hospital-based curative medicine led to the devaluation of the *hakima* and the stillbirth of female professional training (Kuhnke 1990).

In the last decades of the century, however, members of an emerging middle class in the region, linked by education and economic interests to Europe, began to raise their voices in favor of female education—an ideological shift that reflected the changing needs of these classes and their emulation of the European life-style. Cole has suggested that a new upper-middle class wanted to cut down on the big outlays connected with the elaborate harem world and rationalize domestic affairs, tasks only accomplished by the education of wives to be good managers and to be able, when necessary, to function in the public sphere (Cole 1981). The Ottoman encyclopedist and lexicographer Semseddin Sami published a book entitled *Kadinlar* (*Women*) in 1880, in which he argued for female education, as did the Egyptian Qasim Amin in *Tahrir al-marʾah* (*Woman's Emancipation*) and *al-Marʾah al-jadidah* (*The New Woman*). The woman question was first raised in North Africa by a Tunisian scholar-scribe attached to the Bey's court in Tunis; in 1856, Ahmad ibn Abi al-Diyaf wrote *Treatise on Woman*, which discussed female status under Islamic law. In Iran as well, such reformers as Malkum Khan and Mirza Fath ʿAli Akhundzadah called for women's rights and, specifically, female education.

The drive for female education generated a demand for female teachers so that girls could learn in an all-female environment. In a second round of activity in female education and training, a Women's Teachers' Training School was founded in Istanbul in 1872, and the government-run Saniyyah secondary school for girls in Cairo opened a teacher-training section in 1900. Throughout the region, teaching was the first profession that not only was open to women, but actively recruited them in order to meet the needs of a sex-segregated educational system. Although few upper-class families sent their daughters through the new public educational system, many were still being educated at home to be cultured—but not professional— women (F. Davis 1986; Tucker 1985; Mahdavi 1985). In 1900 in Tunis, a novel experiment in female education was initiated by both Tunisian nationalists and liberal French protectorate authorities. Paid for by funds from the *hubus* (*awqaf*), the first secular primary school for Muslim girls was established with a curriculum that stressed the study of Qurʾan and Arabic as well as French and modern subjects. This school educated both the first female physician, Tawhida ben Cheikh, and the spouses of many male Tunisian nationalists. The public school system was supplemented, especially in the field of female education, by an increasing number of missionary schools that recruited female students, including the American College for Girls in Istanbul and the American Presbyterian Missionary School in Iran. Although only small numbers of female teachers were trained in all institutions, public and private combined, in the course of the nineteenth century, a precedent for educating women for professional work had been established and would be drawn upon in the twentieth century to widen female opportunities.

Women's economic activities, then, were profoundly affected by nineteenth-century developments. The economic changes of the period did not necessarily spell improvement for women or raise their level of participation in the economy. Indeed, in the case of peasant women, at least in regions where commercialized agriculture came to dominate, the erosion of the family economy and the rise of wage labor could lead to their economic marginalization. Some women also lost their means of livelihood as the indigenous textile industry faltered in the face of European competition. Certain crafts that employed women, however, probably expanded in the course of the century, and women were recruited to work in the light industries established in the nineteenth century. Overall, the sexual division of labor appeared to be remarkably fluid: women were often drawn into industries that had not previously been dependent on female labor. Although women were very much a part of the work force, they could expect to be remunerated at a rate far lower than that of men. The evolution of upper-class women's economic roles was equally complex and often contradictory. The loci of their economic activities, the *waqf* and long-distance trade, shrank dramatically in many parts of the region. The glimmerings of other opportunities, specifically in the professions, began to appear, however, as a delicate blend of indigenous needs and Western models worked to change the attitudes of the middle and upper classes toward women's work.*

Political Change

In the political realm, women's history in the nineteenth century was colored by particularities of the process of state formation in the region, both in the obvious ways in which state policies encroached on women and in the less direct ways in which changes in the political system affected both male and female participation. In addressing the question of women and politics, the more recent literature is careful to avoid viewing society as a public/private dichotomy in which politics belongs to the public world of men, and family belongs to the private world of women. Indeed, a striking feature of political life in the region, at least in the nineteenth century, is the permeability of the boundaries between public and private spheres. Whereas formal politics—the public institutions that have the power to make and enforce decisions about society—generally excluded women, a range of "informal" political activities, undertaken at the family or community level, were critical to the political system. Despite the fact that the ideal of female seclusion and the practice of sexual segregation permeated the Middle East, women were not entirely closed off from political power, thanks to a multiplicity of ways in which they were

*In addition to the works cited within this section, see Badran 1995; Tucker 1979; Vallet 1911.

able to influence power relations—using, most often, techniques of influence-mongering and manipulation. As members of families, neighborhoods, and communities, women could translate their positions within these basic social units into political influence.

The first striking political feature of the nineteenth century was the rather rapid emergence of "modern" states with agendas of reform. We have the most detailed information, once again, on Egypt. During the Muhammad 'Ali period, the Egyptian state, newly centralized and streamlined, directed its attention to the task of strengthening the country vis-à-vis Europe. Although state policies did not address the question of women explicitly, the task of developing the country called forth state initiatives in, among other areas, the fields of health care and education. The new schools for girls established in the period included a school of midwifery, a clear attempt to address the issues of maternal and child health as well as underpopulation. The problems of endemic disease were tackled through public health campaigns to clean up Cairo and the deployment of public health officials, including newly trained women, to carry out general sanitation measures and programs of immunization against smallpox. In health and education, the state's ambitions of widespread social reform dictated the training and mobilization of women as well as men (Tucker 1985). The Ottomans followed a similar path: from the 1840s onward, the state set up courses for midwives, issued certificates, and attempted to regulate entry into the profession (F. Davis 1986). Beginning in 1839, Tunisia embarked upon a state centralization and modernization program, in imitation of Egypt and of the Ottoman *tanzimat* reforms. Some of the changes had an impact upon women's lives, particularly in the capital city. For example, an urban police was instituted in 1858, extensive public works projects transformed the nature of city life, and special female prisons were created in the early 1860s. Thus, the state and indigenous governing elites claimed even greater jurisdictional controls over female Muslim subjects (Clancy-Smith 1998a). The limitations of state resources, and disruptions in the process of state-formation produced by the debt crises of the second half of the century and growing European control, meant that only a small number of women were actually affected by these policies. The number of women trained, as well as the number who benefited from their services, remained modest. Still, these sorts of reforms marked a new type of state commitment to the education and care of women, a harbinger of the later and more thoroughgoing intervention of the twentieth century.

By the end of the nineteenth century, as most states in the region succumbed to European control in one form or another, the relationship of state power to women is posed more in terms of European colonial or semi-colonial policies. In Egypt and Algeria, colonial authorities claimed that the advancement of women was a special concern of, and even a justification for, their rule. Colonial officials did, at least at the level of rhetoric, pay special attention to women. Lord Cromer in Egypt, for example, was of the opinion that "the East can never really advance unless some thorough—but, of course, gradual—change be made in the position of women" (quoted in Tucker 1985: 125). A major theme in the justification of colonial rule, continually sounded by British and French colonial officials alike, was the degradation of women in "native" society, a condition to be ameliorated only through the good offices of the European governors (Sayigh 1981). In fact, colonial states did not actively pursue policies that promoted women's issues. In Egypt, for example, scant attention was paid to women's education, on the grounds of fiscal constraint. In the few schools for girls the state did sponsor, the curriculum, modeled after that of Europe, tracked females into courses of study that emphasized a future as wives, mothers, or "native governesses." The examination for a primary school certificate included, for girls alone, tests in cooking, laundering, needlework, hygiene, and "housewifery" (Tucker 1985). Outside its rather limited programs in education and health, the colonial state shied away from reform (in the legal status of women, for example) usually on the grounds that such tampering would enrage the "traditional" elements in the country and risk internal destabilization.

In Algeria, constant official criticism of indigenous views of women did not, in practice, spawn any concrete policies or programs aimed at correcting views or realities. French policy eschewed most interference with Islamic personal law, and an unreformed *shariʿah* thus remained more or less intact. At the end of the nineteenth century, after some seventy years of French rule, there was a grand total of 1,984 girls enrolled in school, including 454 in kindergarten. Indeed, after 1861, colonial officials had successfully lobbied against state-supported modern instruction for Muslim females, arguing that such schools were too costly and, worse, formed women who were accepted by neither society; some even went so far as to argue that Western education for Muslim girls produced native prostitutes (Clancy-Smith 1998b). Nowhere has the criticism of French rule been so virulent, however, as on the subject of prostitution. While prostitution had existed before French rule and was even regulated by Ottoman state elites in both Algeria and Tunisia, the growth of European tourism after 1850 in Algeria produced a sort of tourist sex trade (Largueche and Largueche 1992; Clancy-Smith 1998). Algerian society knew, before the French, a form of traditional prostitution practiced by the "Daughters of the Nail" after the Nail tribe, which allowed its young women to become entertainers and prostitutes in the Saharan caravan cities on a temporary basis. After some years as ritual dancers and occasional prostitutes, these young women would return to tribal life to marry, using their earnings as a form of dowry. Under French rule, this traditional prostitution became solely a tourist attraction, with the inevitable loss of its ritual character. Although such commercialization may have been inevitable in view of the overall commercialization of Algerian society, French officials endorsed it by refusing to extend to Algeria the ban on prostitution in metropolitan France (Gordon 1968).

Colonial officials could also actively oppose any woman who seemed to challenge their ideas of the proper place of the native female. Lalla Zaynab, the saintly Algerian woman who in 1897 succeeded her father as head of the Rahmaniyya *zawiya* (Sufi lodge) in al-Hamil, Algeria, was able by virtue of her reputation for piety and learning to retain her hold on this important center of economic power and political influence, despite protests from her male cousin, the chosen candidate of the French authorities. Clancy-Smith has studied Zaynab's ability to outmaneuver French colonial officials, one of whom found her to be an exasperating woman:

> This affair demonstrates that Zainab is a dangerous woman whose intrigues and activities should be closely surveyed. She knows that a woman is always treated with circumspection and she takes advantage of this in order to cause problems for the local [colonial] authority which she believes is favoring her cousin in the matter of succession. (Quoted in Clancy-Smith 1991: 264)

Despite repeated attempts to remove the troublesome Zaynab from power, the French had to wait for her death in 1904 to secure the succession for her cousin. The space that Sufi organizations provided for women to exercise political and spiritual influence was hardly recognized, much less promoted, by colonial officials who liked to pride themselves on their enlightened views on women.

Women were not only the object of evolving state policy in the period. They also participated in the political system, not as rulers and officials in the formal political institutions, but as wielders of political power behind the scenes and as soldiers in the informal politics of the street. Formal politics were indeed male-defined and male-run. Nonetheless, the importance of the family to the political system—both in the form of hereditary rule as the primary legitimizing principle for the Ottomans and Qajars (Iranian dynasty, 1794–1925) and in the central role family and clan solidarity played in more local politics—provided an avenue for female participation. In the rarefied circles of the Ottoman and Qajar ruling groups, the political activities of the royal harem are now recognized. The concubines, sisters, daughters, and, in particular, mother (*valide sultan*) of the Ottoman sultan, for example, who lodged in the imperial harem where the sultan passed much of his time, might exercise considerable influence over the affairs of state. Peirce, in her path-breaking study of women in the Ottoman imperial harem, has demonstrated how royal women were both symbols and wielders of political power. Their ceremonial displays, acts of philanthropy, and real influence over domestic and foreign policy colored Ottoman rule from the sixteenth century on (Peirce 1993). Such influence persisted into the nineteenth century. Selim II's mother, Mihrisah, was a key supporter of his reform program in the early nineteenth century: she built a mosque for the reformed military troops and founded a medical school. Commanding considerable wealth derived from a generous state allowance and, later in the century, from their privately owned property, various women of the harem could extend their influence beyond the palace as important contributors to the social and economic life of Istanbul. They built mosques, tombs, and schools, and involved themselves in social services. Their power was mediated by the chief eunuch, who exercised considerable power by dint of his relation to the harem and the sultan. After Mahmud II's administrative reforms in the 1830s, however, the chief eunuch's political role was curtailed and his control over the imperial *awqaf* brought to an end (F. Davis 1986). The streamlining and rationalization of the administration may have had broader effects on the activities of the harem; the extent to which such reforms narrowed the field for informal influence remains to be studied.

In the Qajar realm, the women of the royal family also emerge as powerful and, at times, rather independent figures. Taj al-Sultana, the daughter of Nasir al-Din Shah, was born in 1884. Her memoirs, written in 1914, cover harem life over the previous thirty years. She was, by all accounts, an unusual woman who eventually took to wearing Western clothes, divorced her husband because he stood in the way of her travel to Europe, and wrote her memoirs about life inside the royal household. In her memoirs, she expressed some rather decided views about women's condition:

> The lives of Persian women consist of two things: the black and the white. When they step outdoors to take a walk, they are frightful images of mourning in black. When they die, they are shrouded in white. I am one of those ill-starred women, and I much prefer the whiteness of the shroud to that hideous figure of mourning; I have always demurred from putting on that garb. The counterpart to this life of darkness is our day of white. In the corner of my house of sorrow, I comfort myself with the thought of that day, yearning for its advent with incalculable joy, as though it were an eagerly awaited lover. (Taj al-Sultana 1993: 285)

At the time of the 1891–92 Tobacco Revolt, the women of the Shah's harem joined the boycott of tobacco, thus lending their prestige to the drive to force the Shah to rescind the controversial tobacco concession (Mahdavi 1985). The political visibility of royal women, who remained in the harem yet managed to take well-recognized political stands, are not unique to the nineteenth century. Such informal exercise of power has a long history. The talents and knowledge of the upper-class harem women, however, would soon seek a more public forum.

Women also participated in the politics of the period outside the ranks of power and prestige. From spontaneous peasant revolts and rural uprisings in the early part of the century to more orchestrated, anti-autocratic, and nationalist movements in the later period, women of various social backgrounds joined in political action. In the series of urban revolts in Cairo beginning in the 1780s and lasting until Muhammad 'Ali consolidated his power, lower-class women took part in street fighting against Mamluks and French occupiers, stoning soldiers from the tops of barricades and taunting them by questioning their manhood and accusing them of effeminacy. Wealthier women might also take to the streets if their interests were threatened. Muhammad 'Ali's abolition of many tax-farms (the prevalent form of revenue collection from the land in Ottoman times) and his interference in *waqf* affairs in 1814 produced a street demonstration by the wealthier women, who were likely to suffer the effects of such measures. In the countryside as well, in the series of rural revolts in Egypt from the 1820s to the 1860s, women were visible participants. In a revolt in Qinah in 1865, for example, women were held as responsible as men, and soldiers sent to repress the revolt raped and massacred women (Tucker 1985). In nineteenth-century Algeria, which witnessed decades of rural revolts and tribal rebellions from 1830 until

1871 and even later, women actively participated in violent collective action, sometimes as combatants and even as leaders of rebellions.

The Babi movement—an Islamic religious movement in Iran which claimed a new revelation within Shiʿa Islam in 1844 and was, eventually, to give rise to the Bahai faith—also mobilized women in the cause of reformist and, from the state's point of view, insurrectionary activities. Here, the commitment to addressing women's conditions emerged as an explicit goal of Babism. Monogamous marriage, education for women, and the lifting of seclusion formed an integral part of the Babist program of social reform. Indeed, a woman leader, Qurrat al-ʿAyn, played a key and formative role in the movement, calling for a deliberate break with the religious norms of the *Shariʿah* and shocking many by removing her own veil. Precisely why the Babis developed such a progressive, and rather unexpected, stand on women has yet to be fully explained (Amanat 1989; Mahdavi 1985; Bayat-Philipp 1978).

Women also joined with men in the various nationalist movements for independence from European imperialism that emerged in the late-nineteenth and early twentieth centuries. In the Ottoman Empire, Egypt, and Iran, middle- and upper-class women, educated at home or in the new government and missionary schools, participated in nationalist politics. Perhaps the best-known female political activist was Halide Edip (Adivar), a writer who used her pen in the service of Turkish nationalism. An early supporter of the Young Turk Revolution, she played an active role in the Turkish War of Independence through her writing on Turkish consciousness and social reform, and, eventually, through extensive public speaking. On June 6, 1919, she stood unveiled in Sultanahmet Square in Istanbul, calling upon the assembled crowd to swear that they would resist the Greek invasion (F. Davis 1986). In the Iranian Constitutional Revolution (1905–1911), women were also much in evidence: they participated in street demonstrations and the political mobilization of other women and were often entrusted with the task of delivering messages and otherwise coordinating political activities because they could move about the cities without provoking suspicions (Bayat-Philipp 1978). They even disguised themselves in order to fight alongside men when the gains of the revolution were under attack, and there are numerous reports of women whose sexual identity was revealed only when they were gravely wounded or killed in battle (Afary 1996). At the time of the 1919 Egyptian Revolution, upper-class women organized all-female demonstrations to protest the ongoing British occupation, much to the consternation of British officials, who did not welcome this activism among the "native ladies." Many of these same "native ladies" gathered in 1920 to form the Wafdist Women's Central Committee, a group attached to the leading nationalist organization and dedicated to furthering the nationalist cause and women's participation in the nationalist struggle. Lower-class women also participated with men in numerous street demonstrations, and harsh repression created numerous female martyrs to the nationalist cause (Badran 1995).

While women made their presence felt in early nationalist movements, only in the newly formed Turkish Republic were they to reap tangible benefits, under the Ataturk program of reform. In Iran, the 1906 Constitution explicitly denied women the right to vote, as did the 1922 Egyptian Constitution. In Egypt, women were even barred from attending the opening of the Parliament they had struggled for, except in the capacity of wives of ministers and high officials (Badran 1995).

Such political exclusion fueled the growth of feminist movements. The emergence of public women's organizations with feminist demands in the early part of the twentieth century is best viewed, however, as the culmination of nineteenth-century developments as well. Economic, political, and social developments of that century—including urbanization, state reforms of education, improved transportation, and an emulation of Western styles in architecture and dress—were slowly transforming the life-style of the upper classes. Upper-class women, still secluded and veiled, began to question the strictures they faced. In Egypt, a young Huda Sha'rawi, daughter of a prominent family and eventual founder of the first Egyptian feminist movement, participated in the first women's salon, organized by Eugénie le Brun, the French-born wife of an upper-class Egyptian. There, women discussed the implications of Islamic modernism, discovering that the veil and female segregation were not, in fact, a necessary or integral part of Islam. Upper- and middle-class Egyptian women writers also began to contribute to the new journals of the 1880s and, in the 1890s, founded women's journals in which feminist issues were raised in the context of both religion and nationalism (Baron 1994). After the turn of the century, middle-class women like Bahitha al-Bad'iyyah (Malak Hifni Nasif) and Nabawiyyah Musa called for increased education and access to work for women as well as legal reform to control divorce and polygamy (Badran 1995).

The exclusion of these women from the benefits of political independence provided the ground for the founding of women's organizations with implicitly feminist agendas. In Egypt, women founded the Mabarrat Muhammad ʿAli in 1909, which provided health care and education to poorer women. According to Huda Shaʿrawi, the upper-class women who ran the organization endowed it with the dual purpose of expanding their own horizons while liberating poorer women. Two other organizations run by middle-class women—Jamʿiyyah al-marʾah al-jadidah (The New Woman Society) and Jamʿiyyah tarqiyyah al-fatah (The Society for the Progress of Young Women)—were founded in 1919 and 1922, respectively, to make education in literacy, hygiene, crafts, and the religious and national heritage available to poor girls (Badran 1993). In the Ottoman Empire, upper-class women organized the Kadinlar Calistirma Cemiyeti (The Society of Women's Work) to encourage poorer women to work outside the home. Other upper-class women, including Halide Edip, also promoted development within their own ranks by organizing an association of women, Teali-i Nisvan Cemiyeti, that arranged courses and conferences for women in Istanbul, inviting male professionals to lecture and providing day care (F. Davis 1986). In Iran, the political climate created by the Constitutional Revolution had opened new doors for discussion and action on women's issues. Women's societies (anjumans) were organized for nationalist political purposes but also for the support of girls' schools, women's clinics, orphanages, and so on. Women's issues, including the right to education and political participation, were vigorously debated in the Iranian press in the second Constitutional period of 1909 to 1911, and a women's press emerged with the publication of the women's journal, Danish, beginning in 1910 (Afary 1996). These sorts of informational and organizational activities mobilized upper- and middle-class women, bringing them into the arena of public service and self-improvement and thus paving the way for the more explicit feminism of the post–World War I period. Due to the much tighter control exerted by France over Algeria and Tunisia, women's associations and organizations, like their nationalist counterparts, were slower to emerge. Nevertheless, the Muslim Union of Tunisian Women was founded in 1936 by Shira ben Mrad, and the Union of Tunisian Women was created in 1944 under the auspices of the Tunisian Communist Party. It is important to note, however, that wealthy women, as endowers of waqf, did have a long tradition of public service. The new service organizations of the late nineteenth and early twentieth centuries constituted, on one level, a means to continue charitable activities in a changing social context.

Women's relationship to political power changed in the course of the nineteenth century. Women had not been strangers to political life. As members of an elite harem or as participants in peasant and urban revolts, women were continuously present in the indigenous political system. The changes of the period, however, did affect political life. As the harem world shrank in size and influence, upper- and middle-class women began to find new ways to exercise some political influence through women's organizations. For lower-class women, the growth in the power and agenda of the state and, in some cases, the introduction of direct colonial rule, tended to curtail the popular revolts in which women had played a prominent role. The extent to which the formalization of political power in the nineteenth century also circumscribed the ways in which women exercised political power at the level of the village, urban neighborhood, or other religious or community organization remains a key area for inquiry.

Culture and Society

We still know very little about the cultural and social worlds of women in the nineteenth century. The historical literature remains thin, and most of the standard sources, such as travelers' reports, Western diplomatic papers, indigenous official records, and contemporary male writers—be they chroniclers, religious thinkers, or various state officials—have nothing very specific to say about the patterns of women's lives. A notable exception lies in the considerable body of writings produced by Western women—travelers, adventurers, pilgrims, missionaries, colonials—who focused much of their attention on indigenous women. Melman has argued that their attitude toward the Eastern "other" was neither unified nor monolithic, but rather a diverse discourse shaped by politics, gender, and class. Read in these multiple contexts, this body of literature can provide us with something of a window on women's worlds (Melman 1992). In a society that to varying degrees (depending on geography and class) practiced rather systematic gender segregation, the rare observations made by male observers about women are considerably more problematic. Overall, we hear a great deal more about the women of the upper class, particularly those in the harem quarters.

Wealthy women of the harem were generally educated at home for most of the nineteenth century. Education, coupled with the substantial personal resources that well-placed women could wield, made them important patrons of the arts and, in at least a few cases, artists in their own right. Female patrons, for example, built or restored thirty-three mosques in the Istanbul area during the eighteenth and nineteenth centuries. Besm-i Alem, a *kadin* (concubine) of Sultan Mahmud II and mother of Abdulmecit, commissioned the Dolmabahce mosque on the Bosphorous shore, the Guraba Hospital and attached mosque in Istanbul, a hospital in Mecca, and some eight fountains (F. Davis 1986). In Egypt, Nafisa Khatun bint 'Abdallah al-Bayda—wife first of 'Ali Bey al-Kabir and, after his death, of Murad Bey, ruler of Egypt at the time of the French invasion in 1798—built a multi-purpose complex in Cairo, finished in 1797, which included an inn and display space for traveling merchants, twenty-five units of low-cost housing, baths for men and women, a Qur'an school, and a water dispensary (Williams 1986). At least one scholar has suggested that women patrons left their mark on their buildings, choosing locations and styles which reflected peculiarly female sensibilities valuing privacy and grace (Bates 1978). The extent to which women patrons influenced architectural styles has yet, however, to be examined in any depth.

Well-educated wealthy women might also become decorative artists in a limited number of genres. Although painting and fine ceramics were apparently not open to women, we do find a number of female calligraphers active in the nineteenth century. The Ottoman women Feride Hanim and Ermine Servet Hanim earned diplomas in calligraphy on the basis of their accomplishments, and a number of other women left devotional books reflecting high levels of calligraphic skill (F. Davis 1986). Most women also embroidered, and the more accomplished produced towels, pillow covers, scarfs, dresses, prayer rugs, and carpets that were veritable works of art. The many fine embroideries of Ottoman and Egyptian origin were designed and stitched by unnamed women (F. Davis 1986). In both Tunisia and Algeria in the early part of the nineteenth century, complex forms of gold thread embroidery for luxury items were taught to young girls of the bourgeois urban classes by *mu'allimat*, women instructors recognized as particularly skilled in needlecraft. The *mu'allimat* also instructed their pupils in a wide array of domestic arts. Thus, an embroidery session was not just a sewing lesson but an organized, pedagogical exercise in inculcating wider social and cultural values. The finished handicraft items were often publicly displayed; in some cities, the girls embroidered their names on the finished pieces (Clancy-Smith 1998b).

Upper-class women also tried their hand at the formal *divan* poetry of high culture, adopting the explicitly male themes of wine, youth, and love. Several poets of the nineteenth century, including Nakiye (1848–1898), Seniye (1836–1905), Mahsah (1864–1902), and Leyla (d. 1824), were widely acknowledged and published in their lifetimes. The last, Leyla, born to a well known *'ulama'* (s. *'alim*, Islamic clergy) family, wrote such lyrical verse that she came to be known as Bulbul (the Nightingale). Her life, which included one brief and unhappy marriage, was not atypical of women poets of the period: many either never married or were divorced after brief, unhappy alliances (F. Davis 1985). Toward the latter part of the century, women writers also participated in the new styles and genres developing in Ottoman and Arabic literature. As poetry of emotion began to replace the more stylized *divan* poetry, such female poets as Nigar Hanim (1856–1918) wrote poetry and prose that revolved around themes of love, joy, and mourning. Nigar, and such Egyptian counterparts as 'Aishah Hanim Isma'il and Sitti Rosa, also held literary salons that promoted the new forms of poetry and supported forays into the writing of prose, including plays and essays.

The written material generated by such women, and a growing audience composed of upper-class and newly educated middle-class women, helped promote the establishment of the women's magazines discussed above in the 1890s in Istanbul and Cairo. These women writers now had a forum in which they could deal with religious, nationalist, and feminist issues, including discussion about the wearing of the veil, the education of children, and the life of European women (Baron 1994; F. Davis 1985; Tucker 1985). For many women, participation in the nationalist and feminist movements intersected with their literary aspirations: Halide Edip's prolific writings, including various essays, novels, and plays, dealt with themes of social reform and Turkish nationalism. As we move into the twentieth century, these women writers still come from a rather narrow segment of society, from the ruling class of high officials or 'ulama' families, where the education of women at home had long been an accepted practice. That these women now engaged in public literary expression did not constitute any real departure from past practice, but the issues they began to tackle moved them far beyond the old themes of love or religious devotion.

We know far less about the cultural world of the majority of women: the peasants and urban poor. Contemporary observers often commented on the rich oral culture of women: the music, songs, dance, and stories that colored all celebrations, particularly weddings (Duff Gordon 1983). Women drummers, singers, and dancers could be hired for festive occasions and earn modest livings as a result. Public performance for money, however, was fraught with ambiguities of status. In Egypt, female entertainers, while much in demand, entered a social netherworld if they performed publicly in front of men. They ran the risk, for example, of being registered as prostitutes and subjected to special taxes and social opprobrium. In 1834, the Egyptian government, which in Ottoman times had recognized and taxed prostitution, banned all prostitutes and public dancers in Cairo, clearly equating the two. Only the *'awalim* (s. *'alimah*), accomplished singers and musicians who performed for the women of the harem, could maintain a flawless reputation and social respect (Tucker 1985). Undoubtedly, music and dance for most women, then as now, was confined to the circles of family and women friends, where accomplished amateurs did not run social risks. Toward the end of the nineteenth century, however, cafés and music halls where both women and men performed did begin to open in Cairo: women could now sing in public, in a setting of commercial entertainment, as respected or at least accepted professionals. The old guilds of *'awalim* were gradually being replaced by a system of professional singers under commercial contract (Danielson 1991).

Lower-class women also participated, to a certain extent, in the rituals associated with the various Sufi *turuq* (s. *tariqah*), the mystical fraternities so important to popular religious culture of the period. We have seen how a woman like Lalla Zaynab in Algeria might attain considerable power and influence in a Sufi organization. Many other women played a more modest part in the Sufi observances. In 1881, for example, the Egyptian state, as part of an effort to exert control over troublesome Sufi orders, issued regulations that attempted, among other things, to limit women's participation in order rituals by forbidding the use of musical instruments when women were present and by insisting on sexual segregation during ritual visits to cemeteries. The obvious presence of women at the Sufi *dhikr*, the ritual of prayer, dance, and chant particular to each order, suggests how little success such regulations had (Tucker 1985). Outside of these sorts of official hints and the fragmentary reports of observers, we still have far too little information on the cultural world of the poorer urban and peasant women to be able to speak to nineteenth-century developments.

The world of the family, in which most women passed their lives, is perhaps just as obscure. Nevertheless, due to Dalenda Largueche's research on nineteenth-century Tunisia, we have a better notion of how families dealt with rebellious female members. Largueche's study of the institution known as *dar jawad*, a sort of domestic prison for "crimes of the heart," reveals the existence of special houses of female obedience that served both upper-class clienteles and ordinary people in such cities as Tunis, though houses for female inmates were segregated by social rank. Sent to *dar jawad* were women who refused to marry spouses chosen by their families or who had fallen out of love with their husbands. Confinement in these special domestic prisons lasted until the women acceded to the wishes of their families (Largueche and Largueche 1992). There is little evidence, however, that such prisons existed in other parts of the Middle East.

The few references made in the historical literature to family life tend to assume that the precepts of Islamic law served to define and describe actual family arrangements that, in addition, allegedly remained virtually unchanged over the course of the nineteenth century. Although work on the history of the family in the Middle East has yet to begin in earnest, there is much evidence to suggest that the nineteenth-century family was not a monolithic institution that conformed to the precepts of Islamic law. We have the most information on the family of the upper classes, where the importance of the household to the wielding of political and economic power was paramount. In the palaces of the ruling group and, to a lesser extent, the lavish houses of the wealthy merchants and '*ulama*', close control of marriage arrangements by marrying off young girls and matching first cousins underscored the importance of the family as a base for political solidarity and alliance, often effected through strategic marriage. The equation of power with a large household establishment underlay the persistence of the institution of the harem, in which the legal wives (up to four under Islamic law) and an unlimited number of concubines, as well as the women's own servants and slaves, lived out their lives. We find such establishments, of course, only in the upper reaches of the ruling group, among the sultans, shahs, and their most powerful officials. Lesser officials and prosperous merchants might support paler versions of the harem by marrying more than one wife or keeping a slave concubine. But wherever the harem prevailed, the drive to preserve control over the all-important household led to the seclusion of women as a fact among the upper classes and as an ideal lower down the social scale. Such a practice did not prevent upper-class women, as we have seen, from leading active lives as economic investors or wielders of political influence, but they had to operate, up to the end of the nineteenth century, largely through intermediaries.

Peasants and the urban poor could not afford the luxury of secluding women, much less of supporting additional wives or concubines. There is evidence to suggest that, as a result, such families operated quite differently from those of the upper class. According to studies of the urban poor in Cairo and the town of Nablus, these families placed far less weight on marriage arrangements, allowing the marriage of women at older ages and countenancing fairly high rates of divorce. Women, of course, could not be secluded because they were involved in work outside the home. In addition, the family as an economic unit was smaller, often resting on relations between a husband and wife bound by a web of debt—usually from money loaned by the woman to her husband, money that then could be used as a kind of leverage. Overall, although the ideal of seclusion might be acknowledged (for example, by restrictive forms of dress, particularly in urban areas), greater flexibility about marriage arrangements, divorce, and women's public activities characterized the lives of lower-class women (Tucker 1993).

Thanks to the work of Duben and Behar, we have the most detailed information on family and household for late-nineteenth-century Istanbul. Among the Muslim population as a whole, we know that the extended family was not the norm: most people lived in small households of four to five people. Polygyny was rare; only 2 percent of married men had more than one wife. Age at marriage was relatively high, at about twenty for women and into the thirties for men. Birth control was practiced extensively and systematically. In other words, most people married late and lived independently of their extended family; their life-style had little in common with that of the upper-class harem dwellers. We do not have enough information on household and family prior to the end of the century to ascertain to what extent this form of family was a new development. On the basis of some earlier work, however, it would appear that at least some of these features were of long standing in Istanbul (Duben and Behar 1991). We do not yet know to what extent these Istanbul patterns were typical of other urban areas of the region in the nineteenth century.

The upper-class family, particularly the institution of the harem, did appear to change in the later part of the century. As political life became more rationalized with the growth of the state, the great houses that had served as the loci for the organization and use of power lost much of their rationale while, at the same time, the old upper class was in economic and political decline. Only the households of the khedive of Egypt, the shah of Iran, and the sultan of the Ottoman Empire preserved elaborate harem quarters, which increasingly came to resemble artifacts of another age. The slave concubines and servants who had peopled the harem gradually became unavailable as the trade in slaves was outlawed in the 1850s by the Ottomans and the Egyptians (although the law was not enforced in Egypt until the late 1870s). Not surprisingly, the institution of the elite family came under scrutiny and the idea of family "crisis" arose in elite circles. Namik Kemal, one of the radical Young Ottomans, attacked the Turkish family in an 1872 article, focusing on the oppression of women and youth as a recipe for conflict and social strife: "The homes in a society are like the rooms in a house. Can one find comfort in a house constantly plagued by hatred and infighting? Could it prosper? Would happiness be possible?" (quoted in Duben and Behar 1991: 196). An end to polygyny and arranged marriage as well as to oppressive male-female relationships was the prescribed solution. In Egypt during the same period, reformers also began to criticize marriage and divorce practices and call for more companionate marriage (Baron 1991). In Iran, Akhundzadeh and Mirza Aqa Khan Kirmani offered criticism of easy male divorce and polygyny, issues that were to be further elaborated by women's groups from 1909 through 1911 (Afary 1996).

We have far less evidence about change in or debates about the lower-class family, although the pressures of economic and political transformation may well have taxed the ability of the institution to provide for all its members: in Egypt, at least, the growth of prostitution and child abandonment in the last quarter of the century suggests some of these strains (Tucker 1985).

Changes in social conditions—the decline of the harem and the problems poorer families faced in coping with new pressures—resonated in the intellectual realm as the ideological battle was joined between the Islamic reformers or "modernists" and the conservative thinkers. The issue of women, or at least the notion that the condition of women called for some special attention and discussion, emerged around mid-century. Religious thinkers, who were after all the society's most prominent intellectuals, first posed the problem as a matter of interpretation of religious law. Rifaʿat al-Tahtawi, in his *Takhlis al-ibriz* (1834) and *al-Murshid al-amin* (1872), discussed the problem of women and society primarily as one of shedding new light on the meaning of the religious law; to a certain extent, the Tunisian Ibn Abi Diyaf presented the same discussion in his *Essai sur la femme* (1856) (Cannon 1985).

The reformist trend they initiated was furthered by the leading Islamic modernist of the century, the Egyptian Muhammad Abduh. In the late nineteenth century, Abduh argued that women's current oppression stemmed, in fact, from the moral disintegration of Muslim society and called for a revitalization that included coming to terms with the inner meaning of Islam. According to Abduh, polygyny, for example, had been allowed in early Islam among righteous believers, but had become, in his day, a corrupt practice lacking justice and equity; therefore, in keeping with the spirit and intent of the law, polygyny should be abolished. For Abduh and other Islamic reformers, women's liberation found its justification as the precondition for a moral and modern society, not as a good in and of itself. While conservative Muslim thinkers were alarmed by the reformist tendency to open the religious law to new interpretations, others, including the journalist and lawyer Qasim Amin, thought Abduh had not gone far enough. In his writings on women's education in al-Mar'ah al-jadidah (1899), Amin appeared to come much closer to supporting the feminist ideas then emerging in women's circles (as discussed above). The freedom to learn, to work, and to grow was a "natural right" of women, the fruit of their intellectual and spiritual equality with men (Stowasser 1993). As Leila Ahmed has pointed out, however, such support arose primarily from his wholehearted embrace of a Western model of development and his desire to emulate a Western gender system. His enthusiasm for, and understanding of, feminist ideas proved to be contingent upon the extent to which they furthered a Western (and colonial) vision of ideal gender relations (Ahmed 1992).

Women's voices also came to be heard in the latter part of the nineteenth century. Elite educated women joined the debate with strong arguments for the end of female seclusion and the expansion of educational opportunities for women. 'A'ishah al-Taimuriyyah, a Cairene of Turkish aristocratic background, typically couched her arguments for female education in the context of the wider social good: women must be educated if society is to advance and prosper. By secluding women and keeping them ignorant, men harm society as a whole:

> Thus, O men of our homelands, O you who control our affairs, why have you left these females behind you for no reason? Why have you neglected the benefits of the maxim: "What you do today you will encounter tomorrow"? Since you have been miserly in extending to these females the true adornment of humanity, and since you have been content to pull them away and isolate them from its brilliant jewel (when they were under your authority, more pliable than a reed pen, when their submission to your control was famous indeed) then why do you raise your hands in confusion, like one who has lost the meanings of things in the hour of need? For you have mocked their situation, and you have made light of their shar-

ing the work with you. You have deemed it best to separate yourselves in every way. Now look: upon whom does the blame accrue?
(Quoted in Badran and Cooke 1990: 132–33)

The arguments for female education came under attack, however, from conservative thinkers. Tal'at Harb, an Egyptian nationalist
and one of the founders of Bank Misr, embraced the conservative
religious argument that men and women were, in fact, unequal, and
that calls for women's liberation were part of the imperialist plot to
weaken Egypt. The Islamic position, as Harb saw it, held that

> Women were created for men's earthly pleasures and in order to
> take care of domestic affairs; God did not create them to attempt to
> defeat the men nor to give opinions or establish policies. If God had
> wanted them to do so, He would have given women courage, intre-
> pidity, chivalry, and gallant audacity, which is not the case. And if
> women wanted to behave like men and carry heavy burdens to be
> his equal . . . would this not be a shirking of the duty assigned them
> by the Almighty? (Quoted in Stowasser 1993: 123)

Thus, rather stark lines were drawn in public religious opinion: the
Islamic reformers argued that women were meant by Islam to play
an active, if not entirely equal, role in society while conservatives
underscored the wide distinctions between the genders, including
disparities in mental, physical, and moral capacities. The heat of this
debate reflected wide disagreement about a series of intersecting political issues. One study has pointed out that lines tended to be drawn
to suit class interests, with those who profited from Western penetration siding with reform and those most injured by the new developments siding with conservatism (Cole 1981). From its beginnings in
the nineteenth century, the "woman question" was intertwined with
issues of Westernization, imperialism, and cultural authenticity, and
strongly linked to religious discourse. Indeed, the issue of gender in
society was to remain, by and large, explicitly "Islamic," a problem
that has dogged discussion right up to the present.

THE TWENTIETH CENTURY

Economic Participation

The growth of a modern capitalist economy and its extension to almost all areas and sectors of the Middle East and the emergence of
states that actively intervened in economic development underlie
many of the changes in women's lives in the twentieth century. His-

torians and anthropologists who have examined women's economic activities in the period have tended to focus on three questions. First, what kind of impact did this particular kind of economic growth have on women's participation in the economy: did the scope or the character of women's economic contributions change in any significant fashion? Second, how has the custom of sexual segregation intersected with the demand for female participation: have distinct patterns of female employment tended to emerge as a result of the pre-existing separation between men and women? Third, as the internationalization of capitalism has brought more women into the labor force, to what extent have women's status and power been enhanced as a result? Again, the assumption, met frequently in the literature, that economic "modernization" gradually brought women into the labor force, eroding the practice of seclusion along the way, is now being questioned as new research suggests the far greater complexity of the process. The dichotomies of private and public or domestic and socialized labor do not allow us to grasp this complexity: whether we look at women in the shrinking world of the pastoral nomads, in rural areas, or in urban settings, we find that the twentieth century is not an era of simple progress, but rather one of change and adaptation.

Among the pastoral nomadic minority of the Middle East region, the basic economic unit was the family. In general, men's and women's economic roles and responsibilities differed, but complementarity rather than subordination seemed to characterize the difference. In a Syrian-Lebanese tribe studied by Chatty (1978) and an Iranian tribe studied by Beck (1978), women had a variety of productive roles, including the care of young and sick animals, the making of butter and cheese, the milking of the camels, sheep, and goats, and the setting up and breaking of camp. In the Syrian-Lebanese tribe, but not in the Iranian, women also controlled the money made through the sale of butter and cheese. In some tribes, such as among the Bayr Ahmad in southwest Iran, women exercised exclusive control over the animals, including the sale of animal products and decisions about what to buy with the money so earned. Although the Bayr Ahmad made important decisions in all-male meetings of the tribe, they were careful to take account of the women's opinions. While the men met, the women assembled within sight and sound of the men to make loud comments on their discussion (Fazel 1977). In the nineteenth and early twentieth centuries, when the power of the state and the reach of the capitalist economy extended only very sporadically into pastoral nomadic redoubts, we can assume that such patterns held:

women often worked with the tribe's animals and enjoyed, as a result, some degree of control over the animals' products, including the cloth spun and woven from wool.

Most authors agree, however, that the twentieth century has gradually brought changes that are having an adverse impact on the productivity and economic power of nomadic women. The increasing strength of the nation state and the growth of the market and money economy draw nomadic groups ever closer to the society outside the tribe. As pastoralists are more integrated into the market economy, the need for cash encourages economic specialization within the tribe and pushes men to seek outside income as shepherds, as sharecroppers, or as wage laborers in towns. New divisions of labor emerge, in which women's work falls more and more into the category of subsistence activities while men earn the money to purchase an ever larger proportion of the tribe's needs. A striking symbol of change lies in the replacement of the camel by the truck among many nomadic peoples: men monopolize the new technology, whereas women lose many of their former economic activities associated with the tribe's animals. When sedentarization increases as a result of state policy and the pull of the market, women may also attempt to assimilate into the village or town milieu by adopting customs of segregation and veiling (Beck 1978; Chatty 1978; Fazel 1977).

In settled agricultural areas as well, the growth of the market and the introduction of new technologies tended to emphasize sexual inequalities. In the Gharb in Morocco, for example, women played an active part in the pre-colonial subsistence economy and enjoyed, as a result, recognized rights to the wealth of the community. Although they could not inherit agricultural land, they could expect material support from male relatives. During the French colonial era, however, land holdings were consolidated at the expense of small peasant holdings, and peasants increasingly, in the twentieth century, went to work as wage laborers on privately owned or state farms. Only men were hired as permanent employees, whereas women worked as seasonal laborers for lower wages at jobs that spared them for unpaid family labor. The cost for women has been great: jolted out of a subsistence agricultural system in which they worked hard but were guaranteed economic security, rural women now work just as hard but enjoy neither permanent, paid jobs like men, nor the benefits of the old family-based system (Mernissi 1983).

Similar trends can be the result of new forms of state intervention. Patterns of national economic development, including industrialization and the modernization of agriculture under the Pahlavis in

Iran (1921–1979), transformed the rural economy, making much peasant-based agriculture unremunerative. Men increasingly joined the wage-labor force, often migrating to large towns at some distance, while women were relegated to the household. The work women had done in the family-based economy—primarily the gathering of food and the care of animals and the processing of their products—no longer existed, and women became totally dependent on the income of male relatives. Deeply ingrained opposition to women working outside the house reduced them to the role of consumers who must try to emulate an urban life-style. Thus women were stripped of their economic activities in agriculture and simultaneously denied access to new kinds of work, trends that were greatly accelerated by the propaganda of the Islamic Revolution after 1979 concerning the proper spheres of female activity (Friedl 1981, 1991). Similarly, in Turkey state policies regarding the dissemination of new agricultural technologies and training have favored men and left rural women outside of the "modern" agricultural sector (Kandiyoti 1977).

Our understanding of rural women's work is hampered, however, by statistical limitations. Mid-twentieth-century statistics show very low rates of female participation in the agricultural labor force. Women constituted 2 percent or less of the labor force in Tunisia, Algeria, and Libya; 4 to 6 percent in Egypt, Iran, and Jordan; and 10 percent in Syria and Morocco. At the same time, women formed anywhere from 40 to 75 percent of agricultural workers reported as "unpaid family labor" (Youssef 1977). Women are undoubtedly undercounted in the wage labor force, and the significance of their contribution to the family farm has been almost completely overlooked. Official sources play a role insofar as they have failed to reflect the nature and scope of the rural woman's productive activities (Badran 1982). Such statistical uncertainty aside, some recent work on rural women does stress the ways in which the capitalization of agriculture has tended, overall, to exclude women from production and transform them into consumers.

On the other hand, certain trends in international capitalism, namely the development of a specialized global economy that transfers labor-intensive production to less-industrialized countries, have raised the numbers of rural women who work in handicraft production oriented toward an export market, particularly since the 1960s. Gunseli Berik, in a detailed study of women carpet-weavers in Turkey, demonstrated the extent to which rural households may become dependent upon the earnings of these women, who contribute anywhere from 25 to 50 percent of household income. Weaving income from their work at home or in ateliers (workshops) has countered both the proletarianization and pauperization of rural households and allowed for some household accumulation. The effects of such activity for women, however, are uneven. There is no evidence that women gain more autonomy: the demands of work, whether in the home or the atelier, inhibit other life choices. Women do appear to be able to exercise at least some control over their earnings. In general, however, women do not gain significantly greater decision-making power but rather remain locked into age and gender hierarchies of the household despite their increased earnings (Berik 1987).

Among urban women, twentieth-century developments had very different consequences for middle-class and lower-class women. The expansion of systems of higher education, which took place at different times in different Middle Eastern countries, tended to open professional opportunities to both men and women of the upper and middle classes. In Egypt, largely thanks to the pressures brought to bear by the Egyptian Feminist Union (founded in 1923), women were admitted to the Egyptian National University in 1928. That same year, Tawhida ben Cheikh became the first Tunisian Arab Muslim woman to be admitted to the Faculty of Medicine in Paris, from which she received a medical degree in 1936. In Turkey, Ataturk's reforms made all education equally accessible, in principle, to males and females. In other areas, such as Kuwait and Saudi Arabia, there were virtually no women in higher education until local universities were opened to them in the 1970s as part of a state push for development. Whether early or late, however, the availability of professional education to women has meant that women of middle-class backgrounds have, in fact, entered professions in significant numbers. Indeed, in a country like Egypt, there was striking feminization of many professions during the 1970s as a result both of government policies under Nasser and Sadat guaranteeing jobs for university graduates and of the departure of men to military service or employment in other Arab countries. This feminization occurred not only in the more traditionally "female" fields of teaching and medicine, but also in such strongly "male" professions as engineering (Howard-Merriam 1979; Moore 1980a). In countries of the Arab Gulf where women were virtually absent from the professions as of the early 1970s, the change has been particularly dramatic. In Kuwait, for example, the number of women in the labor force rose from some 1,000 in 1965 to almost 25,000 in 1985. Of those 25,000, over 50 percent were to be found in the professions (al-Kazi 1986). In other countries of the Arab Gulf as well, better-educated women are much more likely to be employed. In Bahrain, for example, 70 percent of employed women have a high-school education or higher (Fakhro 1990).

This meteoric rise in the admission of women to urban professions was based, in part, on the perceived need to train women to minister to members of their own sex. The focus on the education and training of female teachers and health-care providers, so evident in the nineteenth century, continued in the twentieth: the expanded commitment of newly independent states like Egypt and Syria to economic development in the post–World War II period greatly enlarged the scope of the project, as did the ambitious development plans of the oil-producing states in the 1970s. In both cases, overall shortages of male professionals also led to policies that drew women into other professions, including engineering. The expansion of employment opportunities for middle-class women may prove, however, to be somewhat ephemeral. The slowing of economic growth in the oil-producing states—with its concomitant fall in demand for both home-grown and imported professionals and the surfeit of professionals in countries like Egypt and Iran, where educational programs outstripped the pace of economic development—has reduced the demand for professionals and, indeed, produced professional underemployment. The stage is set, therefore, for a "back to the home" movement for professional women, already apparent in the popular press of the 1980s and 1990s, in which women are portrayed as supplemental workers whose primary role is that of wife and mother. Still, educated upper- and middle-class women do enjoy a long history of work in many parts of the Middle East region, a history which will not, one suspects, be easily forgotten.

Among lower-class women, the choices of urban occupation have been narrower. Although women sometimes were recruited for factory labor in the early part of the century, the large-scale industrialization schemes of the twentieth century have not, by and large, involved the use of female labor: women's participation in industrial production has been minimal (Sullivan 1981; Youssef 1974). Cultural and economic factors both seem to be at work here. Whether in a poor quarter of Cairo or in a Moroccan village, the ideal woman has been the woman who remains at home caring for her husband and children; women who work for wages outside the household lose status. If women had to work, the most acceptable occupations were those which kept women out of public view and away from unrelated men: clothes-washing, spinning and weaving, the raising of small animals, and other home-based activities constituted acceptable forms of female labor in the Moroccan village or the Cairo quarter (S. Davis 1978; Rugh 1985). Post-1962 socialist Algeria also demonstrates these attitudes. Willy Jensen's study of Algerian women during the 1970s and 1980s showed that those who earned a living, moved freely in public places, and were politically active tended to be "women without men"—widowed, divorced, or orphaned females. Working as bathhouse attendants, washers of the dead, religious leaders, sorcerers, healers, servants, or local politicians, these women were socially marginalized, since they were regarded as breaking gender norms regarding women and work (Jensen 1987).

In the more traditional and stable poor quarters of Cairo, however, women have been well integrated into economic and social life. These women, the *banat al-balad*, worked as dressmakers and shop assistants, as nurses and government employees, or even as butchers, peddlers of hashish and other consumption items, and coffeehouse keepers. They did not lose status by conducting such activities; on the contrary, women who worked to support their families were highly regarded in the quarter (el-Messiri 1978).

The marked difference in attitudes toward women's work in the case of two different quarters of Cairo has been explained on the grounds of significant differences in their respective economics. In the poor quarters of the city, relatively newly populated by rural migrants, the new rural pattern of men going into wage labor and women staying in subsistence production at home was transferred wholesale to the city. In the older urban neighborhoods, however, a vestigial pre-capitalist economy in which the family functioned as the unit of production was preserved, the boundaries between home and workplace were blurred, and women's work remained a normal part of the neighborhood scene (Gran 1977). The implications of the developments of the twentieth century are clear: the growth of capitalist enterprise and wage labor in urban areas, insofar as it demarcated the home and the workplace in a powerful new way, introduced questions about the propriety of work for lower-class women that had been largely absent before.

Many women in Middle Eastern cities, however, have entered the labor force, like their rural counterparts, by engaging in small-scale production at home or in neighborhood ateliers. In the poorer working-class neighborhoods of Istanbul in the 1980s, for example, some 65 percent of poor women were estimated to be engaged in some paid activity, mostly piecework knitting or stitching oriented toward an export market. As Jenny White has pointed out in her study of them, these working women constituted a body of cheap labor requiring neither infrastructural investment nor material benefits on the part of their employers or middlemen. Furthermore, their labor was viewed by their communities and by themselves as part of their household labor: they worked in the context of social, often familial, groups where systems of obligations and reciprocity bound them together. Such work gave them the flexibility they needed to run households and raise children while they earned a (small) wage, but the embedding of such work in traditional settings ensured that they would not gain greater individual control over their economic lives (White 1994). Women have entered the labor force in large numbers via this route, but they remain a poorly remunerated, unorganized, and highly gendered segment of that labor force.

The history of women's economic participation in the region began to change in the 1960s as a result of state expansion, economic development, and new levels of demand for labor in the oil-producing states. As male workers migrated to the Gulf from Egypt, Jordan, and the Occupied Territories (the West Bank and Gaza), women entered factories as replacement labor: social constraints proved weaker than the economic imperatives of development. Egypt, Jordan, and Turkey all experienced a marked expansion in women's participation. It is far from clear, however, that such expansion brought women into the factory labor force on a permanent basis: indeed, much of the literature suggests that the higher levels of female participation may well prove to be transitory as the demand for migrant labor diminishes and the men return home (Layne 1981; Abadan-Unat 1977). In the oil-producing states themselves, the indigenous working class is almost entirely male. The dramatic entry of middle-class Kuwaiti women into the professions, for example, has no parallel in the lower class: over 67 percent of Kuwaiti women in the labor force are to be found in jobs requiring at least a high-school education (al-Kazi 1986).

Nor did increased rates of female participation in industry necessarily spell greater access to the privileges enjoyed by the organized working class. Although the number of female industrial workers grew significantly in Iran in the 1950s and 1960s, most of this growth took place in small workshops, particularly those in the textile and food industries where many jobs were low-skilled, poorly paid, and often temporary. Enterprises of nine or fewer workers were also exempt from the provisions of Iran's Labor Law, so that the many women workers of the small workshops did not have rights to equal pay, maternity leave, health care, and day-care services as specified by the Labor Law (Moghissi 1991: 214).

The expansion of a modern capitalist economy in the twentieth century appears to have had significantly different effects on the economic participation of middle- and lower-class women. Opportunities for educated women definitely multiplied as the demand for female teachers and doctors increased, and an overall shortage of professionals encouraged the education and employment of all middle-class candidates, be they men or women. The options for lower-class women, however, appear to have shrunk. As the pre-capitalist systems of family-based farming and crafts production gradually gave way to a wage-labor market, women were largely excluded from the new skilled occupations. They continued to work, but as laborers doing piece-work at very low wages. How much this exclusion owed to social constraints, particularly religious and customary opposition to women working in jobs that could expose them to public view or association with men, remains a subject of some debate. Moghadam has argued that ambivalence on the part of state managers, economic crisis in the region, and the general low level of industrialization have been the major impediments to female employment in the large and modern firms (Moghadam 1993). The relative ease with which women have been brought into the labor force when needed, as in the period of heavy male migration, suggests how quickly social constraints can be overridden. On the other hand, the tenuous position of women, demonstrated by the current "return to the home" campaigns, shows how social constraints can also be resurrected at will. The definition of women's labor as supplemental and temporary undergirds their current economic participation and minimizes the significance of that participation for the achievement of power and autonomy.

Political Life

The history of women's political life in the twentieth century is intertwined with the major political developments of the period, including the movements and wars of national liberation and the emergence of post-independence state structures. It is widely acknowledged that, while women participated actively in the political agitation and even violent confrontations surrounding national liberation, they were not necessarily to reap rewards in the form of increased levels of participation in the formal politics of the post-independence state. Indeed, much of the literature concerned with women and politics attempts to address the questions of why and how women were excluded from political power even though they had been a part of political change. The history of the feminist movement, and the ways in which it developed first in the service of the nationalist movements and then under the aegis of the bureaucracies of post-independence states, has also been a major concern of historians. Finally, the history of women's political life in the period is not complete without some consideration of the effects of political development on the long-established role women had played in the informal politics of influence and intrigue.

The past and present nationalist movements of the region—the Turkish War of Independence (1919–1923), the Iranian Constitutional Revolution (1906–1911), the Egyptian Revolution of 1919, the Algerian War of Independence (1954–1962), and the ongoing Palestinian conflict, to name just a few—all depended on the mobilization of women as demonstrators, organizers, speech-makers, and even fighters. In Turkey, as we have seen above, such women as Halide Edip were major political figures of the movement, writing and speaking in support of the nationalist cause. In Iran, women participated in demonstrations that proved critical to the newly formed parliament's protection from attack, however fleeting. In Egypt, women of all backgrounds participated in street demonstrations protesting the arrest of nationalist leaders by the British in 1919. The Wafdist Women's Central Committee was then founded in 1920 and began to play an important role in the nationalist movement, organizing boycotts of British goods, banks, and personnel. In Algeria, women became cadres in the FLN (Algerian Front for National Liberation), serving first as messengers and intelligence gatherers and later as actual combatants in the urban guerilla war. The Palestinian movement has also mobilized women and incorporated them in both civilian and military roles. In all cases, the traditional views of women were eroded in the process, but such change did not necessarily make any permanent or revolutionary difference in women's position and power (Danforth 1984). Nor was nationalist ideology gendered in any one specific way. As Moghadam has pointed out, nationalist movements have constructed and used gender in different fashions:

> In some historical instances, representations of modernity and national progress include the unveiled, educated, and emancipated modern woman, whereas the woman who is veiled signifies cultural and economic backwardness. In other movements, the search for authenticity, cultural revival, and reproduction of the group seems to be incumbent upon re-veiling and family attachment for

women. This variability may be explained in terms of the different types of nationalist movements (right-wing, left-wing; religiously oriented, secular) and in terms of a shifting relationship between nationalist goals and the struggle for women's rights. (Moghadam 1994: 2–3)

We might also add that, as the twentieth century wore on, nationalist ideologies in the Middle East tended to veer away from the left-wing and secular and toward the fairly conservative and ostensibly religious constructions of gender.

In some cases, as in Iran under Reza Shah, nation-building entailed the creation of a strong executive power that brooked no challenges from independent or even quasi-independent political movements. Iran's independent women's organizations, many of which got their start from women's activities in the Iranian nationalist movement of the 1910s and 1920s in association with communist or socialist parties, came under fire as Reza Shah consolidated his power in the early 1930s and launched attacks against socialism in general, including women's organizations with affiliations to leftist movements. One after the other, these groups—the Patriotic Women's League associated with the Socialist Party, the pro-communist Messengers for Women's Prosperity, the Awakening of Women, and the Women's Society—were all banned and disappeared from Iranian political life. The independent women's press also was proscribed. After the "last semi-independent activity undertaken by women," the Congress of Oriental Women in Teheran in 1932, Reza Shah's political autocracy rang down the curtain on some two decades of a flourishing independent women's movement and ushered in an era in which only state-sponsored programs of reform were found acceptable (Paidar 1995).

Algerian nationalism developed along very different lines, but the outcome was to prove similar for women. In the Algerian War of Independence, women were involved in both rural and urban resistance. In 1956, as the guerilla warfare tactics of the FLN faced ever more sophisticated French counterinsurgency, the FLN came to rely more on its urban cells and decided to involve women more actively in response to the new demands of urban operations: it was Algerian women wearing Western dress who could carry the messages, money, grenades, revolvers, and bombs through French checkpoints without arousing suspicion. Some of the most publicized combatants of the FLN were women: Jamilah Buhrayd, for example, was only twenty-two when arrested while operating as a liaison agent. She was wounded during her arrest, tortured in interrogation, and condemned to death in 1957. Her execution was never carried out, but she spent the remainder of the war incarcerated in France. While *al-Mujahid*, the organ of the FLN, recognized her in 1959 as the most famous Algerian woman, she was not alone: other women, such as Jamilah Bupasha, Zohrah Drif, and Djohar Akru were jailed and tortured as FLN urban agents (Amrane 1991; Fernea and Bezirgan 1977; Gordon 1968).

Public recognition of women's new roles, however, sent mixed signals. The FLN, and Algerian society in general, developed its views of women within the context of French colonialism. French colonists had long justified themselves by pointing to the inferior status of Algerian women as the badge of a backward culture sorely in need of French tutelage, and the French strategy to undermine Algerian resistance included winning Algerian women to European ways. The Algerian response was the perhaps inevitable politicization of tradition: the promotion of women's veiling, for example, as a symbol of the besieged indigenous culture and a gesture in defiance of the French. *Al-Mujahid* proclaimed proudly in 1958 that "On the very first day of the revolution, they [women] attained full dignity as citizens . . . more women are wearing the veil than ever before . . . a sign of quiet affirmation of their patriotism" (quoted in Benallegue 1983: 707). The FLN came to publicize women's participation in the war as evidence of their freedom and dignity under Islam, as validation not of any fundamental change in women's position but of the strength and diversity of their "traditional" roles as defined by religion and custom. When faced with internal economic and political problems after the war, the new government of Algeria tended to undercut the gains women had made in the revolutionary period through the theme of cultural continuity. The officially sanctioned National Union of Algerian Women was instructed to serve the woman's interest as "wife and mother" and not to abandon "the ethical code deeply held by the people" (quoted in Minces 1978: 167–69).

In the Palestinian nationalist movement, as well, women have a long, well-documented history of active participation in the demonstrations, strikes, and military operations that have characterized the different phases of the movement. In 1929, Palestinian women held the Palestine Arab Women's Congress in Jerusalem, which issued protests to the British government against continued Jewish immigration, the practice of collective punishment, and the harsh treatment of Arab prisoners. The upper- and middle-class women of the Arab

Women's Association (variously called the "Arab Women's Committee" and the "Arab Ladies Committee") continued, under the British Mandate, to criticize British rule, write detailed memoranda on political and social conditions, provide support to nationalist prisoners and their families, and take part in street demonstrations, including the wave of protests against the U.N. Partition Plan of 1947 (Fleischmann 1996). During the Arab Revolt against the policies of the British Mandate government from 1936 to 1939, peasant women carried arms and food to guerilla fighters in the hills, hid wounded fighters and engineered their escapes, and smuggled explosives hidden in milk cans or vegetable baskets into urban areas. Since 1948, women have been involved in all the major confrontations, including Palestinian battles with the Lebanese army for control of the refugee camps in Lebanon in 1969, the civil war in Jordan in 1970, the siege of Tal al-Za'tar (Lebanon; 1975–1976), and the 1989 Battle for the Camps in Lebanon (Sayigh 1993; Peteet and Sayigh 1987). In the *intifada* spring of the late 1980s, Palestinian women of the West Bank and Gaza demonstrated against and stoned Israeli soldiers in protest of Israeli policies of occupation (Giacaman and Johnson 1989). Upper- and middle-class Palestinian women, whether in the West Bank and Gaza or in Jordan and Lebanon, have continued to be active in the realm of private voluntary associations geared toward the provision of health and child care, female literacy programs, and emergency aid for the dispossessed. Of the sixty women's charitable societies on the West Bank today, some fifty-four were established prior to 1967 (Dajani 1993).

The critical role women have played in many aspects of the nationalist movement has not translated, however, into formal political power. Women have been encouraged to organize within their own ranks: among the various Palestinian resistance organizations active in Lebanon between 1969 and 1982, women of political commitment and talent could expect to rise to the head of a women's section—an important post, but one which involved tasks of organizing and implementing a strategy formulated at higher levels by men (Sayigh 1993). While the atmosphere of crisis and siege in Lebanon did break down many traditional barriers (leading families to permit unmarried daughters, for instance, to attend mixed-gender political meetings, work in unsupervised settings such as clinics, or even perform guard duty alone at night) such innovations did not, by all accounts, lead to basic change in the way power was structured. Indeed, most observers remark on the extent to which women have served as the bearers of cultural continuity through emphasis on their traditional roles: the woman who gives her sons to the cause, the "mother of martyrs," remains a central symbol (Peteet 1991).

Whether the context was the Egyptian nationalist movement of the 1910s and 1920s, the Algerian War of Independence in the 1950s, the Palestinian nationalist movement from the 1930s to the present, or revolutionary movements in the region (a good example of which was the Sudan Communist Party [Hale 1996]), the women's role was perceived, and constructed, as auxiliary to the primary national or revolutionary task at hand. The prevalence of separate but subordinate women's organizations, the women's associations and unions founded to advance the goals enunciated by a male leadership, did, however, bring many women into the political arena as organizers and activists whose talents and skills were formally recognized. In the process, some traditional constraints on women's freedom of movement and contact with unrelated men were relaxed, and women took a more active part in these movements than they did or as yet do in establishment politics. It was the "unveiled, educated, and emancipated woman" who represented national progress. In general, however, these organizations and movements did not confront directly the issue of women's power and place in society: if discussed at all, change in such realms was assumed to be something that would evolve naturally, after the national or revolutionary struggle was won.

Established state powers in the region have been more apt to intervene in areas directly affecting women's position and power—an intervention variously described as "state feminism" or "state patriarchy," depending on one's evaluation of both the intent and the outcome of state policies. In the drive for development in the newly independent states of the region, certain reforms affecting women were legislated by state powers in an attempt to emulate Western arrangements on the one hand and respond to pressures from upper- and middle-class groups at home on the other. In the early days of the Turkish Republic, female literacy and participation in the labor force were a priority of state policy, and women were granted full political rights in 1933—a reform that did enable women to enter the sphere of formal politics, if only in limited numbers (Abadan-Unat 1981a). In Iran, Reza Shah, after a visit to Turkey, sponsored a 1936 law banning the wearing of the veil, a reform that met with approval from the upper and upper-middle classes but was largely ignored by others in urban areas. The policies of Reza Shah were not buttressed by any social, economic, or legal reforms aimed at empowering women, however, so they could be largely ignored after his abdication in 1941. The drive for development and reform under Muhammad Reza Shah entailed broader measures. Women were granted the right to vote in 1963 as part of the "White Revolution" program. State encouragement of women's education and employment, which coincided with the rapid expansion of the Iranian economy in the early 1970s, had dramatic effects on women of upper- and middle-class backgrounds. By 1978, one-third of all students enrolled in institutions of higher education were female. Women had also penetrated the sphere of formal politics: in the same year, two cabinet posts, two senatorial posts, three deputy ministerial posts, one ambassadorship, and nineteen seats in the parliament were held by women, and women won the right to be judges (Nashat 1983).

Egypt followed a similar path of reform in the context of the revolutionary government brought to power in 1952. The new constitution of 1956 first gave women the vote. Small numbers of women subsequently began to enter the political system: in the first election to the National Assembly in 1957, two women were among the 350 elected deputies, the first women to serve in an Arab parliament. In subsequent parliamentary elections, few of which have involved open campaigning and legal activity by political parties, women have won anywhere from two to eight seats. In 1979, as part of broad alterations in political institutions in Egypt, thirty seats in the new parliament, the People's Assembly, were reserved for women, and by 1983, forty-six women actually served in parliament. Many spheres of the formal political system remained, however, monopolized by men. It took until 1979 for the first woman to be appointed ambassador, and there has never been a female judge. There have been only three women in cabinet-level posts, all of whom have held the position of Minister of Social Affairs (Sullivan 1986). As in Iran before the Islamic Revolution, the state has supported women's access to the political system, but that support has come, by and large, at the level of tokenism.

It is in the realm of the law that state policies in the twentieth century have provoked the most discussion. As secular law codes, largely of Western inspiration, became the law of the land in most countries of the region, the one area retained under the jurisdiction of religious law, the Shari'ah for Muslims, was the area of personal status (that is, laws governing inheritance, marriage, divorce, child custody, and family relations in general). The Turkish Republic did dispense altogether with the Shari'ah, but all other states have retained it, either in pristine form as in Saudi Arabia, or, more commonly, incorporating some rather minor reforms. Insofar as the state became the underwriter of the Islamic courts, the employer of the judges, and the enforcer of their judgments, the state has assumed the role of upholding a certain vision of the Islamic order as far as women are concerned.

While almost all states have reformed the law they apply, any reform that has threatened to change the law significantly has met with resistance. In Iran, the Reza Shah period saw the fixing of a minimum marriage age (absent in Islamic law). Under Muhammad Reza Shah, the Family Protection Act of 1967 curtailed a man's unlimited right to divorce his wife and gave the court new powers of discretion in matters of divorce, child custody, and marriage to a second wife (Nashat 1983b). Amendments to the law in 1975 included the regulation of polygyny by making the court's agreement to the taking of a second wife contingent upon the first wife's consent, or proof of her refusal of sex, mental illness, barrenness, or disappearance. In addition, a first wife had the right to divorce if she disapproved of the court's decision on a second wife (Paidar 1995). Similar sorts of reforms—the institution of a minimum marriage age, the placing of at least some conditions on the man's right of unilateral repudiation, and the limiting of polygyny—were promulgated in states as diverse as Egypt, Syria, Iraq, and the Peoples' Democratic Republic of Yemen in the course of the 1950s, 1960s, and 1970s. In terms of social legislation to improve the legal, economic, and civil status of women, Tunisia stands alone. The 1956 Code of Personal Status, enacted with Tunisia's independence from France that year, outlawed polygyny and repudiation and made marriage, divorce, and child custody solely the purview of secular courts of law. Subsequent legislation guarantees equal pay for equal work, regardless of sex.

The history of reform, however, is not one of steady progress toward a liberalization of the *Shariʿah*. On the contrary, the 1980s was a decade of "re-Islamicization" of the legal structure: in such countries as Egypt, Sudan, and Algeria, reaffirmations of the centrality and immutability of the *Shariʿah* have eroded the basis of legal reform (Hatem 1993). In 1984, the Algerian government, despite vocal protests from Algerian women (including some of the historic female figures of the war of independence, like Jamilah Bourayd and Jamilah Boupasha), promulgated a Code of Personal Status that took a conservative position on woman's place in society. Although the principle of legal equality between the sexes had been clearly stated in

Algeria's Constitution (1963) and National Charter (1976), the 1984 code institutionalized gender inequality by recognizing the rights of male guardianship in marriage arrangement, allowing polygyny, giving the husband unilateral rights of divorce as long as a judge approves, and privileging the father in child custody. A long history of struggle over personal status law in which debates between conservative and liberal views had derailed codification in the 1960s and 1970s had finally been resolved by the triumph of the conservative interpretation in 1984 (Knauss 1987).

Iran has moved the furthest in this direction in the wake of the Islamic Revolution of 1979: not only was the Family Protection Act revoked, but all divorces obtained under its provisions were declared void (Ramazani 1980). In the early years of the Islamic Revolution, conservative legal interpretations that lowered the marriage age, removed restrictions on polygyny, and eroded women's rights in marriage gained ground. In practice, however, courts and judges functioned in a somewhat eclectic fashion, utilizing the old Iranian Civil Code (1931) as a legal source but supplementing it by reference to *fatwa*s issued by Ayatollah Khomeini or even by regulations found in the supposedly abrogated Family Protection Law. Finally, in 1989, an authoritative collection of family laws was produced that formalized the actual situation: legally valid sources for family law included the Civil Code and the Family Protection Law, along with related legislation from the Majles, regulations issued by the High Council of the Judiciary, and *fatwa*s issued by the Ayatollahs Khomeini and Montazeri. Under these laws, women have won back some rights, such as the right to have a marriage contract that gives them the power to initiate divorce in a number of situations, including the taking of a second wife (Paidar 1995). Laws in other areas have followed a similar pattern. In the early days of the Revolution, new "Islamic" laws were promulgated that mandated Islamic "cover" for all women in public places, segregated women in workplaces, outlawed abortion (legalized in 1977), and closed nearly 140 university fields of study to women (Afkhami 1994b). Over time there has been softening on some of these positions. A husband cannot prevent his wife from working unless he can prove that her job is contrary to the interest and reputation of the family, and even the touchy subject of abortion has been reopened, with respected ayatollahs opining that early abortion is countenanced by Islam (Paidar 1995). Most of these improvements have been modest, however. Like other late-twentieth-century Middle Eastern brands of nationalism, Iran has focused on a cultural revival that tends to present the veiled and domesticated woman as the key to rejuvenation based on cultural authenticity.

The Egyptian feminist movement fastened on legal reform early on as central to the feminist agenda. In addition to their struggle for political rights and educational opportunities for women, the upper- and middle-class women of the Egyptian Feminist Union (EFU), led by Huda Shaʿrawi, lobbied for reform of personal status laws, especially those governing divorce and polygyny, in the 1920s and 1930s. They argued within the framework of Islamic modernism for reforms that would preserve the intent of the law and remove what had come to be legalized oppression of women, including the institution of restrictions on marriage age, polygyny, and divorce, and reforms of child custody and inheritance law (Badran 1995). Although many of their campaigns to open new educational and work opportunities to women did bear fruit in the interwar period, the issue of legal reform, as we have seen, proved particularly thorny, and it took some fifty years for the changes they advocated to be introduced into Egypt (Badran 1993).

The EFU early on joined the International Women's Suffrage Alliance (based in Europe), thereby stressing the universal aspects of women's oppression and emphasizing the commonality of European and Egyptian women. It was upon their return from an International Women's Suffrage conference in 1923 that leaders of the EFU removed their veils in the Cairo train station to dramatize their rejection of this form of seclusion for upper- and middle-class Egyptian women. In the 1930s, however, the EFU gradually moved out of its alliance with European feminism and began to develop an Arab nationalist context. In 1937, an Arabic-language magazine, *al-Misriyyah*, replaced the French-language *L'Égyptienne* as the organ of the EFU. Finally, in 1945, members helped found the Arab Feminist Union, which sought to develop an Arab feminism with nationalist resonance (Badran 1995).

Elsewhere in the region, women's organizations emerged in the 1930s and 1940s primarily to undertake activities of a charitable nature with nationalist overtones. In the course of promoting female literacy, establishing workshops to provide jobs for poor women, or running day-care centers, many of these organizations developed implicit feminist agendas as well, although they might not raise the questions of dress and legal reform. In pre-1948 Palestine, for example, the Women's Union, run by a small group of women from the better-known families, looked after orphans, did emergency relief work, and represented Palestinian women at international conferences (Sayigh 1993). The League of Sudanese Women, organized in 1946 by urban, educated women (many of whom were associated with the Sudanese Communist Party) pursued a similar course, establishing a night school for women with an associated nursery to train them in literacy, sewing, home economics, and health care (Hale 1996). The 1940s brought a new emphasis on the responsibility of educated women to reach out to their sisters in Egypt as well: the Daughters of the Nile Union, founded by Duriyya Shafiq in 1948, placed great emphasis on the teaching of literacy and hygiene to poor women, whereas the Egyptian Feminist Union came to incorporate a left wing that focused on the organization and concerns of working-class women (Badran 1993).

Increasingly in the 1950s and 1960s, however, as the various states of the region expanded their power, independent women's organizations were brought to heel. In Egypt, although the revolutionary government gave women the vote and new opportunities to receive decent education and health care, the banning of independent political organizations effectively meant the end of the EFU and all other organized feminist groups (Badran 1993). Women could organize only under the wing of the state-controlled Arab Socialist Union. The High Council of Iranian Women, founded in 1961, was also a clear attempt at state control: women's organizations had to join the High Council, headed conveniently enough by the Shah's sister, in order to have any legal standing. In 1966, the High Council was replaced by the Women's Organization of Iran, also headed by the Shah's sister, which was subservient to the ruling Rastakhiz Party (Sansarian 1982).

In other parts of the region, particularly in the conservative states of the Arab Gulf, women still struggled for basic rights, including the right of political participation. In Kuwait, the Arab Women's Development Society was founded by Kuwaiti women in the 1960s with the goal of helping to "modernize" Kuwaiti women. As the organization developed and came into contact with other Arab women's groups, its goals shifted toward the achievement of gender equality. In 1971, it helped to place an equal rights bill before the Kuwaiti Assembly calling for, among other things, female enfranchisement, gender equality in employment, and the restriction of polygyny. Such demands sparked heated debate in the Assembly, but ended rather ignominiously without a vote being taken. The issue of the female vote was raised again in the 1980s, shortly after the Kuwaiti parliamentary system was restored after a long hiatus, but it was twice defeated in the Assembly. After the Gulf War of 1991, the heroic record of Kuwaiti women in war and an atmosphere of political reform encouraged women to demonstrate, once more to no avail, for women's suffrage (al-Mughni 1993).

The growing power of political parties and nationalist movements also had an effect on women's ability to organize independently. The Women's Union of the Sudan Communist Party, for example, although benefiting from the remarkable strength and organization of the party in Sudan, found itself engaged primarily in providing "women-as-Greek-chorus" for the Party's policies (Hale 1993). The General Union of Palestinian Women's lack of autonomy vis-à-vis its parent Palestine Liberation Organization has been identified as a key problem insofar as feminist issues were effectively shelved in the face of the demands of the nationalist movement (Peteet and Sayigh 1987). The resources and organization of states and parties also brought certain benefits: the official women's groups were more successful in reaching large numbers of women, particularly in rural areas and poor urban quarters. On the other hand, any explicitly feminist agenda was either lost or co-opted in a modified form by the state. In this context we understand the move in the 1980s toward the establishment of a number of new women's groups strongly jealous of their independence (Hatem 1993).

Did all the political developments of the twentieth century—the growth of state power, the institution of new political structures, and the emergence of well-organized nationalist movements and parties— obliterate the informal politics of intrigue and influence in which women had played such an active role? There is evidence that the politics of influence did persist, at least in part, in the nomadic camps and peasant villages removed from the new centers of power. First, in an environment where family solidarity and alliance continued to undergird local power relations, women could continue to exercise considerable control as the arrangers of marriages by virtue of the fact that they, when given in marriage, were often the actual glue of the alliance. Second, women might form powerful social groups among themselves that could bring coordinated influence to bear on male relatives. Third, women controlled popular religious practices: they were the ones who could intercede for good or ill with the supernatural (C. Nelson 1974). A study of women's roles in a Moroccan village also concluded that women, relying on a strong network of ties, exercised considerable control over the flow of information in the village and, as a result, over political decisions (S. Davis 1983). Certainly the male fear of women's power at these levels was enshrined in folk traditions like the following Egyptian proverb:

> Women's intrigues are mighty
> To protect myself I keep running
> Women are belted with serpents
> And bejewelled with scorpions
> (Malik, n.d.)

As the political isolation of the camp and the village has decreased, however, the local politics in which informal arrangements play such a major part have been shrinking in significance. The difficulty women have faced in the region in entering the formal political sphere means that there is likely to be little immediate compensation for losses in informal power.

Culture and Society

Women's contributions to the development of cultural life in the Middle East, at least in the realm of high culture (including written poetry, novels, and song), have been extensive. The upper-class tradition of educating women, which produced the many "women of letters" in the nineteenth century, laid the foundations for women to play a central role in the development of new art forms in the twentieth century, including free verse poetry, the novel, and painting and sculpture. Although women writers and artists have focused, to a great extent, on the themes of national liberation and the existential crisis of the region in the post-independence period, as have their male counterparts, the work of some women also has reflected feminist sensibilities: the ways in which custom and the family weigh upon women recurs as a central concern of many women writers.

One of the best known poets of the century is an Iraqi, Nazik al-Mala'ika. Her mother, Salma al-Kazimiyyah, was herself a poet and a veiled activist in the Iraqi nationalist movement against British colonialism. Born to a privileged family in Baghdad in 1923, al-Mala'ika attended college in Iraq and later studied in the United States as well. She pioneered the use of free verse in Arabic poetry in the 1940s and, indeed, is credited by many as being the first to break away from the classical form of the Arabic *qasida*. Her own evaluation of the influences on her work blended themes of nation and gender:

> A basic fear of death, an innate freedom I lacked,
> wounds I suffered as a result of the women's
> humiliating state in the Arab world, consecutive
> national setbacks and political defeats: these are
> the elements that have painted my poetry with sorrow
> (Quoted in Boullata 1978: 15)

Some of her poetry has dealt very directly with the oppression women have faced. In "Washing Off Disgrace," a young woman is stabbed to death by a male relative, in the wake of some actual or imagined sexual transgression on her part, to "wash the disgrace" off the family name. The poem, in part, laments for all women:

> Women of the neighborhood
> women of the village
> we knead our dough with our tears
> > that they may be well-fed
> we loosen our braids
> > that they may be pleased
> we peel the skin of our hands washing their clothes
> > that they may be spotless white.
> No smile
> No joy
> No rest
> for the glitter of a dagger
> > > of a father
> > > of a brother
> > is all eyes.
> > > > (Boulatta 1978: 21)

Another of the most important women poets of the century, Fadwa Tuqan, born in Nablus, Palestine, in 1917, wrote primarily love poetry in the late 1950s and early 1960s; from 1967 on, however, most of her poems have focused on the Palestinian national struggle. In a region where poetry has been an important and widely read form of political expression, such women as Tuqan or Etel Adnan of Lebanon have been not only artistic innovators but also very much part of their country's political life.

Many women poets have gradually, in the course of the twentieth century, developed a more explicitly female voice. The renowned Iranian poet, Parvin E'tessami (1907–1941), was praised for her "manly" poems precisely because they did not sound like women's poems. Although it is true that E'tessami wrote very few poems that addressed women's issues per se, pleas for women's emancipation were scattered throughout her work (Milani 1992). The foremost woman poet of the next generation, Forugh Farrokhzad (1935–1967), wrote more confessional poetry in which private ideas and feelings of a sensual, erotic nature featured prominently. Her explorations of love and the female self departed dramatically from male models of poetic themes, suggesting new possibilities for women's poetry (Milani 1992).

Women have also figured as important novelists in the region. The themes their novels address appear to parallel the development of women's poetry: an overwhelming concern with the existential issues of personal freedom in the 1950s and early 1960s gave way to a more focused treatment of women's oppression and the possible political solutions to this oppression. Most recently, the limitations of nationalist politics and male-authored solutions have emerged as themes. In North Africa, some women novelists, such as the Algerian Assia Djebar, were the heirs of a bicultural French-Arabic cultural tradition. Written in French, Djebar's first novel, *La soif* (*The Thirst*), published in 1957, traced a woman's individual revolt; since then, her novels have continued to treat the issue of woman's position but with increasing attention to the political context as well as the concrete social and sexual problems women face. Nawal El-Sa'adawi, the Egyptian physician who also wrote a number of novels in the 1970s, has been frank and unrelenting in the description of women's oppression her novels supply. In *Woman at Point Zero* (1977), the central figure is a woman subjected to clitoridectomy, who is forced to marry an old and abusive husband and escapes into prostitution and new cruelties at the hands of a pimp; she manages to overcome all these difficulties only to fall in love with a "good" man, who deserts her to marry a wealthy woman. Arab society, for El-Sa'adawi, can never be healthy as long as it treats women so horribly (Accad 1993).

Many other women writers have made distinctive contributions to literary life and style in the twentieth century. Their marginal social position has encouraged them to write subversively. The Lebanese women writers who lived the civil war, for instance, developed an alternative "female" approach to war writing. These "Beirut Decentrists," as Miriam Cooke christened them, deconstructed the Lebanese nation through their criticisms of tribalism and the seductive power of violence and death. Their poems and novels focus, instead, on the importance of life-sustaining quotidian acts and the construction of a new patriotism built on the values of communal responsibility, not exclusion and violence (Cooke 1987). Similarly, Fedwa Malti-Douglas has studied the ways in which contemporary Arab women novelists have subverted gender discourse. Working within a literary tradition that has viewed the woman as imprisoned in a (defective) physicality, women writers confront and even flaunt that physicality by exploring female sexuality; at the same time, they may emphasize the corporeality of the male (Malti-Douglas 1991).

Not all women writers have been so openly confrontational in their writing. In her study of contemporary women writers in Saudi Arabia, Saddeka Arebi found that although Saudi women poets, novelists, and essayists are engaged in critiques of the social institutions that shape their lives, they retain basic loyalty to these institutions. Arranged marriage, veiling, and sexual segregation are part of the tradition they generally accept as their own; they focus on the abuses of these traditions, such as the arrangement of clearly incompatible marriages for ignoble ends, but they usually recognize and support the importance of the family role in marriage decisions. We need to understand that Saudi women writers do not accept Western definitions of their problems, including, for example, the "problem" of veiling. As Arebi observes:

> The institution of physical concealment in public, as manifested in veiling, is criticized even less than segregation. The *abaya* [black concealing garment] is not portrayed as a restriction on their freedom but rather as key to women's accessibility to the public field. But other reasons account for why women have not severely criticized the institution of concealment. Judging by my own experience with veiling in Saudi Arabia, I can attest to the sense of power and control a woman feels in having the advantage of being the seer not the seen. Both men and women recognize this advantage of the *abaya*, and it has led women writers to frequently assert its existence in their texts, either to indicate a setting (i.e., that events are talking place in Saudi Arabia) or to symbolize oppression in relation to its black color, rather than to complain about its restrictive function. (Arebi 1994: 279–80)

This is but one of many ways in which Saudi women writers are fashioning their own cultural discourse on women's issues that in local history, social tradition, and Islam are not rejected, but rather subjected to subtle forms of reinterpretation.

In the field of popular music, the undisputed towering personality of the century was Umm Kulthum, an Egyptian woman born about 1910 in a small village. She received a basic education in the local mosque school and began to sing religious songs at local celebrations. Her audience and fame grew until she became the best-known singer in the Arab world, one who kept her listeners riveted to their radios listening to songs about love, national feeling, or religion—which could last for several hours. Her funeral in 1975 was a state occasion in Cairo, attended by dignitaries from all the Arab countries and some four million Egyptians who came to mourn her in person (Fernea and Bezirgan 1977).

Although a small number of women have thus succeeded in penetrating the realm of high culture dominated by men, most women inhabit a rather different world. Women's society in the city or village has developed a rich oral culture, distinct from that of men, which has served to express women's perceptions and desires, or simply to entertain. The elaborate lullabies sung by women in Tunisia, for example, incorporate the mother's fantasies and desires about what the child will be or do when grown. Many lullabies focus on the sex of the baby, discussing in musical form the virtues of girls and boys. The mother of a girl might sing:

> A girl child is better than ten thousand boys;
> If she's far away she asks after her mother;
> If she's near she brings me her love
> And gives me part of her food.
> (Fernea and Bezirgan 1977: 89)

A study of the improvised poetry of Bedouin women in Egypt has revealed how they use this oral form to express feelings and insights that might otherwise be socially unacceptable. Many women of this community are also consummate story tellers whose tales not only illustrate how they negotiate the social complexities of their community but also reflect their sense of the universal (Abu-Lughod 1986, 1993). In a coastal Tunisian town, women's stories have traditionally had fantasy plots, as opposed to real-life narratives, both reflecting and helping them cope with the narrowness of a secluded life. As more and more girls attend school and women go out to work and even travel, women's stories have increasingly come to be real-life narratives similar to those that are told by men relating their adventures outside the home. Here we see how some of the particularities of women's culture are disappearing as women's lives change (Webber 1985).

Other aspects of women's culture have not only been preserved in the twentieth century, but have received special encouragement as their commercial value has risen. Women in the town of Akhmim in Egypt, for example, set up an embroidery and weaving cooperative in the 1960s, which has not only promoted women's crafts but has been a resounding commercial success (Williams 1986). Similar schemes for the encouragement and marketing of women's embroideries can be found all over the region: in Lebanon, the West Bank and Gaza, and Jordan, embroidery has been an important source of income for displaced Palestinian women. The work is creative: the traditional patterns are continually being supplemented by new designs, new colors, and the use of new materials. The overall rhythm of popular culture has clearly changed, however, as the erosion of the "woman's world" and the market orientation of women's crafts gives much wider scope to external influences.

The discussion about women's role in society has also expanded in the twentieth century, incorporating elements of the nineteenth-century debate about seclusion and the proper level of women's participation in society outside the family. In some areas of the region, notably many of the Gulf states, women's lives are still lived out of the public domain in an all-female world composed of relatives and friends. The ways in which women, in a country like North Yemen, have used their separate sphere to develop women's networks and, ultimately, to gain considerable power by means of behind-the-scenes manipulations has been the theme of recent studies: extremes of sexual segregation can, it seems, provide a space for women to experience connectedness and psychological strength (Makhlouf 1979; Dorsky 1986).

The debate about the proper role of women has nowhere been as heated and dramatic as in Iran. To a certain extent, the debate crystallized around the issue of dress, of the need for women to wear a "veil" in the sense of the modest covering provided by the *chador*; the *chador* in turn came to be the symbol of a cultural authenticity to be preserved in the face of Western cultural imperialism. The reforms of Reza Shah, which included the short-lived outlawing of the veil in 1936, first politicized the veil, associating campaigns against it with an unpopular pro-Western regime. In the 1950s, 1960s, and 1970s, as the cultural impact of the West, alongside its economic clout and political meddling, was felt in Iran, the wearing of the *chador* or a head scarf came to be promoted as an alternative to Western clothes and make-up, as a statement, in brief, of opposition to Western influence as a whole. Such influential Islamic thinkers as Ali Sharia'ti called for the promotion of qualities of family loyalty and modesty along with education and social activity for women (Betteridge 1983). Khomeini, in his exile, encouraged women to help overthrow the Shah's regime and foresaw that under a new regime they would be involved in "every aspect of life" while not free to do anything "against chastity or harmful to the nation" (quoted in Tabari and Yeganeh 1982: 98–103). Once the new Islamic government was in power, these vague pronouncements took more concrete shape in the form of, among other things, the compulsory wearing of the veil. Opposition to veiling, including the two women's demonstrations held in 1979 and 1980, was denounced as Western imperialism. Women's position in society, as symbolized by covering in public space, had become inextricably intertwined with Western influence and the movement against the Shah, as well as the construction of a society faithful to Islamic beliefs and indigenous culture. And, moving full circle, opposition to forced veiling is now a key position of those opposed to the Islamic regime.

"Veiling" has become, certainly in the Western view, a touchstone for women's issues. In the 1980s and 1990s, many women in different parts of the Middle East, particularly in urban areas, have donned a new form of "Islamic" dress that includes a long dress or coat and a head scarf often worn with a turban. Although social pressure cannot always be ruled out, many young women appear to choose this form of dress over the alternatives of Western-style dress or various indigenous styles worn by older women. Several explanations have been offered for this trend. First, sociological reasons include the advantages such dress provides for women who study or work in mixed-sex environments. By wearing Islamic dress, women can proclaim their seriousness and avoid the tensions produced by the rapid erosion of sexual segregation while maintaining access to public space. Second, women, like men, have found that the post-independence promises of progress through Western versions of liberalism or socialism have not borne fruit; they signal a "return" to indigenous culture and authenticity as a guide to a better future. Third, there is a rising tide of religiosity in the region which translates, for women and men, into changing dress styles (Macleod 1991; Zuhur 1992).

Another way of understanding the move on the part of at least some women toward social and religious conservatism is by reference to the "patriarchal bargain." Deniz Kandiyoti has argued that the breakdown of classic patriarchy in the region, the result of new market forces and capitalist penetration, often meant an emancipation fraught with dislocation and loss. As men could no longer effectively control their property and their families in the face of immiseration, women encountered difficulties collecting on their share of the patriarchal bargain—that is, the support and protection by male family members in return for their obedience. Some women seek to affirm their rights to this support and protection under the old normative order by emphasizing their submissiveness and propriety, by wearing the veil, for example, as a bid for the security and stability of the old (and somewhat mythic) order. Islamism in this approach takes its place as champion of the former patriarchal bargain, and veiling becomes a potent symbol of women's bid for dignity under the old terms (Kandiyoti 1991).

The move toward veiling must also be located within particular contexts of class. In Egypt, for example, the wearing of marked Islamic dress has evolved from an urban, largely middle-class protest movement into a much broader phenomenon: working women of the lower-middle classes often adopt this dress, as do some rural village girls who find it a respectable way to distinguish themselves from other, less-educated rural women who wear traditional dress that is equally modest but tarred by its association with the limitations of village life. Another striking development has been the highly publicized conversion of a number of prominent and privileged actresses, belly dancers, and singers to the Islamic path, dramatically demonstrated not only by their exits from stage and screen, but also by their assuming Islamic garb. Lila Abu-Lughod has pointed out how other women have reacted to these "born again" stars: feminist intellectuals and political activists have been very critical but for many ordinary Egyptian women, such conversions make these exotic and fascinating stars seem less distant and more accessible, inhabitants of a familiar world of religion and morality. In the process, however, the real chasms between women's lives in a poor Egyptian village or urban quarter and in a wealthy Cairo suburb are invariably obfuscated; the veil can produce false feelings of solidarity and similarity as well (Abu-Lughod 1995).

Not all discussion of women's oppression has focused on the problem of dress. The private sexual oppression of women, long a taboo subject, was broached in the 1970s in the form of an attack on the practice of clitoridectomy. The genital mutilation of young girls, thought to be necessary in order to control an otherwise rampant sexuality, has long been widely practiced in Egypt, Sudan, and some Red Sea coastal regions, although not elsewhere in the region. Nawal El-Saʿadawi, in her book *Woman and Sex* (*al-Marʾah wa jins*) (1975), deplored the physical and psychological harm done to women by this operation and called for its eradication. Sudanese feminists have launched a systematic campaign to convince people that the operation, done in the name of Islam, is not, in fact, sanctioned by the religion and brings psychic scarring, permanent injury, and even death to girls who undergo it (El Dareer 1982).

The question of what Islam does or does not expect or require of women has been hotly debated throughout the period. The Islamic modernist discourse has had its spokesmen, notably Mahmud Shaltut,

a rector of al-Azhar University in Cairo in the early 1960s and a political ally of Nasser. Shaltut argued that women's equality in religious obligations translated into a religious right to be educated. In
addition, Shaltut supported women's suffrage on the grounds that
women had been early supporters of the Prophet Muhammad. A much
more conservative interpretation has also had its supporters. Conservative religious thinkers in Egypt, Jordan, and Syria called on wom-
en to wear the veil, in the form of clothing covering all parts of the
body but the hands and face. The best veil for a woman, however, is
her home: conservatives argue for female domesticity. Women should
work outside the home only out of dire necessity, because work ex-
poses women to unrelated men and disrupts the natural order of the
family, in which men serve as women's guardians. Nor should women
seek any form of political participation: the practice of the early Islamic community is cited as grounds for excluding women from all
political life, including the holding of political office and suffrage rights.
The activist-fundamentalist groups in the region, which emerged in
force mainly in the 1970s, share this conservative view of women but
have given it new life by making it the centerpiece of an Islamic authenticity locked in conflict with Western imperialism. The colonial
and imperialist powers have used the woman issue to attempt to undermine the Muslim family and, as a result, Muslim society as a whole.
The fundamentalists are also very critical of Muslim feminists who,
by virtue of their campaigns for women's rights, objectively aid foreign powers in their sabotage of Muslim society (Stowasser 1993).

The conservative and fundamentalist voices have gained importance in the 1970s and 1980s as disillusionment with "Arab socialism" and a general sense that the secular strategy had failed swelled
the more conservative ranks. Many young women, as we have seen—
particularly those of lower-middle-class background who were studying or working in urban areas and were exposed, as a result, to the
ambiguities surrounding women in public space—were drawn to the
styles of dress and behavior prescribed by the conservatives, while
others actually joined the fundamentalist movements. Ironically
enough, these movements appeared, at times, to enable young women
to feel more secure and comfortable in public space and to sanction
their work and school life when properly conducted (El Guindi 1983).

Despite the dominance of an explicitly Islamic discourse where
women's issues are concerned, the role religion has played in the
perceptions or actualities of women's lives is not so clear. For rural or
poorer urban women, many of the debates about Islamic roles seem
almost irrelevant. In a collection of five oral histories of impoverished

urban Egyptian women, religion figures hardly at all (Atiya 1982). Even in the heat of the Islamic Revolution in Iran, the women of an Iranian village were little concerned by the pronouncements of religious authorities (Friedl 1989). As they tell their life stories, the women cite custom and the need to preserve a good reputation as the main considerations circumscribing their activities: nowhere is there explicit reference to what is or is not religiously prescribed behavior for women. When religion does enter, it is usually in the form of the charms and oaths anathema to the religious establishment and the fundamentalists alike. These women, so bowed down with problems of survival, still seem sure of their place in society, a society of their relatives and friends, where they come and go without much recourse to religious opinion.

CONCLUSION

It has proved extremely difficult to generalize about the impact of change on women in the modern period or about the ways in which women themselves have shaped, and continue to shape, the history of the Middle East. We have seen striking variations by region and class in the ways women have experienced developments in the nineteenth and twentieth centuries, and the ongoing discussion of gender underscores the absence of agreement about what the roles and power of women and men were, are, and should be. Still, we can hazard a few conclusions concerning major patterns of change in the economic, political, and social spheres.

The changes in women's economic participation have varied by class. Among the rural and urban lower classes, capitalist development seems, by and large, to have restricted and devalued women's work by demarcating the home from the workplace and defining appropriate women's work as work at home. Economic need, however, whether produced by rapid industrialization or male labor shortages, could pull women into the modern labor force whenever they were needed. Modern capitalist development has entailed the recruitment of many women into piecework at home or in small ateliers where they are very poorly remunerated. Among the educated middle class, on the other hand, the modern period has been one of expanding educational and occupational opportunities as the demands of rapid development mobilized the resources and skills of the entire middle class, men and women alike. Women's position in the economic system continues to be precarious, however, and fraught with a social ambiguity that gives no assurances about the future.

In politics, women have been active participants in the many popular movements of the period, from the spontaneous peasant uprisings of the nineteenth century to the nationalist movements and wars of the twentieth. Such activity has not translated, however, into formal political power, and "women's issues" have, by and large, been subordinated to the "larger" national or revolutionary task. As the state has become more and more powerful, it has intervened in the regulation and definition of gender by insisting, in many cases, on at least token female participation in the political arena while, at the same time, serving as guarantor of patriarchal law. Women have, however, been active on their own behalf, both in a number of feminist movements and as behind-the-scenes wielders of influence. The formalization of much political life may have eroded, however, certain other avenues of female influence, such as the intrigues of the harem or the informal women's lobbies of the tribe or village.

Finally, women's position in society in the modern period has been shaped by the drive for cultural authenticity in the face of cultural imperialism and the relative ease with which an "Islamic" culture can be asserted on the basis of its distinctive views of gender roles. Although much of the discussion of gender has taken an explicitly religious form, women themselves have tended to focus on constraints imposed by custom and tradition. Increasingly, over the course of the twentieth century, the rich oral culture of women has been supplemented by the proliferation of women poets and novelists whose voices are raised in praise or, more often, in blame of the dominant definitions of gender roles, whether buttressed by religion or by custom that promotes female seclusion. As studies of women in the modern period multiply, and the work and writings of Middle Eastern women themselves become more accessible to us, we can expect to understand better the complex ways in which indigenous cultural and political patterns have interacted with external pressures to change the role gender plays in Middle East society.

SOURCES: 8000 B.C.E.–C.E. 1800

Abbott, Nabia. 1941. "Women and the State on the Eve of Islam." *American Journal of Semitic Languages and Literatures* 58 (January–October): 259–84.

———. 1942a. "Women and the State in Early Islam. I. Muhammad and the First Four Caliphs." *Journal of Near Eastern Studies* 1: 106–26.

———. 1942b. "Women and the State in Early Islam. II. The Umayyads." *Journal of Near Eastern Studies* 1: 341–61.

———. 1974. *Two Queens of Baghdad: Mother and Wife of Harun al-Rashid.* Chicago: Midway Reprints. Originally published 1946.

———. 1985. *Aishah, the Beloved of Muhammad.* London: Al Saqi Books. Originally published 1942.

Abu-Said, Abeer. 1984. *Qatari Women Past and Present.* Harlow: Longman.

Adams, Robert M. 1962. "Agriculture and Urban Life in Early Southwestern Iran." *Science* 136, no. 3511: 109–22.

Adams, Robert M., and Hans J. Nissen. 1972. *The Uruk Countryside: The Natural Setting of Urban Societies.* Chicago: University of Chicago Press.

Ahmed, Leila. 1986. "Women and the Advent of Islam." *Signs* 11, no. 4 (Summer): 665–91.

———. 1989. "Arab Culture and Writing Women's Bodies." *Feminist Issues* 9, no. 1: 41–56.

———. 1991. "Gendering the Ungendered Body: Hermaphrodites in Medieval Islamic Law." In Keddie and Baron, *Women in Middle Eastern History.*

———. 1992. *Women and Gender in Islam: Historical Roots of a Modern Debate.* New Haven: Yale University Press.

Ahsan, Muhammad Manazir. 1979. *Social Life under the Abbasids.* London: Longman.

Ali, Muhammad. 1983. *A Manual of Hadith.* Guilford, Surrey, England: Curzon Press.

Anawati, George. 1958. "Islam and the Immaculate Conception." In O'Connor, *The Dogma of the Immaculate Conception.*

Angerman, Arina, et al., eds. 1989. *Current Issues in Women's History.* London: Routledge and Kegan Paul.

Ashtor, E. 1976. *A Social and Economic History of the Near East in the Middle Ages.* Berkeley and Los Angeles: University of California Press.

Austin, R. W. J. 1984. "The Feminine Dimensions in Ibn ʿArabi's Thought." *Journal of the Muhyiddin Ibn ʿArabi Society* 2: 5–14.

Badran, Margot. 1989. "The Origins of Feminism in Egypt." In Angerman, *Current Issues in Women's History*.

Baer, Gabriel. 1983. "Women and Waqf: An Analysis of the Istambul Tahrir of 1546." *Asian and African Studies* 17, nos. 1–3: 9–28.

Bagnall, Roger, and B. Frier. 1994. *The Demography of Roman Egypt*. Cambridge: Cambridge University Press.

Balkan, Kemal. 1986. "Betrothal of Girls during Childhood in Ancient Assyria and Anatolia." *Assyriological Studies* 23: 1–9.

Batto, B. F. 1974. *Studies on Women at Mari*. Baltimore: Johns Hopkins University Press.

Bayani, Shirin. 1352/1973a. *Hasht Maqaleh dar Zamineh-yi Tarikh* (Eight articles on history). Tehran: Tus Publications.

———. 1352/1973b. *Zan-i Irani dar ʾAsr-i Mughul* (Iranian women during the Mongol period). Tehran: Tehran University Press.

———. 1980. "Land Tenure and Women at Mari." *Journal of the Economic and Social History of the Orient* 23: 209–39.

Beck, Lois, and Nikki Keddie, eds. 1978. *Women in the Muslim World*. Cambridge: Harvard University Press.

Becker, Gary S. 1985. "Human Capital, Effort, and the Sexual Division of Labor." *Journal of Labor Economics* 3, no. 1, pt. 2: S33–S59.

Beeston, F. 1952. "The So-called Harlots of Hadramaut." *Oriens* 5: 16–17.

Berkey, Jonathan P. 1991. "Women and Islamic Education in the Mamluk Period." In Keddie and Baron, *Women in Middle Eastern History*.

Blau, Francine D., Marianne A. Ferber, and Anne E. Winkler. 1998. *The Economics of Women, Men, and Work*. Englewood Cliffs, N.J.: Prentice Hall.

Boserup, Esther. 1970. *Women's Role in Economic Development*. New York: St. Martin's Press.

Bosworth, E. C., et al., eds. 1989. *The Islamic World from Classical to Modern Times: Essays in Honor of Bernard Lewis*. Princeton, N.J.: Darwin Press.

Bouhdiba, Abdelwahab. 1985. *Sexuality in Islam*. Trans. Alan Sheridan. London: Routledge and Kegan Paul.

Bowen, Donna Lee. 1981. "Muslim Juridical Opinions concerning the Status of Women as Demonstrated by the Case of ʾAzl." *Journal of Near Eastern Studies* 41: 323–29.

Boyle, J. A. 1968. *Cambridge History of Iran*. Vol. 5. Cambridge: Cambridge University Press.

Braidwood, Linda S., and Robert Braidwood. 1986. "Prelude to the Appearance of Village-Farming Communities in Southwestern Asia." In Canby, *Ancient Anatolia*.

Bridenthal, Renate, Susan M. Stuart, and Merry E. Wiesner, eds. 1998. *Becoming Visible*. 3rd ed. Boston and New York: Houghton Mifflin.

Brock, Sebastian P., and Susan Ashbrook Harvey, trans. 1987. *Holy Women of the Syrian Orient*. Berkeley and Los Angeles: University of California Press.

Bullough, Vern L. 1973. *The Subordinate Sex*. Urbana, Ill.: University of Illinois Press.

Bürgel, J. C. 1979. "Love, Lust, and Longing: Eroticism in Early Islam as Reflected in Literary Sources." In al-Sayyid-Marsot, *Society and the Sexes in Medieval Islam*.

Cameron, Averil, and Amelie Kuhrt, eds. 1983. *Images of Women in Antiquity*. London: Croom Helm.

Canby, J. Vorys, ed. 1986. *Ancient Anatolia: Aspects of Change and Cultural Development*. Madison: University of Wisconsin Press.

Combs-Schilling, M. E. 1989. *Sacred Performances: Islam, Sexuality, and Sacrifice*. New York: Columbia University Press.

Crawford, Harriet. 1991. *Sumer and the Sumerians*. Cambridge: Cambridge University Press.

Dengler, Ian C. 1978. "Turkish Women in the Ottoman Empire: The Classical Age." In Beck and Keddie, *Women in the Muslim World*.

Dickson, H. R. P. 1951. *The Arab of the Desert*. London: George Allen and Unwin.

Donner, Fred M. 1981. *The Early Islamic Conquest*. Princeton: Princeton University Press.

Edwards, I. E. S., et al. 1970. *Cambridge Ancient History*. Cambridge: Cambridge University Press.

Elias, Jamal J. 1988. "Female and Feminine in Islamic Mysticism." *Muslim World* 77, nos. 3–4: 209–24.

Eyre, C. J. 1984. "Crime and Adultery in Ancient Egypt." *Journal of Egyptian Archaeology* 70: 101–102.

Farah, Madelain. 1984. *Marriage and Sexuality in Islam*. Vol. 1, pt. 1. Salt Lake City: University of Utah Press.

Fensham, F. Charles. 1962. "Widow, Orphan, and the Poor in Ancient Near Eastern Legal and Wisdom Literature." *Journal of Near Eastern Studies* 21: 129–39.

Finkelstein, J. J. 1966. "Sex Offence in Sumerian Laws." *Journal of the American Oriental Society* 86: 355–72.

Firestone, Reuven. 1990. "Sarah's Identity in Islamic Exegetical Tradition." *Muslim World* 80, no. 2: 65–71.

Flannery, Kent V. 1965. "The Ecology of Early Food Production in Mesopotamia." *Science* 147, no. 3663: 1247–56.

Gelb, I. J. 1967. "Approaches to the Study of Ancient Society." *Journal of American Oriental Society* 87: 3–9.

———. 1972. "From Freedom to Slavery." *Bayerische Akademie der Wissenschaften* 75, Series A/6: 81–92.

———. 1973. "Prisoners of War in Early Mesopotamia." *Journal of Near Eastern Studies* 32: 70–98.

Gerber, Haim. 1980. "Social and Economic Position of Women in an Ottoman City: Bursa, 1600–1700." *International Journal of Middle East Studies* 12, no. 3: 231–44.

Ghazali, Abi Hamid. 1968. *Al-Tibar Al-Masbuk fi Nasihat al-Muluk* (Advice to Kings). Cairo: Al-Azhar University Press. See also Ghazali's *Book of Council for Kings*. Trans. F. R. Bagley. Oxford: Oxford University Press, 1964.

Gibb, H. A. R. 1972. *Mohammedanism*. 2d ed. Oxford: Oxford University Press.

Girshman, R. 1978. *Iran from the Earliest Times to the Islamic Conquest*. Harmondsworth: Penguin.

Glassner, J. J. 1989. "Women, Hospitality, and the Honor of the Family." In Lesko, *Women's Earliest Records from Ancient Egypt*.

Goitein, S. D. 1967–1978. *A Mediterranean Society*. 3 vols. Berkeley and Los Angeles: University of California Press.

———. 1979. "The Sexual Mores of the Common People." In al-Sayyid-Marsot, *Society and the Sexes in Medieval Islam*.

Goldziher, Ignaz. 1971. *Muslim Studies*. Trans. C. R. Barber and S. M. Stern. London: George Allen and Unwin.

Goody, Jack. 1990. *The Oriental, the Ancient, and the Primitive: Systems of Mar-*

riage and the Family in the Pre-Industrial Societies of Eurasia. Cambridge, England.

Hallaq, Wael B. 1984. "Was the Gate of Ijtihad Closed?" *International Journal of Middle East Studies* 16, no. 1: 3–41.

Hallo, William H. 1976. "Women of Sumer." *Bibliotheca Mesopotamica* 4: 23–40.

Hambly, Gavin R. G. 1998. *Women in the Medieval Islamic World.* New York: St. Martin's Press.

Harris, Rikvah. 1989. "Independent Women in Ancient Mesopotamia?" In Lesko, *Women's Earliest Records.*

Harvey, Susan Ashbrook. 1983. "Women in Early Syrian Christianity." In Cameron and Kuhrt, *Images of Women in Antiquity.*

Haug, M., and E. W. West, eds. and trans. 1872. *The Book of Arda Viraf.* Bombay: n.p.

Herlihy, David. 1975. "Life Expectancies for Women in Medieval Society." In Morewedge, *The Role of Women in the Middle Ages.*

Hermansen, Marcia. 1983. "Fatimeh as a Role Model in the Works of Ali Sharicati." In Nashat, *Women and Revolution in Iran.*

Herrin, Judith. 1983. "In Search of Byzantine Women: Three Avenues of Approach." In Cameron and Kuhrt, *Images of Women in Antiquity.*

Al-Hibri, Azizah, ed. 1982. *Women and Islam.* Oxford: Pergamon Press.

Hodgson, M. G. S. 1974. *The Venture of Islam.* 3 vols. Chicago: University of Chicago Press.

Hole, Frank, ed. 1987. *The Archeology of Western Iran.* Washington, D.C.: Smithsonian Institution Press.

Hussain, Freda, ed. 1984. *Muslim Women.* New York: St. Martin's Press.

Hussein, Aftab. 1987. *Status of Women in Islam.* Lahore: Law Publishing Company.

Ibn Battuta, Abu ʾAbdallah Muhammad. 1395/1977. *Rihlat Ibn Battata* (Travels of Ibn Battuta). Ed. Ali A Kittani. 2 vols. Beirut: n.p. See also *Travels of Ibn Battuta.* Trans. H. A. R. Gibb. London: Hakluyt Society, 1958.

Ibn Ishaq, Muhammad. 1955. *Sirat Rasul Allah* (The life of Muhammad). Trans. A. Guillaume. Karachi: Oxford University Press.

Ibn Khaldun. 1967. *Al-Muqaddimah* (The Muqaddimah: An introduction to history). Trans. F. Rosenthal; ed. and abridged by N. J. Dawood. Princeton: Bollingen Series.

Imber, Colin. 1983. "Zina in Ottoman Law." In Bacqué-Gramont and Dumont, *Contributions à l'histoire économique.*

Jacobsen, Thorkil. 1970. *Toward the Image of Tammuz and Other Essays on Mesopotamian History and Culture.* Ed. William L. Moran. Cambridge: Harvard University Press.

Jastrow, M. 1921. "Veiling in Ancient Assyria." *Revue Archeologique* 14: 209–38.

Jennings, Donald C. 1975. "Women in Early Seventeenth Century Ottoman Judicial Records: The Shariʿa Court of Anatolian Kayseri." *Journal of the Economic and Social History of the Orient* 18, pt. 1: 53–114.

Juynboll, G. H. A. 1989. "Some Isnad-Analytical Methods Illustrated on the Basis of Several Woman-Demeaning Sayings from Hadith Literature." *Al-Qantara* 10: 343–84.

Kandiyoti, Deniz. 1991. "Islam and Patriarchy: A Comparative Perspective." In Keddie and Baron, *Women in Middle East History.*

Keddie, Nikki R., and Beth Baron, eds. 1991. *Women in Middle Eastern History: Shifting Boundaries in Sex and Gender.* New Haven: Yale University Press.

Keddie, Nikki R., and Lois Beck, eds. 1978. *Women in the Muslim World.* Cambridge: Harvard University Press.

Khan, Muhammad M. 1981. *The Translation of the Meanings of Sahih al-Bukhari (in Arabic and English).* 9 vols. Medina: Dar al-fikr.

Kister, M. J. 1988. "Legends in Tafsir and Hadith Literature: The Creation of Adam and Related Stories." In Rippin, *Approaches to the History of the Interpretation of the Qur'an.*

Knapp, A. Bernard. 1988. *The History and Culture of Ancient Western Asia and Egypt.* Chicago: Dorsey Press.

Kramer, Samuel Noah. 1953. "The Myth of Inanna and Bilulu." *Journal of Near Eastern Studies* 12: 160–71.

———. 1976. "Poets and Psalmists, Goddesses and Theologians: Literary, Religious and Anthropological Aspects of the Legacy of Sumer." *Bibliotheca Mesopotamica* 4: 3–21.

Kramer, S. N., and Diane Wolkstein. 1983. *Inanna, Queen of Heaven and Earth.* New York: Harper and Row.

Kritovoulos. 1954. *History of Mehmed the Conqueror.* Trans. C. T. Riggs. Princeton: Princeton University Press.

Kuhrt, Amelie. 1989. "Non-Royal Women in the Late Babylonian Period: A Survey." In Lesko, *Women's Earliest Records from Ancient Egypt and Western Asia.*

Laiou, Angeliki E. 1981. "The Role of Women in Byzantine Society." *Jahrbuch der Österreichischen Byzantinistik* 31, no. 1.

Lambton, Ann K. S. 1953. *Landlord and Peasant in Persia.* London: Oxford University Press.

———. 1988. *Continuity and Change in Medieval Persia: Aspects of Administrative, Economic and Social History, Eleventh to Fourteenth Centuries.* Albany: State University of New York Press.

Lane, Edward William, trans. N.d. *The Thousand and One Nights, Commonly Called the Arabian Nights' Entertainment.* 4 vols. New York: Bigelow, Brown.

Lapidus, Ira Marvin. 1988. *A History of Islamic Societies.* Cambridge: Cambridge University Press.

Larsen, Mogens Trolle. 1982. "Your Money or Your Life: A Portrait of an Assyrian Businessman." In Postgate, *Societies and Languages of the Ancient Near East.*

Lassner, J. 1965. "Why Did the Caliph al-Mansur Build ar-Rusafa?" *Journal of Near Eastern Studies* 24: 95–99.

Lerner, Gerda. 1986. *The Creation of Patriarchy.* New York: Oxford University Press.

Lesko, Barbara S. 1998. "Women of Ancient Egypt and Western Asia." In Bridenthal et al., *Becoming Visible.*

Lesko, Barbara S., ed. 1989. *Women's Earliest Records from Ancient Egypt and Western Asia.* Atlanta: Scholars Press.

Lev, Yaaco. 1987. "The Fatimid Princess Sitt al-Mulk." *Journal of Semitic Studies* 32, no. 2 (Autumn): 319–28.

Lewis, Bernard. 1966. *The Arabs in History.* New York: Harper and Row.

Lichtenstadter, Ilse. 1935. *Women in Ayyam al-Arab: A Study of Female Life during Warfare in Pre-Islamic Arabia.* London: Royal Asiatic Society.

138   Sources

Lutfi, Huda. 1981. "Al-Sakhawi's Kitab al-Nisa' as a Source for the Social
    and Economic History of Muslim Women during the Fifteenth Cen-
    tury A.D." *Muslim World* 71, no. 2: 104–24.
———. 1983–1984. "A Study of Six Fourteenth Century Iqrars from Al-Quds
    relating to Muslim Women." *Journal of the Economic and Social His-
    tory of the Orient* 26, pt. 3: 246–91.
———. 1991. "Manners and Customs of Fourteenth-Century Cairene Wom-
    en: Female Anarchy versus Male Shar'i Order in Muslim Prescrip-
    tive Treatises." In Keddie and Baron, *Women in Middle Eastern His-
    tory.*
Mahdi, Muhsin. 1984. *Kitab Alf Laila wa Laila* (The book of the thousand-
    and-one nights). Leiden: E. J. Brill.
Makdisi, George. 1981. *The Rise of Colleges: Institutions of Learning in Islam and
    the West.* Edinburgh: Edinburgh University Press.
Malcolm, John. 1845. *Sketches of Persia.* London: John Murray.
Manniche, Lise. 1987. *Sexual Life in Ancient Egypt.* London: KPI.
Marcus, Abraham. 1973. "Men, Women and Property: Dealers in Real Estate
    in Eighteenth Century Aleppo." *Journal of the Economic and Social
    History of the Orient* 26, pt. 2: 136–63.
Marmon, Shaun. 1982–1989. "Concubinage, Islamic." In Strayer et al., *Dic-
    tionary of the Middle Ages.*
Al-Mawdudi, Abu l-A'la. 1972. *Terjuman al-Qur'an. 1939.* Trans. al-Ash'ari
    under the title *Purdah and the Status of Women in Islam.* Lahore: Is-
    lamic Publications.
Mazaheri, Aly. 1951. *La Vie Quotidienne des Musulmans au Moyen Age Xe au
    XIIIe Siècle.* Paris: Librairie Hachette.
McAuliffe, Jane Dammen. 1981. "Chosen of All Women: Mary and Fatima
    in Qur'anic Exegesis." *Islamochristiana* 7: 26–27.
Mellaart, James. 1975. *The Neolithic of the Near East.* New York: Charles Scrib-
    ner's Sons.
Moore, Andrew M. 1985. "The Development of Neolithic Societies in the
    Near East." *Advances in World Archeology* 4: 1–68.
Morewedge, Rosemarie T., ed. 1975. *The Role of Women in the Middle Ages.*
    Albany: State University of New York Press.
Al-Mulk, Nizam. 1978. *The Book of Government.* Trans. Hubert Darke. Lon-
    don: Routledge.
Musallam, B. F. 1983. *Sex and Society in Islam.* Cambridge: Cambridge Univer-
    sity Press.
Nashat, Guity. 1983. "Women in Pre-Revolutionary Iran: A Historical Per-
    spective." In Guity Nashat, ed., *Women and Revolution in Iran.* Boul-
    der: Westview Press.
Al-Nashkhi, Muhammad b. Ja'far. 1954. *The History of Bukhara.* Trans. Rich-
    ard Frye. Cambridge: Harvard University Press.
O'Connor, E. D., ed. 1958. *The Dogma of the Immaculate Conception: History and
    Significance.* Notre Dame, Ind.: University of Notre Dame.
Parsay, Farrukhru, et al. 1977. *Zan dar Iran-i Bastan* (Women in ancient Iran).
    Tehran: Offset Press. Originally published 1346.
Patai, Raphael. 1951. "Nomadism: Middle Eastern and Central Asian." *South-
    western Journal of Anthropology* 7: 401–14.
Peirce, Leslie P. 1993. *The Imperial Harem Women and Sovereignty in the Otto-
    man Empire.* New York: Oxford University Press.
Pellat, Charles. 1969. *The Life and Works of Jahiz.* Berkeley and Los Angeles:
    University of California Press.

Perikhanian, A. 1983. "Iranian Society and Law." In Yarshater, *Cambridge History of Iran*, vol. 3.

Peters, F. E. 1994. *Mecca: Literary History of the Muslim Holy Land.* Princeton: Princeton University Press.

Petrushevsky, I. P. 1968. "The Socio-Economic Condition of Iran under the Il-Khans." In Boyle, *Cambridge History of Iran.*

Petry, Carl F. 1983. "A Paradox of Patronage during the Later Mamluk Period." *Muslim World* 73, nos. 3–4: 182–207.

———. 1991. "Class Solidarity versus Gender Gain: Women as Custodians of Property in Later Medieval Egypt." In Keddie and Baron, *Women in Middle Eastern History.*

Pigulevskaja, N. 1963. *Les Villes de l'état Iranien aux epoches Parthe et Sassanide.* Paris: Mouton and Co.

Pomeroy, Sarah B. 1984. *Women in Hellenistic Egypt: From Alexander to Cleopatra.* New York: Schocken.

Postgate, J. N. 1982. *Societies and Languages of the Ancient Near East: Studies in Honour of I. M. Diakanoff.* Warminster: Aris and Phillips, Ltd.

Powers, David S. 1986. *Studies in Qur'an and Hadith: The Formation of the Islamic Law of Inheritance.* Berkeley and Los Angeles: University of California Press.

Pritchard, James B. 1958. *The Ancient Near East: An Anthology of Texts and Pictures.* 2 vols. Princeton: Princeton University Press.

Rahman, Fazlur. 1983. "Status of Women in the Qur'an." In Nashat, *Women and Revolution in Iran.*

Rahmatalla, Maleeha. 1963. *The Women of Baghdad in the Ninth and Tenth Centuries as Revealed in the History of Baghdad of al-Hatib.* Baghdad: Times Press.

Rippin, Andrew, ed. 1988. *Approaches to the History of the Interpretation of the Qur'an.* Oxford: Clarendon.

Roth, Martha T. 1987. "Age of Marriage and the Household: A Study of Neo-Babylonian and Neo-Assyrian Forms." *Comparative Studies in Society and History* 29, no. 4: 715–47.

Roux, George. 1980. *Ancient Iraq.* 2d ed. Harmondsworth: Penguin.

Rowton, M. 1967. "The Physical Environment and the Problem of the Nomads." *Les Congres et Colloque de l'Université de Liege* 42: 109–21.

Saggs, H. W. 1965. *Everyday Life in Babylonia and Assyria.* London: B. T. Batsford.

Sanders, Paula. 1989. "From Court Ceremony to Urban Language: Ceremonial in Fatimid Cairo and Fustat." In Bosworth et al., *The Islamic World.*

Saunders, J. J. 1965. *A History of Medieval Islam.* London: Routledge and Kegan Paul.

Savory, Roger. 1980. *Iran under the Safavids.* Cambridge: Cambridge University Press.

Al-Sayyid-Marsot, Afaf Lutfi, ed. 1979. *Society and the Sexes in Medieval Islam.* Malibu, Calif.: Undena.

Schacht, Joseph. 1984. *An Introduction to Islamic Law.* Oxford: Clarendon.

Schimmel, Annemarie. 1975. *Mystical Dimensions of Islam.* Chapel Hill: University of North Carolina Press.

———. 1982. "Women in Mystical Islam." In Al-Hibri, *Women and Islam.*

Schub, Michael B. 1991. "The Male Is Not Like the Female: An Eponymous Passage in the Qur'an." *Zeitschrift für Arabische Linguistik* 23: 102–104.

Seibert, Ilse. 1974. *Women in the Ancient Near East*. Trans. Marianne Herzfeld. Leipzig: Edition Leipzig.

Shatzmiller, Maya. 1995. "Women and Property Rights in al-Andalus and the Maghrib: Social Patterns and Legal Discourse." *Islamic Law and Society* 2, no. 3: 219–57.

Silver, Morris. 1985. *Economic Structures of the Ancient Near East*. Totowa, N.J.: Barnes and Noble Books.

Smith, Jane I. 1975. "Women in the Afterlife: The Islamic View as Seen from Qur'an and Tradition." *Journal of the American Academy of Religion* 43: 39–50.

———. 1989. "The Virgin Mary in Islamic Tradition and Commentary." *Muslim World* 79: 161–87.

Smith, Jane I., and Yvonne Y. Haddad. 1982. "Eve: Islamic Image of Woman." In Al-Hibri, *Women and Islam*.

Smith, Margaret. 1928. *Rabi'a the Mystic and Her Fellow-Saints in Islam*. Cambridge: Cambridge University Press.

Smith, W. Robertson. 1903. *Kinship and Marriage in Early Arabia*. Boston: Beacon Press.

Sourdel-Thomine, Janine, and Dominique Sourdel. 1973. "Biens fonciers constitues waqf en Syrie Fatimide pour une famille de Sarifs Damascains." *Journal of the Economic and Social History of the Orient* 15: 269–96.

Spellberg, Denise A. 1988. "Nizam al-Mulk's Manipulation of Tradition: 'A'isha and the Role of Women in the Islamic Government." *Muslim World* 67, no. 2: 111–17.

———. 1990. "The Politics of Praise: Depictions of Khadija, Fatima and 'A'isha in Ninth-Century Muslim Sources." *Literature East and West* 26: 130–148.

———. 1991. "Political Action and Public Example: 'A'isha and the Battle of the Camel." In Keddie and Baron, *Women in Middle Eastern History*.

———. 1994. *Politics, Gender, and the Islamic Past: The Legacy of 'A'isha bint Abi Bakr*. New York: Columbia University Press.

———. 1996. "Writing the Unwritten Life of the Islamic Eve: Menstruation and the Demonization of Motherhood." *International Journal of Middle Eastern Studies* 28: 305–24.

Sprengling, M. 1938–1939. "From Persian to Arabic." *American Journal of Semitic Languages* 55–56: 175–225.

Stephan, St. H. 1944. "An Endowment Deed of Khësseki Sultën, Dated the 24th May 1552." *Quarterly of the Department of Antiquities in Palestine* 10: 170–99.

Stern, Gertrude H. 1939a. "The First Women Converts in Early Islam." *Islamic Culture* 8: 290–305.

———. 1939b. *Marriage in Early Islam*. London: Royal Asiatic Society.

Stowasser, Barbara Freyer. 1984. "The Status of Women in Early Islam." In Husain, *Muslim Women*, pp. 11–43.

———. 1994. *Women in the Qur'an, Traditions, and Interpretation*. Oxford: Oxford University Press.

Strayer, J. J., et al. 1982–1989. *Dictionary of the Middle Ages*. Vol. 3. New York: Scribner.

Al-Tabari, Abu Ja'far Muhammad. 1954–1968. *Jami' al-Bayan 'an Ta'wil al-Qur'an* (The complete elucidation in interpretation of the Qur'an). 3d ed. 30 vols. Cairo: Mustafa al-Babi al-Halabi.

————. 1964. *Tarikh al-Rusul wa al-Muluk* (The history of prophets and kings). Ed. M. J. De Goeje. Series 3, vol. 1. Leiden: E. J. Brill.

Tusi, Nasir al-Din. 1964. *The Nasirean Ethics.* Trans. G. M. Wickens. London: George Allen and Unwin.

Van De Mieroop, Marc. 1989. "Women in the Economy of Sumer." In Lesko, *Women's Earliest Records from Ancient Egypt and Western Asia.*

Veyne, Paul. 1987. *A History of Private Life from Pagan Rome to Byzantium.* 2 vols. Trans. Arthur Goldhammer. Cambridge: Belknap Press of Harvard University Press.

Walther, Wiebke. 1981. *Woman in Islam.* Trans. C. S. V. Salt. Princeton and New York: Markus Wiener.

Watt, W. Montgomery. 1953. *Muhammad at Mecca.* Oxford: Oxford University Press.

————. 1956. *Muhammad at Medina.* Oxford: Clarendon.

Watt, W. Montgomery, and M. V. McDonald, trans. 1987. *The Foundations of the Community.* Vol. 7 of *The History of Tabari (Tarikh al-Rusul wa'l-muluk), Bibliotheca Persica.* Ed. Ehsan Yarshater. SUNY Series in Near Eastern Studies, edited by Said Arjomand. Albany: State University of New York Press.

Wegner, Judith Romney. 1982. "The Status of Women in Jewish and Islamic Marriage and Divorce Law." *Harvard Law Journal* 5, no. 1: 1–33.

Yaron, Reuven. 1969. *The Laws of Eshnunna.* Jerusalem: Hebrew University Press.

Yarshater, Ehsan. 1983. "Mazdakism." In Yarshater, *Cambridge History of Iran.*

Yarshater, Ehsan, ed. 1983. *Cambridge History of Iran.* Vol. 3 (2 parts). Cambridge: Cambridge University Press.

SOURCES: THE NINETEENTH AND TWENTIETH CENTURIES

The following bibliography focuses on readily available books and periodicals in western languages. It is not intended to be a comprehensive listing of the literature, but instead cites the books and articles found to be of most use in the construction of an overview of women's history in the modern period.

An asterisk (*) marks novels and autobiographies written by Middle Eastern women.

Abadan-Unat, Nermin. 1977. "Implications of Migration on Emancipation and Pseudo-Emancipation of Turkish Women." *International Migration Review* 11, no. 1: 31–58.

———. 1978. "The Modernization of Turkish Women." *Middle East Journal* 32, no. 3: 291–306.

———. 1981a. "Women in Government as Policy-Makers and Bureaucrats: The Turkish Case." In Rendel, *Women, Power, and Political Systems.*

———. 1981b. *Women in Turkish Society.* The Hague, Netherlands: Brill.

*Abouzeid, Leila. 1989. *Year of the Elephant.* Austin: Center for Middle Eastern Studies, University of Texas at Austin.

Abu-Lughod, Lila. 1986. *Veiled Sentiments: Honor and Poetry in a Bedouin Society.* Berkeley and Los Angeles: University of California Press.

*———. 1993. *Writing Women's Worlds: Bedouin Stories.* Berkeley and Los Angeles: University of California Press.

———. 1995. "Movie Stars and Islamic Moralism in Egypt." *Social Text* 42 (Spring): 53–67.

Accad, Evelyn. 1993. "Rebellion, Maturity, and the Social Context: Arab Women's Special Contribution to Literature." In Tucker, *Arab Women.*

Adas, Michael, ed. 1993. *Islamic and European Expansion.* Philadelphia: Temple University Press.

*Adivar, Halide Edip. 1926. *Memoirs of Halide Edip.* Chicago: The Century Co.

*———. 1928. *The Turkish Ordeal; Being the Further Memoirs of Halide Edip.* Chicago: The Century Co.

———. 1930. *Turkey Faces West: A Turkish View of Recent Changes and Their Origins.* New Haven: Yale University Press.

*Adnan, Etel. 1982. *Sitt Marie Rose: A Novel.* Translated by Georgina Kleege. Sausalito, Calif.: Post-Apollo Press.

Afary, Janet. 1996. *The Iranian Constitutional Revolution, 1906–1911*. New York: Columbia University Press.

Afkhami, Mahnaz. 1994. "Women in Post-Revolutionary Iran: A Feminist Perspective." In Afrkhami and Friedl, *In the Eye of the Storm*.

Afkhami, Mahnaz, and Erika Friedl, eds. 1994. *In the Eye of the Storm: Women In Post-Revolutionary Iran*. Syracuse, N.Y.: Syracuse University Press.

Ahmed, Leila. 1982. "Western Ethnocentrism and Perceptions of the Harem." *Feminist Studies* 8, no. 3 (Fall): 521–24.

———. 1992. *Women and Gender in Islam: Historical Roots of a Modern Debate*. New Haven: Yale University Press.

Alloula, Malek. 1986. *The Colonial Harem*. Manchester, England: Manchester University Press.

Altorki, Soraya. 1986. *Women in Saudi Arabia: Ideology and Behavior among the Elite*. New York: Columbia University Press.

Amanat, Abbas. 1989. *Resurrection and Renewal: The Making of the Babi Movement in Iran, 1844–1850*. Ithaca, N.Y.: Cornell University Press.

*Amir, Dayzi. 1994. *The Waiting List: An Iraqi Woman's Tale of Alienation*. Translated by Barbara Parmenter. Austin: Center for Middle East Studies.

Amrane, Djamila. 1991. *Les femmes Algeriennes dans la guerre*. Paris: Éditions Plon.

*Amrouche, Fadhma. 1988. *My Life Story: The Autobiography of a Berber Woman*. London: Woman's Press.

Anderson, David, ed. 1998. *Africa's Urban Past*. Cambridge: Cambridge University Press.

Arebi, Sadeeka. 1994. *Women and Words in Saudi Arabia: The Politics of Literary Discourse*. New York: Columbia University Press.

*Atiya, Nayra. 1982. *Khul-Khaal: Five Egyptian Women Tell Their Stories*. Syracuse, N.Y.: Syracuse University Press.

*Attar, Samar. 1994. *Lina: Portrait of a Damascene Girl*. Colorado Springs: Three Continents Press.

Badran, Margot. 1982. "Women and Production in the Middle East." *Trends in History* 2, no. 3: 59–88.

———. 1985. "Islam, Patriarchy, and Feminism in the Middle East." *Trends in History* 4, no. 1: 49–71.

———. 1993. "Independent Women: More than a Century of Feminism in Egypt." In Tucker, *Arab Women*.

———. 1995. *Feminists, Islam, and Nation: Gender and the Making of Modern Egypt*. Princeton, N.J.: Princeton University Press.

Badran, Margot, and Miriam Cooke, eds. 1990. *Opening the Gates: A Century of Arab Feminist Writing*. Bloomington: Indiana University Press.

Baer, Gabriel. 1983. "Women and Waqf: An Analysis of the Istanbul Tahrir of 1546." *Asian and African Studies* (Jerusalem) 17, nos. 1–3: 9–28.

*Bakr, Salwa. 1993. *The Wiles of Men and Other Stories*. Translated by Denys Johnson-Davies. Austin: University of Texas Press.

Baron, Beth. 1991. "The Making and Breaking of Marital Bonds in Modern Egypt." In Keddie and Baron, *Women in Middle Eastern History*.

———. 1994. *The Women's Awakening in Egypt: Culture, Society, and the Press*. New Haven: Yale University Press.

Basu, Amrita, ed., with the assistance of C. Elizabeth McGrory. 1995. *The Challenge of Local Feminisms: Women's Movements in Global Perspective*. Boulder, Colo.: Westview Press.

Bates, Ulku. 1978. "Women as Patrons of Architecture in Turkey." In Beck and Keddie, *Women in the Muslim World*.

Bayat-Philipp, Mangol. 1978. "Women and Revolution in Iran, 1905–1911."
In Beck and Keddie, *Women in the Muslim World*.

Beck, Lois. 1978. "Women among Qashqaʾi Nomadic Pastoralists in Iran." In
Beck and Keddie, *Women in the Muslim World*.

Beck, Lois, and Nikki Keddie, eds. 1978. *Women in the Muslim World*. Cambridge: Harvard University Press.

Benallegue, Nora. 1983. "Algerian Women in the Struggle for Independence
and Reconstruction." *International Social Science Journal* 35, no. 4:
703–17.

Bendt, Ingela, James Downing, and Ann Henning. 1982. *We Shall Return:
Women of Palestine*. Westport, Conn.: Lawrence Hill.

Berik, Gunseli. 1987. *Women Carpet Weavers in Rural Turkey: Patterns of Employment, Earnings, and Status*. Geneva, Switzerland: International
Labour Office.

Betteridge, Anne H. 1983. "To Veil or Not to Veil: A Matter of Protection or
Policy." In Nashat, *Women and Revolution in Iran*.

Boals, Kay. 1976. "The Politics of Cultural Liberation: Male-Female Relations in Algeria." In Carroll, *Liberating Women's History*.

Boals, Kay, and Judith Stiehm. 1974. "The Women of Liberated Algeria."
Center Magazine 7, no. 3: 74–76.

Boullata, Kamal, ed. 1978. *Women of the Fertile Crescent: Modern Poetry by Arab
Women*. Washington, D.C.: Three Continents Press.

Bowlan, Jeanne. 1998. "Civilizing Gender Relations in Algeria: The Paradoxical Case of Marie Bugéja, 1919–39." In Clancy-Smith and Gouda,
Domesticating the Empire.

Brown, L. Carl, and Matthew S. Gordon, eds. 1996. *Franco-Arab Encounters:
Studies in Memory of David C. Gordon*. Syracuse, N.Y.: Syracuse University Press.

Cannon, Byron D. 1985. "Nineteenth-Century Arabic Writings on Women
and Society: The Interim Role of the Masonic Press in Cairo (al-
Lataʾif, 1885–1895)." *International Journal of Middle East Studies* 17:
463–84.

Carroll, Berenice, ed. 1976. *Liberating Women's History*. Urbana and Chicago:
University of Illinois Press.

Chatty, Dawn. 1978. "Changing Sex Roles in Bedouin Society in Syria and
Lebanon." In Beck and Keddie, *Women in the Muslim World*.

Chaudhuri, Nupur, and Margaret Strobel, eds. 1992. *Western Women and Imperialism: Complicity and Resistance*. Bloomington: Indiana University
Press.

Clancy-Smith, Julia. 1991. "The House of Zainab: Female Authority and
Saintly Succession in Colonial Algeria." In Keddie and Baron, *Women in Middle Eastern History*.

———. 1992. "Passionate Nomad: A European Woman in l'Algérie Française
(Isabelle Eberhardt, 1877–1904)." In Chaudhuri and Strobel, *Western Women and Imperialism*.

———. 1996. "The Colonial Gaze: Sex and Gender in the Discourses of French
North Africa." In Brown and Gordon, *Franco-Arab Encounters*.

———. 1998a. "Gender in the City: Women, Migration, and Contested Spaces
in Tunis, 1850–1881." In Anderson, *Africa's Urban Past*.

———. 1998b. "Islam, Gender, and Identities in the Making of French Algeria, 1830–1962." In Clancy-Smith and Gouda, *Domesticating the Empire*.

———. 1999. "A Woman without Her Distaff: Gender, Work, and Handicraft

Production in Colonial North Africa." In Meriwether and Tucker, *A Social History of Women and the Family*.

Clancy-Smith, Julia, and Frances Gouda, eds. 1998. *Domesticating the Empire: Race, Gender, and Family Life in French and Dutch Colonialism*. Charlottesville: University Press of Virginia.

Cole, Juan Ricardo. 1981. "Feminism, Class, and Islam in Turn-of-the-Century Egypt." *International Journal of Middle East Studies* 13: 394–407.

Cooke, Miriam. 1987. *War's Other Voices: Women Writers on the Lebanese Civil War*. Cambridge: Cambridge University Press.

Dajani, Suad. 1993. "Palestinian Women under Israeli Occupation: Implications for Development." In Tucker, *Arab Women*.

Daleb, Nuha. 1978. "Palestinian Women and Their Role in the Revolution." *Peuples Mediterraneans* 5: 35–47.

Danforth, Sandra. 1984. "The Social and Political Implications of Muslim Middle Eastern Women's Participation in Violent Political Conflict." *Women and Politics* 4, no. 1 (Spring): 35–54.

Danielson, Virginia. 1991. "Artists and Entrepreneurs: Female Singers in Cairo during the 1920s." In Keddie and Baron, *Women in Middle Eastern History*.

El Dareer, Asthma. 1982. *Women, Why Do You Weep? Circumcision and Its Consequences*. London: Zed Books.

Davis, Fanny. 1986. *The Ottoman Lady: A Social History from 1718 to 1918*. New York: Greenwood Press.

Davis, Susan Schaeffer. 1978. "Working Women in a Moroccan Village." In Beck and Keddie, *Women in the Muslim World*.

———. 1983. *Patience and Power: Women's Lives in a Moroccan Village*. Cambridge, Mass.: Schenkman.

*Djebar, Assia. 1957. *La soif*. Paris: Julliard.

———. 1985. *Fantasia: An Algerian Cavalcade*. London: Quartet Books.

*———. 1987. *A Sister to Scheherazade*. Portsmouth, N.H.: Heinemann.

Dodd, Peter C. 1968. "Youth and Women's Emancipation in the United Arab Republic." *Middle East Journal* 22, no. 2: 159–72.

Dorsky, Susan. 1986. *Women of 'Amran: A Middle East Ethnographic Study*. Salt Lake City: University of Utah Press.

Duben, Alan, and Cem Behar. 1991. *Istanbul Households: Marriage, Family and Fertility, 1880–1940*. Cambridge: Cambridge University Press.

Duff Gordon, Lucy. 1983. *Letters from Egypt*. London: Virago Press.

Early, Evelyn Aleene. 1993. "Getting It Together: *Baladi* Egyptian Businesswomen." In Tucker, *Arab Women*.

Eliraz, Giora. 1982. "Egyptian Intellectuals and Women's Emancipation, 1919–1939." *Asian and African Studies* (Jerusalem) 16, no. 1: 95–120.

Fakhro, Munira A. 1990. *Women at Work in the Gulf: A Case Study of Bahrain*. London: Kegan Paul International.

Fay, Mary Ann. 1996. "The Ties That Bound: Women and Households in Eighteenth-Century Egypt." In Sonbol, *Women, the Family, and Divorce Laws*.

———. 1997. "Women and Waqf: Property, Power and the Domain of Gender in Eighteenth-Century Egypt." In Zilfi, *Women in the Ottoman Empire*.

Fazel, G. Reza. 1977. "Social and Political Status of Women among Pastoral Nomads: The Bayr Ahmad of Southwest Iran." *Anthropological Quarterly* 50: 77–89.

Fernea, Elizabeth Warnock. 1965. *Guests of the Sheik*. New York: Doubleday.
———. 1976. *A Street in Marrakech*. Garden City, N.J.: Anchor Books.
———. 1985. *Women and the Family in the Middle East*. Austin: University of Texas Press.
Fernea, Elizabeth Warnock, and Basima Bezirgan, eds. 1977. *Middle Eastern Muslim Women Speak*. Austin: University of Texas Press.
Fleischmann, Ellen. 1996. "The Nation and Its 'New' Women: Feminism, Nationalism, Colonialism, and the Palestinian Women's Movement, 1920–1948." Ph.D. dissertation, Georgetown University.
Fletcher, Yaël Simpson. 1998. "'Irresistible Seductions': Gendered Representations of Colonial Algeria around 1930." In Clancy-Smith and Gouda, *Domesticating the Empire*.
Friedl, Erika. 1981. "Women and the Division of Labor in an Iranian Village." *MERIP Reports* 95: 12–18.
———. 1989. *Women of Deh Koh: Lives in an Iranian Village*. Washington: Smithsonian Institution Press.
———. 1991. "The Dynamics of Women's Spheres of Action in Rural Iran," In Keddie and Baron, *Women in Middle Eastern History*.
Gadant, Monique. 1981. "Les femmes, la famille, et la nationalité Algerienne." *Mediterranean Peoples* 15: 25–56.
Giacaman, Rita, and Penny Johnson. 1989. "Building Barricades and Breaking Barriers." In Lockman and Beinin, *Intifada: The Palestinian Uprising against Israeli Occupation*.
Gordon, David. 1968. *Women of Algeria: An Essay on Change*. Harvard Middle East Monographs XIX. Cambridge: Center for Middle Eastern Studies, Harvard University.
Graham-Brown, Sarah. 1988. *Images of Women: The Portrayal of Women in Photography of the Middle East, 1860–1950*. New York: Columbia University Press.
Gran, Judith. 1977. "Impact of the World Market on Egyptian Women." *MERIP Reports* 58: 3–7.
El Guindi, Fadwa. 1983. "Veiled Activism: Egyptian Women in the Contemporary Islamic Movement." *Mediterranean Peoples* 22–23: 79–89.
Haim, Sylvia G. 1981. "The Situation of Arab Women in the Mirror of Literature." *Middle Eastern Studies* 17, no. 4: 510–30.
Hajaiej, Monia. 1996. *Behind Closed Doors: Women's Oral Narratives in Tunis*. New Brunswick, N.J.: Rutgers University Press.
Hale, Sondra. 1986. "The Wing of the Patriarch: Sudanese Women and Revolutionary Parties." *MERIP Middle East Report* 16, no. 1: 25–30.
———. 1993. "Transforming Culture or Fostering Second-Hand Consciousness? Women's Front Organizations and Revolutionary Parties—the Sudan Case." In Tucker, *Arab Women*.
———. 1996. *Gender Politics in Sudan: Islamism, Socialism, and the State*. Boulder, Colo.: Westview.
Hammam, Mona. 1980. "Women and Industrial Work in Egypt: The Chubra El-Kheima Case." *Arab Studies Quarterly* 2, no. 1: 50–69.
Hansen, Henny. 1961. *The Kurdish Woman's Life*. Copenhagen, Denmark: Nationalmuseet.
Hatem, Mervat. 1993. "Towards the Development of Post-Islamicist and Post-Modernist Feminist Discourses in the Middle East." In Tucker, *Arab Women*.
Heggoy, Alf Andrew. 1972. "Cultural Disrespect: European and Algerian Views

on Women in Colonial and Independent Algeria." *Muslim World* 62, no. 4: 323–35.

———. 1974. "Algerian Women and the Right to Vote: Some Colonial Anomalies." *Muslim World* 64, no. 3: 228–35.

Hegland, Mary Elaine. 1986. "Political Roles of Iranian Village Women." *MERIP Middle East Report* 16, no. 1: 14–19, 46.

Helfgott, Leonard M. 1994. *Ties That Bind: A Social History of the Iranian Carpet.* Washington, D.C.: Smithsonian Institution Press.

Howard-Merriam, Kathleen. 1979. "Women, Education, and the Professions in Egypt." *Comparative Education Review* 23: 256–70.

Iglitzin, Lynne, and Ruth Ross, eds. 1976. *Women in the World.* New York: Clio Books.

Jennings, Ronald C. 1975. "Women in the Early Seventeenth Century Ottoman Judicial Records: The Sharia Court of Anatolian Kayseri." *Journal of the Economic and Social History of the Orient* 28: 53–114.

Jensen, Willy. 1987. *Women without Men: Gender and Marginality in an Algerian Town.* Leiden, The Netherlands: E. J. Brill.

Kandiyoti, Deniz. 1977. "Sex Roles and Social Change: A Comparative Study of Turkey's Women." *Signs: Journal of Women in Culture and Society* 3, no. 1: 57–73.

———. 1991. "Islam and Patriarchy: A Comparative Perspective." In Keddie and Baron, *Women in Middle Eastern History.*

———, ed. 1991. *Women, Islam, and the State.* London: Macmillan.

al-Kazi, Lubna Ahmad. 1986. "The Transitory Role of Kuwaiti Women in the Development Process." Unpublished Paper Presented at the CCAS Annual Symposium, April.

Keddie, Nikki, and Beth Baron, eds. 1991. *Women in Middle Eastern History.* New Haven: Yale University Press.

Knauss, Peter. 1987. *The Persistence of Patriarchy: Class, Gender, and Ideology in Twentieth Century Algeria.* New York: Praeger.

*Kordi, Gohar. 1991. *An Iranian Odyssey.* London: Serpent's Tail.

Kuhnke, Laverne. 1990. *Lives at Risk: Public Health in Nineteenth Century Egypt.* Berkeley and Los Angeles: University of California Press.

Largueche, Dalenda. 1996. "Confined, Battered, and Repudiated Women in Tunis since the Eighteenth Century." In Sonbol, *Women, Family, and Divorce Laws.*

Largueche, Dalenda, and Abdelhamid Largueche. 1992. *Marginales en terre d'Islam.* Tunis: CERES Productions.

Layne, Linda. 1981. "Women in Jordan's Workforce." *MERIP Reports* 95: 19–23.

Lazreg, Marnia. 1994. *The Eloquence of Silence: Algerian Women in Question.* New York: Routledge.

Lockman, Zachary, and Joel Beinin, eds. 1989. *Intifada: The Palestinian Uprising against Israeli Occupation.* Boston: South End Press.

Macleod, Arlene Elowe. 1991. *Accommodating Protest: Working Women, the New Veiling, and Change in Cairo.* New York: Columbia University Press.

Mahdavi, Shireen. 1983. "Women and the Shii Ulama in Iran." *Middle Eastern Studies* 19, no. 1: 17–27.

———. 1985. "Women and Ideas in Qajar Iran." *Asian and African Studies* (Jerusalem) 9: 187–97.

Maher, Vanessa. 1974. *Women and Property in Morocco: Their Changing Relation* to the Process of Stratification in the Middle Atlas. Cambridge: Cambridge University Press.

Makhlouf, Carla. 1979. *Changing Veils: Women and Modernization in North Yemen*. London: Croom Helm.

Malik, Ibn Anan. N.d. *al-Muwattah*. Cairo: Mustafa al-Babi al-Hakabi.

Malti-Douglas, Fedwa. 1991. *Woman's Body, Woman's Word: Gender and Discourse in Arabo-Islamic Writing*. Princeton: Princeton University Press.

Marcus, Abraham. 1983. "Men, Women and Property: Dealers in Real Estate in Eighteenth-Century Aleppo." *Journal of the Economic and Social History of the Orient* 26, no. 2: 137–63.

Marshall, Susan E. 1984. "Politics and Female Status in North Africa: A Reconsideration of Development Theory." *Economic Development and Cultural Change* 32, no. 3: 499–524.

Marsot, Afaf Lutfi al-Sayyid. 1978. "The Revolutionary Gentlewomen in Egypt." In Beck and Keddie, *Women in the Muslim World*.

Melman, Billie. 1992. *Women's Orients: English Women and the Middle East, 1718–1918*. Ann Arbor: University of Michigan Press.

Meriwether, Margaret. 1993. "Women and Economic Change in Nineteenth Century Syria: The Case of Aleppo." In Tucker, *Arab Women*.

Meriwether, Margaret, and Judith Tucker, eds. 1999. *A Social History of Women and the Family in the Middle East*. Boulder, Colo.: Westview.

———. 1999. *The Kin Who Count: Family and Society in Ottoman Aleppo*. Austin: University of Texas Press.

Mernissi, Fatima. 1975. *Beyond the Veil: Male-Female Dynamics in a Modern Muslim Society*. Cambridge, Mass.: Schenkman.

———. 1983. "Women and the Impact of Capitalist Development In Morocco, Part II." *Feminist Issues* 3, no. 1: 61–112.

*———. 1989. *Doing Daily Battle: Interviews with Moroccan Women*. New Brunswick, N.J.: Rutgers University Press.

———. 1991. *The Veil and the Male Elite: A Feminist Interpretation of Women's Rights in Islam*. Reading, Mass.: Addison-Wesley.

el-Messiri, Sausan. 1978. "Self-Images of Traditional Urban Women In Cairo." In Beck and Keddie, *Women in the Muslim World*.

Milani, Farzanah. 1992. *Veils and Words: The Emerging Voices of Iranian Women Writers*. Syracuse, N.Y.: Syracuse University Press.

Miller, Susan G. 1996. "Gender and the Poetics of Emancipation: The Alliance Israélite Universelle in Northern Morocco, 1890–1912." In Brown and Gordon, *Franco-Arab Encounters*.

Minces, Juliette. 1978. "Women in Algeria." In Beck and Keddie, *Women in the Muslim World*.

Moghadam, Valentine M. 1993. *Modernizing Women: Gender and Social Change in the Middle East*. Boulder, Colo.: Lynne Rienner Publishers.

———, ed. 1994. *Gender and National Identity*. London: Zed Books.

Moghissi, Haideh. 1991. "Women, Modernization and Revolution in Iran." *Review of Radical Political Economics* 23, no. 3, 4: 205–23.

Moore, Clement Henry. 1980. "Sexual Equality and Professional Impoverishment." In Moore, *Images of Development*.

———, ed. 1980. *Images of Development*. Cambridge: M.I.T. Press.

M'rabet, Fadela. 1969. *La Femme Algerienne suivi de les Algeriennes*. Paris: F. Maspero.

al-Mughni, Haya. 1993. *Women in Kuwait: The Politics of Gender*. London: Saqi Books.

Nashat, Guity, ed. 1983a. *Women and Revolution in Iran*. Boulder, Colo.: Westview.

———. 1983b. "Women in Pre-Revolutionary Iran: A Historical Overview."
In Nashat, *Women and Revolution in Iran*.

Nelson, Barbara J., and Najma Chowdhury, eds. 1994. *Women and Politics
Worldwide*. New Haven: Yale University Press.

Nelson, Cynthia. 1974. "Public and Private Politics: Women in the Middle
Eastern World." *American Ethnologist* 1: 551–63.

———. 1996. *Doria Shafik, Egyptian Feminist*. Gainesville: University Press of
Florida.

*Out el Kouloub. 1994. *Ramza*. Translated by Nayra Atiya. Syracuse, N.Y.:
Syracuse University Press.

Paidar, Parvin. 1995. *Women and the Political Process in Twentieth Century Iran*.
Cambridge: Cambridge University Press.

Peirce, Leslie P. 1993. *The Imperial Harem: Women and Sovereignty in the Ottoman Empire*. New York: Oxford University Press.

Peteet, Julie. 1986. "No Going Back: Women and the Palestinian Movement."
MERIP Reports 16, no. 1: 20–24.

———. 1991. *Gender in Crisis: Women and the Palestinian Resistance Movement*.
New York: Columbia University Press.

Peteet, Julie, and Rosemary Sayigh. 1987. "Between Two Fires: Palestinian
Women in Lebanon." In Ridd, *Caught Up in Conflict*.

Petek-Salom and Pinar Hukum. 1983. "Après Kemal Ataturk, Qu'en est-il
de l'émancipation des femmes?" *Mediterranean Peoples* 22–23: 161–
80.

Phillip, Thomas. 1977. "Women in the Historical Perspective of an Early Arab
Modernist (Gurgi Zaidan)." *Welt des Islam* 18, no. 1–2: 65–83.

Quataert, Donald. 1991. "Ottoman Women, Households, and Textile Manufacturing, 1800–1914." In Keddie and Baron, *Women in Middle Eastern History*.

———. 1993. *Ottoman Manufacturing in the Age of the Industrial Revolution*. Cambridge: Cambridge University Press.

Ramazani, Nesta. 1980. "Behind the Veil: Status of Women In Revolutionary
Iran." *Journal of South Asia and Middle Eastern Studies* 4, no. 2: 27–36.

Rendel, M. ed. 1981. *Women, Power, and Political Systems*. New York: St. Martin's
Press.

Ridd, R., ed. 1987. *Caught Up in Conflict*. New York: Macmillan.

Roded, Ruth. 1994. *Women in Islamic Biographical Collections*. Boulder, Colo.:
Lynne Rienner Publishers.

Rugh, Andrea. 1979. *Coping with Poverty in a Cairo Community*. Cairo Papers in
Social Science 2, no. 1, Cairo: American University in Cairo Press.

———. 1985. "Women and Work: Strategies and Choices in a Lower-Class
Quarter of Cairo." In Fernea, *Women and the Family*.

*El Saadawi, Nawal. 1982. *The Hidden Face of Eve: Women in the Arab World*.
Translated by Sharif Hetata. Boston: Beacon Press.

*———. 1983. *Woman at Point Zero*. Translated by Sharif Hetata. London: Zed
Books.

*———. 1986a. *Memoirs from the Women's Prison*. Translated by Marilyn Booth.
London: Women's Press.

*———. 1986b. *Two Women in One*. Translated by Osman Nusairi and Jane
Gough. Seattle: Seal Press Feminist.

Sabbah, Fatna. 1984. *Women in the Muslim Unconscious.* Translated by Mary Jo Lakeland. New York: Pergamon Press.

Sansarian, Elizabeth. 1982. *The Women's Rights Movement in Iran: Mutiny, Appeasement and Repression from 1900 to Khomeini.* New York: Praeger.

Sayigh, Rosemary. 1981. "Roles and Functions of Arab Women." *Arab Studies Quarterly* 3, no. 3: 258–74.

———. 1993. "Palestinian Women and Politics In Lebanon." In Tucker, *Arab Women.*

Seager, Joni. 1997. *The State of Women in the World Atlas.* 1986. Revised, New York: Penguin.

Seghdi, Hamideh. 1982. "Women and Class in Iran, 1900–1978." Ph.D. dissertation, City University of New York.

*Sha'rawi, Huda. 1987. *Harem Years: The Memoirs of an Egyptian Feminist.* Translated by Margot Badran. New York: The Feminist Press.

*al-Shaykh, Hanan. 1986. *The Story of Zahra.* London: Quartet.

*———. 1989. *Women of Sand and Myrrh.* Translated by Catherine Cobham. London: Quartet.

Smith, Jane I. 1980. *Women in Contemporary Muslim Societies.* Lewisburg, Pa.: Bucknell University Press.

Sonbol, Amira El Azhary, ed. 1996. *Women, the Family, and Divorce Laws in Islamic History.* Syracuse, N.Y.: Syracuse University Press.

*Souief, Ahdaf. 1992. *In the Eye of the Sun.* London: Bloombury.

Stiehm, Judith. 1976. "Algerian Women: Honor, Survival, and Islamic Socialism." In Iglitzin and Ross, *Women in the World.*

Stowasser, Barbara. 1993. "Women's Issues in Modern Islamic Thought." In Tucker, *Arab Women.*

Sullivan, Earl L. 1981. *Women and Work in the Arab World.* Cairo Papers in Social Science, 4, no. 4, Cairo, Egypt: American University in Cairo Press.

———. 1986. *Women in Egyptian Public Life.* Syracuse, N.Y.: Syracuse University Press.

Tabari, Azar, and N. Yeganeh. 1982. *The Shadow of Islam: The Women's Movement in Iran.* London: Zed Books.

*Taj al-Sultana. 1993. *Crowning Anguish: Memoirs of a Persian Princess from the Harem to Modernity, 1884–1914.* Washington, D.C.: Mage Publishers.

Tessler, Mark, and Ina Warriner. 1997. "Gender, Feminism, and Attitudes toward International Conflict: Exploring Relationships with Survey Data from the Middle East." *World Politics* 49, no. 2 (January): 250–81.

Tahon, Marie-Blanche. 1992. "Women Novelists and Women in the Struggle for Algeria's National Liberation (1957–1980)." *Research in African Literatures* 23, no. 2 (Summer): 39–50.

Tucker, Judith E. 1979. "Decline of the Family Economy in Mid-Nineteenth Century Egypt." *Arab Studies Quarterly* 1, no. 3: 245–71.

———. 1983. "Problems in the Historiography of Women in the Middle East: The Case of Nineteenth Century Egypt." *International Journal of Middle East Studies* 15, no. 3: 321–36.

———. 1985. *Women in Nineteenth Century Egypt.* Cambridge: Cambridge University Press.

———. 1993a. "The Arab Family in History: 'Otherness' and the Study of the Family." In Tucker, *Arab Women.*

————. 1993b. "Gender and Islamic History." In Adas, *Islamic and European Expansion*.

————. 1994. "Muftis and Matrimony: Islamic Law and Gender in Ottoman Syria and Palestine." *Islamic Law and Society* 1, no. 3: 265–300.

————. 1998. *In the House of the Law: Gender and Islamic Law in Ottoman Syria and Palestine*. Berkeley and Los Angeles: University of California Press.

————, ed. 1993. *Arab Women: Old Boundaries, New Frontiers*. Bloomington: Indiana University Press.

*Tuqan, Fadwa. 1990. *A Mountainous Journey: A Poet's Autobiography*. St. Paul, Minn.: Greywolf Press.

Vallet, Jean. 1911. *Contribution a l'étude de la condition des ouvriers de la grande industrie au Caire*. Paris: Imprimerie Valentinoise.

Webber, Sabra. 1985. "Women's Folk Narratives and Social Change." In Fernea, *Women and the Family*.

White, Jenny B. 1994. *Money Makes Us Relatives: Women's Labor In Urban Turkey*. Austin: University of Texas Press.

Wikan, Unni. 1982. *Behind the Veil in Arabia: Women in Oman*. Baltimore, Md.: Johns Hopkins University Press.

Williams, Caroline. 1986. "Women and the Arts: An Historical Survey." Unpublished paper presented at the CCAS Annual Symposium, April.

Youssef, Nadia Haggag. 1974. *Women and Work in Developing Countries*. Berkeley: Institute of International Studies.

————. 1977. "Women and Agricultural Production In Muslim Societies." *Comparative International Development* 3, no. 1: 41–88.

Zilfi, Madeline C., ed. 1997. *Women in the Ottoman Empire: Middle Eastern Women in the Early Modern Era*. Leiden, The Netherlands: Brill.

Zuhur, Sherifa. 1992. *Revealing Reveiling: Islamist Gender Ideology in Contemporary Egypt*. Albany: State University of New York Press.

NOTES ON CONTRIBUTORS

Cheryl Johnson-Odim is professor of history and chairs the Department of History at Loyola University, Chicago. She co-authored *For Women and the Nation: Funmilayo Ransome-Kuti of Nigeria* and co-edited *Expanding the Boundaries of Women's History*. She has published many articles and chapters on African women's history and on feminist theory. She is a past member of the board of directors of the African Studies Association and the American Council of Learned Societies and serves on the editorial boards of the *Journal of Women's History* and *Chicago Women, 1770–1990: A Biographical Dictionary*.

Guity Nashat is associate professor of Middle Eastern history at the University of Illinois at Chicago and senior research fellow at the Hoover Institution, Stanford University. She has published *The Origins of Modern Reform in Iran* and edited a collection of articles, *Women and Revolution in Iran*. Currently, she is studying the evolution of the role of the state in the Middle East.

Margaret Strobel is professor of women's studies and history at the University of Illinois at Chicago. Her book *Muslim Women in Mombasa, 1890–1975* won the African Studies Association's Herskovits Award in 1980. She is author of *European Women and the Second British Empire* and co-editor of *Three Swahili Women, Life Histories from Mombasa, Kenya*; *Western Women and Imperialism: Complicity and Resistance*; and *Expanding the Boundaries of Women's History*. She serves on the editorial board of *Chicago Women, 1770–1990: A Biographical Dictionary*, and is working on a book about the Chicago Women's Liberation Union.

Judith E. Tucker is professor of history and director of Academic Programs in Arab Studies at Georgetown University. She authored *Women in Nineteenth-Century Egypt* and *In the House of the Law: Gender and Islamic Law in Ottoman Syria and Palestine* and edited *Arab Women: Old Boundaries, New Frontiers*.

INDEX

Names in this index are alphabetized in two ways: (1) by the first letter of the first word, and (2) in the more recent period, by the "last" name, when that has been used as a "family" name.